Measuring the Impact of the Nonprofit Sector

NONPROFIT AND CIVIL SOCIETY STUDIES
An International Multidisciplinary Series

Series Editor: Helmut K. Anheier

> London School of Economics and Political Science
> London, United Kingdom

CIVIL SOCIETY AND THE PROFESSIONS IN EASTERN EUROPE
Social Change and Organizational Innovation in Poland
S. Wojciech Sokolowski

MEASURING THE IMPACT OF THE NONPROFIT SECTOR
Edited by Patrice Flynn and Virginia A. Hodgkinson

NEIGHBORHOOD SELF-MANAGEMENT
Experiments in Civil Society
Hillel Schmid

PRIVATE FUNDS, PUBLIC PURPOSE
Philanthropic Foundations in International Perspective
Edited by Helmut K. Anheier and Stefan Toepler

A Continuation Order Plan is available for this series. A continuation order will bring delivery of each new volume immediately upon publication. Volumes are billed only upon actual shipment. For further information please contact the publisher.

Measuring the Impact of the Nonprofit Sector

Edited by

PATRICE FLYNN

Flynn Research
Harpers Ferry, West Virginia

and

VIRGINIA A. HODGKINSON

Center for the Study of Voluntary Organizations and Service
The Georgetown Public Policy Institute
Washington, D.C.

KLUWER ACADEMIC/PLENUM PUBLISHERS
NEW YORK, BOSTON, DORDRECHT, LONDON, MOSCOW

Library of Congress Cataloging-in-Publication Data

Measuring the impact of the nonprofit sector/edited by Patrice Flynn
and Virginia A. Hodgkinson.
     p. cm. — (Nonprofit and civil society studies)
     Includes bibliographical references and index.
     ISBN 0-306-46547-7—ISBN 0-306-46548-5 (pbk.)
     1. Nonprofit organizations—Evaluation. 2. Organizational effectiveness. 3. Evaluation
research (Social action programs) I. Flynn, Patrice. II. Hodgkinson, Virginia Ann. III.
Series.

HV41 .P73 2001
361.7'63—dc21

                                                2001029578

ISBN 0-306-46557-7 (Hardbound)
ISBN 0-306-46548-5 (Paperback)

©2001 Kluwer Academic/Plenum Publishers, New York
233 Spring Street, New York, N.Y. 10013

http://www.wkap.nl/

10 9 8 7 6 5 4 3 2 1

A C.I.P. record for this book is available from the Library of Congress.

sensitive to both quantitative and qualitative research methods. The participants voiced concern that what could currently be counted may not measure what truly is the value added to society by nonprofit organizations and citizen participation.

The group concluded that the time has come for the nonprofit sector to initiate a long-term research agenda to formally identify, quantify, and self-assess those qualities that make the sector unique. It is our hope that this volume will spark interest not only in setting such an agenda, but also in planting the seeds for the development of the theoretical and empirical research to begin the process of measurement.

Finally, we want to thank the very talented and hardworking Susan Wiener for her devotion to both the topic of this volume and its editors and for shepherding the book through the production process at Independent Sector.

PATRICE FLYNN
VIRGINIA A. HODGKINSON

Preface

One of the major tasks facing nonprofit sector researchers and practitioners is the development of empirical tools to measure the inherent worth of nonprofit organizations and the sector as a whole over time. This effort will be demanding and complex but necessary as the sector is called upon to demonstrate its accomplishments and impact in an era of greater accountability to the public.

Toward this end, Independent Sector commissioned a group of renowned scholars to write a series of papers on the state of the art of performance measurement in the nonprofit sector. The papers were presented at a conference held on September 5–6, 1996, at the Carnegie Corporation in Washington, D.C. Each scholar was asked to reflect upon three central questions. (1) Should we attempt to measure the impact of the nonprofit sector and why? (2) What is the state of the literature on measuring the effectiveness or performance of the sector? (3) What are the inherent dangers, impediments, and/or political implications in developing such measures?

A serious dialogue ensued among the 80 conference participants, who included directors of nonprofit academic centers and other private research facilities, selected donors, and leaders from organizations with an interest in this research agenda. At the end of the two-day conference, the mandate was loud and clear. First, it was recognized that the development of a conceptual framework for measuring the impact of the nonprofit sector on society would serve the vital needs of many researchers, practitioners, and funders of nonprofit organizations. Second, such an effort has never been attempted on the national level because of the methodological, financial, and political challenges inherent in the exercise. Third, the results of this kind of research have the potential to expand our existing knowledge about the sector if approached methodically and in a collaborative manner that includes not only researchers but also individuals on the front lines of nonprofit sector work. Last, the effort must be

Contributors

Colin Campbell • University Professor in Public Policy, The Georgetown Public Policy Institute, Washington, DC 20007

Jim Castelli • President, Castelli Enterprises, Inc., Burke, Virginia 22015

Clifford W. Cobb • Senior Fellow, Redefining Progress, Sacramento, California 95816

James P. Connell • President, Institute for Research and Reform in Education, Toms River, New Jersey 08753

Susan Cutcher-Gershenfeld • Quality Consultant, Executive Office of Elder Affairs, Commonwealth of Massachusetts, Boston, Massachusetts 02108

Paul DiMaggio • Professor, Department of Sociology, Princeton University, Princeton, New Jersey 08544

Patrice Flynn • Economist and Chief Executive Officer, Flynn Research, Harpers Ferry, West Virgina 25425

Bradford H. Gray • Director, Division of Health and Science Policy, New York Academy of Medicine, New York, New York 10029

Martha Taylor Greenway • Executive Director of Planning, Research and Policy, Fulton County Schools, Atlanta, Georgia 30315

Virginia A. Hodgkinson • Research Professor of Public Policy and Director, Center for the Study of Voluntary Organizations and Service, The Georgetown Public Policy Institute, Washington, DC 20007

Adena M. Klem • Research Associate, Institute for Research and Reform in Education, Toms River, New Jersey 08753

Kenneth C. Land • John Franklin Crowell Professor, Department of Sociology and Senior Fellow, Center for Demographic Studies, Duke University, Durham, North Carolina 27708

John D. McCarthy • Professor, Department of Sociology, Pennsylvania State University, University Park, Pennsylvania 16802

Kathleen D. McCarthy • Professor of History and Director, Center for the Study of Philanthropy, Graduate School and University Center, City University of New York, New York, New York 10016

David Mathews • President and Chief Executive Officer, Charles F. Kettering Foundation, Dayton, Ohio 45459

Melissa M. Stone • Associate Professor, Hubert H. Humphrey Institute of Public Affairs, University of Minnesota, Minneapolis, Minnesota 55455

Burton A. Weisbrod • John Evans Professor of Economics and Faculty Fellow, Institute for Policy Research and Chair, Philanthropy, Voluntarism, and Nonprofit Organizations Program, Northwestern University, Evanston, Illinois 60208

Julian Wolpert • Henry G. Bryant Professor of Geography, Public Affairs, and Urban Planning, Woodrow Wilson School of Public and International Affairs, Princeton University, Princeton, New Jersey 08544

Robert Wuthnow • Professor of Sociology and Director, Center for the Study of Religion, Princeton University, Princeton, New Jersey 08544

Margaret Jane Wyszomirski • Director, Arts Policy and Administration Program, Ohio State University, Columbus, Ohio 43210

Contents

Measuring the Impact of
the Nonprofit Sector

Part **I**

Introduction

Chapter 1

Measuring the Contributions
of the Nonprofit Sector

PATRICE FLYNN AND VIRGINIA A. HODGKINSON

Over the past two decades, researchers have made progress measuring the size, scope, and dimensions of the nonprofit sector. These efforts have resulted in the development of a national classification system (e.g., the National Taxonomy for Exempt Entities), measures of sectoral inputs (e.g., staff, volunteers, financial resources), and indicators of organizational outputs (e.g., program activities, persons served, units of service delivered). The information provides key insights and the background needed to develop a national statistical portrait of the nonprofit sector, nationally and internationally (Hodgkinson & Weitzman, 1996; Salamon & Anheier, 1996). More recently, however, there is new interest in measuring the benefits of the sector and the overall impact that nonprofit organizations have on society over time. This effort is demanding and complex, but necessary, as the sector and its institutions will be called upon to demonstrate their accomplishments and inherent worth in an era of greater accountability to the public.

To date, the nonprofit sector has relied on anecdotal evidence and general good will to argue for its many successes and tax-exempt status. There is no body of scholarly literature assessing the roles, functions, and contributions of

PATRICE FLYNN • Economist and Chief Executive Officer, Flynn Research, Harpers Ferry, West Virginia 25425.   VIRGINIA A. HODGKINSON • Research Professor of Public Policy and Director, Center for the Study of Voluntary Organizations and Service, The Georgetown Public Policy Institute, Washington, DC 20007.

Measuring the Impact of the Nonprofit Sector, edited by Patrice Flynn and Virginia A. Hodgkinson, New York, Kluwer Academic/Plenum Publishers, 2002.

the nonprofit sector beyond evaluation research at the institutional level. Hence, in public deliberations, nonprofit professionals are unable to clearly articulate the myriad activities performed by 501(c)(3) organizations and any ensuing, greater societal good. While both government and business have clear and consistent bottom lines (i.e., elections and profits, respectively), the bottom line for nonprofits is vague (i.e., the production of collective goods that would not otherwise be provided in society). Until we develop a useful methodology to describe and measure the sector, we are reduced to operating on beliefs about the value added by nonprofit organizations as well as their contemporary roles and functions.

Many pitfalls prevent an accurate assessment of the impacts that nonprofit organizations and the sector as a whole have on society. Nevertheless, we are persuasively coaxed down this research path by the guest authors of this volume. Eighteen scholars collectively explore research approaches, methodologies, conceptual frameworks, and fundamental issues associated with measuring the effectiveness of the sector and its impact on community and society. At the heart of the exercise is a desire to gain a deeper understanding of the uniqueness of nonprofit organizations in improving the quality of life in communities and the roles nonprofits play in preserving and strengthening citizen participation in democratic societies.

THE GROWING IMPORTANCE OF MEASURING IMPACT

The primary purpose of this volume is to explore the potential to develop precise empirical tools to measure the impact of the charitable nonprofit sector, or specific subsectors, on society. In the increasingly competitive world in which nonprofits operate, there are new demands for impact analysis. Foundations want to know whether the programs they fund are making a difference. Private donors inquire as to how donations serve targeted audiences. Board members ask for detailed information on organizational activities and performance.

Attention to measurement has also become more important among government agencies with the increased privatization of social welfare and the devolution of federal government decision-making powers to the states. Following the passage of the Government Performance and Results Act of 1993, the Personal Responsibility and Work Opportunity Reconciliation Act of 1996, and the Balanced Budget Act of 1996, organizations receiving government funds are required to conduct internal performance evaluations. Over the past decade, performance contracting quickly became the way local and state governments sought service delivery. This has led to new levels of both competition and collaboration among the three sectors—government, business and nonprofits—depending upon the approach of government (Egan, Cross, & Marger, 1999; Weisbrod, 1997).

Existing measures provide a valuable statistical profile of the size of the nonprofit sector relative to government and commercial sectors. The nonprofit sector represented nearly 7 percent of national income in the United States in 1996, up from 5.5 percent in 1977. The sector also accounted for an estimated 7 percent of total paid employment, up from 5.3 percent in 1977. When volunteer time is included (93 million Americans, representing the equivalent of 5.7 million full-time employees), the charitable nonprofit sector represents approximately 10.8 percent of total employment in the United States (Hodgkinson & Weitzman, 1998).

Such measures offer a much better idea of *inputs* to the sector rather than specific *outcomes* achieved in the long term. To be explored more fully is the other side of the accountability ledger, capturing the benefits that the sector produces to improve the quality of life in communities. As discussed in the following chapters, some outputs are available in their simplest forms, such as the number of hospital beds filled or the number of students enrolled. There is little evidence, however, that organizations can reliably measure organizational performance at the institutional level, much less at the community and/or sectoral levels at a time when sophisticated assessment methodologies are in demand.

Increased demand for rigorous measurement tools is not limited to nonprofits in the United States. With the growth of foundation-sponsored foreign aid and the popular belief that nonprofit organizations are important vehicles to develop democracy and to offset poverty, efforts are being made to measure the impact of nonprofit organizations abroad. But the data systems and empirical tools to assess socio-economic development and democracy formation are primitive compared to those available for assessing business activities (Edwards & Hulme, 1996; World Bank, 1998).

Moreover, as the authors in this volume point out, the current focus on measuring service delivery of nonprofit organizations sometimes distracts from the other key roles and functions of the sector, such as providing avenues for affiliation; bringing about social change, advocacy, research, and experimentation; empowering citizens; engaging in arts and culture; and promoting and strengthening democracy and religious participation. The fall of Communism has generated an interest in the power of the third sector to offset the power of government and to empower citizen action in Eastern Europe and other developing nations. The term "civil society," selected by Eastern European scholars to name this third sector of organizations and associations between government and business, has led to an explosive amount of research worldwide. Civil society and civic renewal have also become important topics in the United States, with an incredible outpouring of research and scholarly disagreement, as well as citizen organization and action, around such issues as quality of life and livable communities (Dionne, 1998; Ehrenberg, 1999; Fullinwider, 1999; O'Connell, 1999; Skocpol & Fiorina, 1999).

Ultimately, the configuration of various types of nonprofit institutions, governance, services, and citizen participation leads to outcomes that can be expressed as the benefits or changes brought about in people, societies, and/or the environment. Progress is being made toward quantifying these changes, using systemic benchmark indicators over the past decades as noted by Kenneth Land (Chapter 4) and most recently with the publication of the *Calvert–Henderson Quality of Life Indicators: A New Tool For Assessing National Trends* (Henderson, Lickerman, & Flynn, 2000). But the publication of this new volume starkly reveals (1) that social science methodology has not advanced to the point of identifying contributions to quality of life indicators by type of institution and (2) the lack of reliable data series that measure citizen contributions to society. The authors reveal that measuring institutional contributions poses major methodological difficulties and that basic information needs to be collected over long periods of time in order to test various theories about institutional or sectoral behavior.

To honestly measure the degree to which organizations with Section 501(c)(3) status are contributing to the betterment of society and, hence, earning tax-free status is a daunting task. We are persuasively coaxed down this path by our guest authors, one of whom, Paul DiMaggio (Chapter 15) states that "the potential of impact analysis for enhancing the reflexivity of the nonprofit sector, encouraging dialogue between researchers and practitioners, and creating more sophisticated ways of thinking about the sector and its goals strikes me as making the quest worthwhile." David Mathews (Chapter 8) warns that "getting the results that we want in the affairs of our communities may not be reducible to simply promulgation standards and measuring results; it may require a process of judging results publicly." In other words, mechanisms need to be developed for citizens to directly examine outcomes of their decisions to determine whether or not these were the desired outcomes. Otherwise, as Burt Weisbrod (Chapter 16) reminds us, "The danger is that easily measured outputs or outcomes will be measured while others remain unmeasured and, in effect, valued at zero. Resources will then be misallocated, too few going into the provision of such subtle outputs as tender loving care in a nursing home, appreciation of art and music, [and] education in cultural values."

LINE OF INQUIRY

The line of inquiry pursued in this volume presumes that the sector is ready and willing to engage in a social and economic accountability study and to make transparent the nature of nonprofit organizations, an honest and self-reflective exercise for those who work in the sector. There are several inherent difficulties in conducting performance studies. For some social scientists, the methodological blocks are the most challenging because there is no clear path in the extant literature on how to measure organizational outcomes or impacts. For others, steeped in the tradition of evaluation research, the lack of a comparison group (or counterfactual) against which progress can be assessed makes the research exercise uninteresting. Still others hesitate for lack of a conceptual or theoretical framework to approach the exercise.

Political dilemmas related to accountability measures must also be considered when attempting such a statistical effort. Empirical measures created to describe the sector will be used by a variety of audiences to applaud or to critique the sector. For example, heated debates between the Reagan administration and environmental groups in the early 1980s resulted in the near abolition of certain programs within the U.S. Environmental Protection Agency (EPA). Environmentalists argued that without EPA data and needs assessments, the public would be deprived of salient information on the condition of the environment. The Administration argued that there were other priorities for the national budget. Recognizing that people measure what is important to them, any and all statistical measures can quickly become politicized.

These challenges not withstanding, we believe that the accumulated knowledge of practitioners and researchers provides a viable foundation on which to begin the process of measurement. We acknowledge that the process will be a crude beginning that necessitates the development of a lexicon for discussing what constitutes a "contribution," a "success," or an "outcome" in each of the subsectors. We also recognize that our initial efforts will require the use of systems analysis if the aim is to move beyond measuring immediate, linear achievements to truly delve into more fundamental, long-term effects.

This volume explores various approaches to measurement ranging from concrete empirical techniques to abstract conceptual arguments on the value of measurement to foster democracy. The insights shed light on various types of measurement that an organization may want to employ, such as downward performance measures (i.e., to customers), upward performance measures (i.e., to bosses, boards, and funders), functional accountability measures (i.e., at the individual project level), and strategic accountability measures (i.e., for wider programmatic goals). The authors examine the potential to measure political objectives in a society devoted to promoting democratic institutions, women's rights, and equal access to services. The methodologies allow for both instrumental rationality (i.e., "bean counting") as well as a more systemic approach (i.e., the unbundling of information). The depth of perception of the authors allows the creative reader to gain insights into the subtlest facets of measurement, such as the tender loving care provided to people, animals, and the earth during times of need, an often unspoken value of private charities.

The volume is also unique in that the papers pertain both to the sector as a whole and to specific subsectors therein, such as religious congregations, arts organizations, and human service agencies. The ideas are conveyed through the disciplinary lenses of political science, economics, humanities, sociology, geography, and journalism. Some authors are extremely pessimistic and others quite optimistic about the potential outcomes of such an exercise. We purposefully cast a wide net to expand our collective horizons on the subject.

COMMON TERMINOLOGY

We learned quickly the importance of developing a common terminology. What we thought would be simple reference terms were actually points of departure. For example, the term "function" has distinct meanings for sociologists and economists. Hence, we begin by carefully defining our terms. Like many other social scientists in the human services subsector, we adopted a set of definitions developed by the United Way of America to differentiate inputs, outputs, and outcomes (Greenway, this volume, Chapter 13; Hatry, 1999). *Inputs* include resources dedicated to or consumed by the program (e.g., money, staff and volunteer time, facilities, equipment, supplies). *Outputs* are direct products of program activities, usually measured in terms of the volume of work accomplished (e.g., number of classes or counseling sessions, educational materials, participants served, performances). Outputs have little inherent value in themselves, but are expected to lead to a desired benefit and/or change for a target audience. *Outcomes*, on the other hand, are the benefits or changes (for individuals, populations, the earth, society) derived from the program, activity, inputs, and/or outputs (e.g., Are participants better off after receiving the service? Is the river cleaner as a result of reduced production by Company X upstream?). Outcomes may relate to behavior, skills, knowledge, attitudes, values, condition, status, or other attributes.

Impacts are inherently more difficult to measure because we must first understand the causal relationships between the measured inputs, outputs, and outcomes and the underlying phenomena leading to the observed results. Impact analysis helps us understand "why" a phenomenon occurred and apportion credit or blame for any change(s). Outcomes, in contrast, tell us "what" has occurred. In order to measure the impact of something, we are required to formulate a theory of behavior (e.g., a hypothesis) and a testable model (e.g., if A then B), to collect reliable data, and to execute formal analysis. One of the outcomes of this special volume on measurement is our conclusion that the nonprofit sector is many years away from being able to measure its impact on society. First, we must make strides toward better measurement of the sector's outputs and outcomes from which a cohesive theory of behavior might emerge.

ORGANIZATION OF THE VOLUME

The authored chapters are presented in four parts to reflect the major themes that emerged from the conference and follow-up discussions and research. Part II is devoted to exploring how we might think about measuring the contributions of nonprofits from a practical or operational perspective. Clifford Cobb (Chapter 2) presents a conceptual model that can be used to assess the degree to which economic and social indicators are value neutral (i.e., mathematically elegant or conforming to a predetermined methodology) or value explicit (i.e., crude estimates of relevant features of our experience). He argues that our society has opted to establish a system of measurement that allows us to deny warning signs of failure and perpetuates dysfunctional and unjust systems. The charge is to develop instrumental, quality measures of success and failure in society that point beyond themselves and truthfully communicate our cultural identity.

Melissa Stone and Susan Cutcher-Gershenfeld (Chapter 3) discuss how mission vagueness, the blurring of lines between for-profit and nonprofit organizations, and loose coupling between donors and beneficiaries compound the problems associated with assessing organizational effectiveness. Measurement is complicated by the fact that we have not reached consensus on causal models that clarify the links between means and ends. The authors present three conceptual models commonly used by academics to assess organizational effectiveness (i.e., natural systems model, goal model, and decision-process model), which further illuminate the lack of consensus on how to think about effectiveness, much less how to proceed with the empirical exercise. Stone and Cutcher-Gershenfeld present an array of examples on how nonprofit practitioners are making headway to measure effectiveness in Minnesota, Massachusetts, and elsewhere.

Kenneth Land (Chapter 4) embeds the exercise of measuring the impact of the nonprofit sector into the historical and contemporary literature on social indicators. He provides rich evidence of both the limitations of such measures and their potential to help illuminate the performance of nonprofit organizations. The paper gives specific meaning to and helpful examples of core terms of measurement. For example, Land differentiates between *objective indicators* that represent social facts independent of personal evaluations and *subjective indicators* that measure individuals' experiences and evaluations. He astutely notes that studies of objective and subjective well-being can inform each other, whereby the domains from the objective social indicators are used to define the objects for subjective ratings, and measures of subjective salience are used to develop weights and scales for objective indicators.

Part III examines the concept of measurement as it relates to the governance and advancement of democratic societies. In recent decades, scholars have revisited the role of associations and all sorts of voluntary organizations as essential ingredients of a democratic society. Another theme important to the study of civil society is the role of government and leadership. Colin Campbell (Chapter 5), studying the role of government and leadership in a civil society, focuses on neoliberalism and its impact on social welfare in Anglo-American states. He argues that the neoliberal view that the role of the state should be minimal in a laissez-faire economy has led to a crisis in leadership and a decline of the welfare state. With the growth of inflation and declining economies during the 1970s, citizens in Australia, New Zealand, Great Britain, Canada, and the United States became convinced that "interventionalist" government could not solve social problems. For Campbell, the measure becomes the ability of leaders and legislatures to define the appropriate role of the state. Also, the measure of public leaders "holding the microphone in public discourse" will determine the future of the not-for-profit sector which could encounter impossible burdens in a minimalist state. He argues that the role of the independent sector rests "not in a mad dash to catch bodies as they fall through safety nets, but rather to contribute to maintaining a vibrant civil society."

One of the most important roles of nonprofit organizations is to advocate causes in the public interest. It is this role that is most identified with the contribution of nonprofit organizations to democracy. John McCarthy and Jim Castelli (Chapter 6) argue that measuring policy advocacy of nonprofit organizations is the major goal of research, but much needs to be done before that goal is achieved. Policy advocacy must be measured across all nonprofit organizations, not simply the small group of organizations that are called advocacy organizations. Furthermore, advocacy efforts need to be compared with those of business, government, and political organizations in order to measure the particular contributions of nonprofit organizations to policy advocacy. The authors outline a broad research agenda for defining advocacy, identifying direct and indirect advocacy activities, and studying both institutions and individuals.

From the role of public leadership, Julian Wolpert (Chapter 7) addresses the question of measuring the impact of various types of nonprofit organizations. He takes a broad approach by focusing on distributional impacts, not just income redistribution. His emphasis is on the ability to measure the "incidence of benefit," that is, who benefits from different types of nonprofit organizations and how. Since the Depression, the government, rather than not-for-profit organizations, has had the primary role in income redistribution and the provision of safety nets for the poor. Nonprofit organizations play a supplementary role in this responsibility and, at times, are partners with government in providing services. In the scant research available on the beneficiaries of nonprofit organizations, there seemed to be little redistribution.

While the measurement of inputs of nonprofit organizations has improved over the last decade, available data on outputs, outcomes, and impact are very primitive or nonexistent. Wolpert argues that measuring outcomes will become even more important in an era of government devolution and cutbacks in funding. He also notes the importance of trying to measure the "distinctive and independent agenda" of nonprofit organizations in their distributory role that is based on enrichment of civic life, ensuring quality and variety in community services, and responding ethically to community needs.

In the last chapter of this section, David Mathews (Chapter 8) wonders whether it is possible to "regenerate public life." Mathews presents a paradigm of what public life looks like in order to perhaps strengthen it. He asserts that no one knows if public life can be renewed, but possibly his set of assumptions built on learnings might eventually be "tested by experience." His research reveals, for example, that strong communities have a "civil infrastructure" or a group of networks, associations, and organizations that provide channels of communication and a form of public space for deliberation among citizens. Practices that become habits include the ability of citizens to name problems, to make decisions together through public discussion about how to act on these problems, to engage in public action, and to evaluate or judge the results of the public action. Communities with successful public lives have different ways of using power, and these are inclusive and lateral, not vertical. Ultimately, a community makes decisions through public deliberation, by taking public action, and by assuming responsibility as citizens in judging results.

Part IV examines the concept of measurement from the vantage of subsectors and special populations. While citing the importance of history, sociology, political science, and economics to women's studies, Kathleen McCarthy (Chapter 9) argues that a multidisciplinary approach is needed to measure women's philanthropy and its impact on society. Research on women has shown the importance of literacy, religion, and independent sources of income upon the development of women and the development of societies in which they lived or live. While she clearly finds intrinsic value in qualitative research, she argues that an important first step for quantitative measures is to collect statistical data by gendered categories in studies of nonprofit organizations and in women's giving. The impact of various special populations is difficult to measure unless statistical systems identify organizations, such as women's organizations, or women separately in statistical systems of individuals.

James Connell and Adena Klem (Chapter 10) argue that traditional approaches to evaluation in education reform efforts have done little to provide the body of evidence necessary to assess the effectiveness, or lack thereof, of education reform to either public or private donors. They present a plan built on the theory of change, a method for collecting data to evaluate whether the implementation of steps to accomplish change is working, and a longer term plan to document the impact of an educational program over time on the lives of children. Measuring outcomes and impact must be comprehensive, but uniquely tailored to each specific change situation and within the confines of existing institutions.

Bradford Gray (Chapter 11) discusses the large sector of health care which is going through rapid change both in ownership characteristics (i.e., public, nonprofit, and for-profit) and in types of institutions (e.g., nonprofit and for-profit health maintenance organizations and home health agencies). He argues that although many traditional measures are useful, such as the number of patients served or number of beds, they do not measure community benefit which might provide the best approach to distinguish between nonprofit, for-profit, and public hospitals and their individual contributions to community. Gray offers a broad definition of the items that might be included in a definition of community benefit. Unfortunately, data covering community benefit items are not widely collected, but Gray suggests that if such data were collected, it could help communities and local governments make better informed decisions when organizations consider converting to for-profit status.

Margaret Jane Wyszomirski (Chapter 12) takes on the challenging task of evaluating what might need to be done to measure the impact of the arts on society. She acknowledges that impact is currently measured in audience surveys, the number of arts agencies, level of expenditures, etc. To better measure the impact of the arts requires both better data collection and the development of indexes to measure economic impact, organizational health, educational impact, and community effect in the art world. Wyszomirski argues that the challenges of such measures are formidable, but the approach might help to overcome the "virtual invisibility" of the impact of the arts on society.

Martha Taylor Greenway (Chapter 13) surveys the efforts of human service organizations among United Way supported agencies to measure program outcomes. On the basis that the fundamental purpose of the human services sector "is to improve the condition of the people," she asserts that measuring the contribution of any particular organization is "tricky" in light of the variety of experiences, organizations, opportunities, and people that affect human lives. However, she also asserts that organizations that attempt the process of assessment have realized other benefits, such as improved performance, better motivated staff, and increased ability to recruit volunteers. She argues that there is no real need to define success, outcomes, and impact among agencies. Rather, she sees a need for organizations, primarily working in isolation, to join together to establish some comparative measures of outcomes among similar programs for the purpose of improvement more so than accountability or sanction. She concludes that even though some progress is being made to develop outcome indicators in individual agencies, much needs to be done to bridge "the achievements of individual programs with the outcomes that we theorize are required for community change."

In the final chapter of this section, Robert Wuthnow (Chapter 14) explores how to document the role of religious institutions in society. While recognizing that the *Giving and Volunteering* series inaugurated by Independent Sector is quite new and not adequately analyzed, he suggests that religious institutions are engaging in a wide range of activities not regularly charted in existing surveys or data series. Groups engaging in these activities include interfaith coalitions, community development partnerships bringing nonprofit and government organizations together, and various volunteer networks. Wuthnow recommends in-depth research at the community level in order to understand the existing complexity of the mix of existing organizations, affiliations, and partnerships. Only by understanding these complex mixes can aggregate data be created based upon a dense base of community data.

THE CHALLENGES AND OPPORTUNITIES OF MEASURING

The final section reminds us of why it is important to develop a research agenda and precise empirical tools to measure the impact of the nonprofit sector. Paul DiMaggio and Burton Weisbrod present ideas on how to approach the exercise, some pitfalls to avoid, and the potential rewards.

Paul DiMaggio (Chapter 15) is cautious about the downside of instrumental rationality, the "sacred cow" of modern culture, which may be ill-suited to measuring the impact of the sector in which organizational goals are heterogeneous. Nonetheless, he finds value in the ritual of trying to calculate the impact of nonprofit subsectors because of its power "to bring people together, to define identities, and to move people to seek change . . . [through] a kind of religiously infused social movement." Specifically, the exercise may help the sector clarify its objectives, focus the attention of managers and trustees on their organizations' missions, provide a nonthreatening context in which different parts of the sector coalesce and generate new potentially valuable research.

Burton Weisbrod (Chapter 16) provides an insightful overview of the need for carefully developed evaluations of the nonprofit sector as a whole, of obstacles in the process, and of proposed approaches. The focus of his inquiry is the degree to which the expansion of the nonprofit sector over the past three decades is economically efficient and desirable. Weisbrod advises caution when attempting to measure sectoral outputs and outcomes. The danger, he argues, stems from the fact that nonprofit organizations are more likely than for-profit firms to provide outputs that are difficult to value and hence measure. A flawed attempt at measurement would yield a systematic underestimation of nonprofits' social contributions.

Despite the difficulties, Weisbrod argues that the exercise is critical for a number of reasons. First, the nonprofit sector has not been granted the justification (or status) held by privately owned, for-profit enterprises throughout American history. Therefore, when nonprofits clash with private firms, the nonprofit organization "is on the defensive to demonstrate its social value." Solid evidence that nonprofits make a difference and that they perform economically viable functions not afforded by private firms or government would clarify the unique role of nonprofits in society. A second rationale stems from the increased blurring of lines between for-profit and nonprofit activities, which begs the question of whether nonprofits are acting more like for-profit firms and, thus, are forfeiting their claims to special status and privilege. Solid evidence on the contributions, successes, and uniqueness of the nonprofit sector could help inform the ongoing debate about the organization of society into the three distinct sectors of government, business, and nonprofits.

CONCLUSIONS AND NEXT STEPS

The authors of this volume understand that measuring the impact of the nonprofit sector on society poses formidable challenges. The danger is that what can be quantified may not be the most valuable contributions of the sector. Furthermore, a focus on short-term, quantifiable outputs may derail the long-term goals of an organization. Issues of impact demand assessment over long periods of time. For example, lowering poverty levels in low-income communities may take multiple strategies from a host of diverse nonprofit organizations, the business community, and government. It will involve job skills, education, capital investment, citizen empowerment, and participation. While some outputs can be measured in the shorter term, reducing poverty and re-building healthy communities is a longer term investment.

If we want to know what works and what the components of successful efforts are, we need to begin to explore measures on several fronts, including program outcomes at the organizational level and community studies.

Program Outcomes. Efforts need to be made to systematically assess progress in measuring program outcomes at the organization level. An evaluation of accumulated learning from several organizations and foundations would be a first step in assessing the progress, pitfalls, and potential replicability of promising work in this area.

Community Studies. Data need to be collected at the community level based upon sets of benchmarks and indicators that communities believe they want to achieve. While many communities collect data, very few, if any, studies collect data from the perspective of institutional contributions across all sectors in order to determine the unique and cumulative contributions of various types of organizations. Furthermore, these studies need to include the types, level, and density of citizen participation in setting and achieving community goals.

In sum, the contribrutors to this volume agree that the effort to measure the impact of the nonprofit sector is valuable even if, in a scientific sense, it is doomed and somewhat risky because of the current inadequacy of social science methodology to provide tools designed to measure those qualities of the sector that add value to society. It is abundantly clear that the real questions that need to be addressed in long-term studies are for the most part not addressed in current research. We have no guiding theories from which to base assessments of the sector's performance and/or effectiveness. Further, experimentation in the design of sophisticated quantitative and qualitative methodological tools to measure performance is encouraged. Ideas about the contributions of the not-for-profit sector are abundant, but data required to address the power of these ideas are scant.

Meanwhile, practitioners in the field are busy collecting measures to tell their unique stories. In the end, we believe that the potential exists for impact analysis to enhance the reflectiveness of the nonprofit sector, to encourage a dialogue between researchers and practitioners, and to create more sophisticated ways to think about the sector and its goals. As Professor DiMaggio reminds us, "assessing the sector's impact is, strictly speaking, impossible. But then alchemists made significant contributions to modern chemistry, even though they never succeeded in turning lead into gold."

REFERENCES

Dionne, E. J., Jr. (Ed.). (1998). *Community works: The revival of civil society in America.* Washington, DC: Brookings Institution Press.

Edwards, M., & Hulme, D. (Eds.). (1996). *Beyond the magic bullet: NGO performance and accountability in the post-cold war world.* West Hartford, CT: Kumarian Press.

Egan, A. H., Cross, A., & Mayer, R. (1999). *Elements for successful inter-sectoral and cross-sectoral strategic collaboration in an era of change, devolution, and institutional rationalization: Findings from applied research and consultation in independent sector.* Working Papers. Washington, DC: Independent Sector.

Ehrenberg, J. (1999). *Civil society: The critical history of an idea.* New York: New York University Press.

Fullinwider, R. K. (Ed.). (1999). *Civil society, democracy, and civic renewal.* Lanhan, MD: Roman and Littlefield Publishers, Inc.

Hatry, H. P. (1999). *Performance measurement: Getting results.* Washington, DC: The Urban Institute Press.

Henderson, H., Lickerman, J., & Flynn, P. (Eds.). (2000). *Calvert-Henderson quality of life indicators: A new tool for assessing national trends.* Bethesda, MD: The Calvert Group, Ltd.

Hodgkinson, V. A. & Weitzman, M. (1996). *Nonprofit almanac 1996–1997.* San Francisco: Jossey-Bass.

Hodgkinson, V. A., & Weitzman, M. (1998). Update and revisions to the *Nonprofit Almanac.* Retrieved from the World Wide Web: http://www.independentsector.org.

O'Connell, B. (1999). *Civil society: The underpinnings of American democracy.* Hanover, NH: University Press of New England.

Salamon, L. M., & Anheier, H. K. (1996). *The emerging nonprofit sector.* Manchester, UK: University Press.

Skocpol, T., & Fiorina, M. P. (Eds.). (1999). *Civic engagement in American democracy.* Washington, DC: Brookings Institution Press and the Russell Sage Foundation.

Weisbrod, B. (1997). The future of the nonprofit sector: Its entwining with private enterprise and government. *Journal of Policy Analysis and Management, 16*(4), 541–555.

World Bank. (1998). *Assessing aid: What works, what doesn't, and why.* A World Bank Policy Research Report. New York: Oxford University Press for the World Bank.

Part **II**

Concerns of Measurement and Evaluation

Part II contains three chapters that address some of the methodological issues that arise when measuring the outcomes, impacts, performance, and successes of nonprofits. We purposely begin with concrete examples of measurement to familiarize the reader with the history of social and economic measurement, place the reader's interests in the context of existing models and methods, and provide the scope of measurement addressed in the volume.

Cobb (Chapter 2) describes economic and social indicators as "second-order pain receptors" that industrial societies established to provide condensed, metaphorical information about their condition or larger reality. In developing a model to conceptualize the degree to which indicators are value neutral (i.e., mathematically elegant or conforming to a predetermined methodology) or value explicit (i.e., crude estimations of relevant features of our experience), Cobb provides insights on developing instrumental, quality measures of success and failure of society. He concludes that our society has opted to establish a system of measurement that allows us to deny warning signs of failure and to perpetuate dysfunctional and unjust systems.

Cobb presents a model of five concentric circles representing a society's ability to move and change. In the simplest model (circle one) are the sterile intellectuals who deny the validity of indicators all together by banishing "all talk of values, purposes, and goals" for the sake of positive rather than normative science. In the second circle are "economists with a penchant for policymaking" who are not willing to admit that they are compromising positivist principles for the numbers they need to set policy. As a result, this group brings "implicit value judgment in through the back door" when denying that certain statistics, such as the gross domestic product, are value laden. The alternative, "to admit that values underlie economic policy," is too embarrassing.

After assigning Republicans to circle two, Cobb argues that Democrats dominate circle three by bringing "feminine" concerns to the table through "hard numbers" (e.g., income distribution, unemployment, home ownership, life expectancy, infant mortality, literacy, and disposable income). Realizing that "masculine" indicators tend to be more credible, New Democrats like former President Clinton "have shifted indicators of compassion to indicators of power and control." By the fourth circle, the underlying values are made explicit and there is less reliance on hard numbers in favor of more subjective, multidimensional data that challenge the status quo. Here the larger picture of our economic, social, and environmental condition begins to emerge at the expense of mathematically elegant methodologies.

The author leaves open the possibility that researchers may eventually reach a fifth circle that will change the way we think about indicators and make the information more broadly accessible. This circle of paradise might treat indicators as metaphors, whereby "rather than pretending to see our condition directly, we might affirm that we are like the figure in Plato's cave, looking at the shadows on the back wall." Indicators then become "numbers that point beyond themselves" and truthfully communicate our cultural identity.

Stone and Cutcher-Gershenfeld (Chapter 3) further enhance our understanding of the "Challenges of Measuring Performance in Nonprofit Organizations," be it implicit or explicit performance. They approach the topic from three viewpoints—theoretical (e.g., organizational effectiveness), empirical (e.g., case studies), and practical (e.g., shifts in power relationships). They argue that the problems associated with assessing organizational effectiveness are compounded by blurring lines that divide for-profit and nonprofit organizations, mission vagueness, and loose coupling between donors and beneficiaries.

From a theoretical perspective, measurement is complicated because multiple definitions are used in the sector and contrasting conceptual frameworks guide different disciplines. In addition, we lack clarity on the link between means and ends (i.e., no causal model) and any bottom-line indicators to measure mission effectiveness. Stone and Cutcher-Gershenfeld present three conceptual models commonly used by academics to assess organizational effectiveness: a natural systems model, a goal model, and a decision-process model. The analysis illuminates the lack of consensus on how to think about effectiveness, much less how to proceed with the exercise.

The chapter closes with valuable insights on best practices and lessons learned from nonprofit practitioners in Minnesota's Human Services Department, the state of Massachusetts, the Hymans and Shawmut Foundations, United Way of America, Communities for People, and Vinfen Corporation. All of these organizations are faced with both internal and external pressure to develop performance measures and recognize that "a move toward performance-based measurement changes the nature of the relationship between funder and grantee." Moreover, the process used to develop empirical measures is critical to their successful implementation.

Land (Chapter 4) embeds the exercise of measuring the impact of the independent sector into the historical and contemporary literature on social indicators. He provides rich evidence of both the limitations of such measures and their potential to help illuminate the performance of nonprofits. Land helps the reader differentiate between social indicators that represent social facts independently of personal evaluations (i.e., objective indicators) from indicators that measure individuals' experiences and evaluations of social circumstances (i.e., subjective indicators). The author astutely notes that studies of objective and subjective well being can inform each other when domains from the objective social indicators are used to define the objects for subjective ratings, and measures of subjective salience are used to develop weights and scales for objective indicators.

The role of and impetus for social reporting has changed considerably since the 1960s. At present, social reporting places quality of life issues on the political agenda, supplies material to the media and public debates, and indirectly affects the political apparatus. The social indicators movement is supplementing the retrospective model-of-old to a prospective model of anticipation or trends. The major research tasks associated with social reporting under the current "model of enlightenment are to monitor or describe social trends, explain these trends, identify relevant relationships between different developments, and investigate the consequences of those and likely future developments in time series of indicators."

Building upon the work of Wolpert (Chapter 7), Land defines major categories of organizations that comprise the nonprofit sector (e.g., service, philanthropy, charity, and fellowship) and describes various approaches and considerations to enable researchers to assess the impact of these organizations on society. Using a slightly different lexicon than that of Greenway (Chapter 13), Land presents a model that differentiates between endogenous output and outcome descriptive indicators and the side-order effects that emerge during the production and delivery of outputs and outcomes. This chapter gives helpful examples of and specific meaning to core terms of measurement.

Chapter **2**

Measuring Failure
to Find Success

CLIFFORD W. COBB

Organizations, from the smallest clubs to federal agencies, often fail to accomplish their mission. This failure may occasion a sense of shame, but it should not, because it implies that the institution aimed high. As Robert Browning said: "Ah, but a man's reach should exceed his grasp. Or what's a heaven for?" Failure can help us grow wiser if we learn from it. Rather than causing shame, falling short of goals should promote reflection and renewal. An agency that fails to help people find jobs might redefine success by the number of clients it advises. A church that fails to offer its members a rewarding spiritual experience might claim success based on the growth of its budget. In this manner, organizations frequently engage in what sociologists call "displacement of goals" in order to deny failure.

Consider the disastrous condition of the nation's education system. National commissions have studied it repeatedly throughout this century, but despite all of the efficiency-minded reforms and increased funding, millions of children are ill served by it. High dropout rates reflect the wholesale abandonment of segments of the population. Functional illiteracy, even among high school and college graduates, remains appallingly high: only 10 percent of high school graduates and half of all college graduates can understand a newspaper editorial, read a bus schedule, or calculate a tip in a restaurant (National Center for Education Statistics, 1990, Table 334).

CLIFFORD W. COBB • Senior Fellow, Redefining Progress, Sacramento, California 95816.

Measuring the Impact of the Nonprofit Sector, edited by Patrice Flynn and Virginia A. Hodgkinson, New York, Kluwer Academic/Plenum Publishers, 2002.

The basic problem of the education system is not that it fails, but paradoxically that schools and students are not allowed to fail. Teenagers are allowed to graduate from high school without the basic skills necessary to function as adults. Others who are falling behind are pressured out of school to avoid the stigma of their failure. By making failure a taboo, which makes it unspeakable, school managers have clogged the information channels that would allow society to know what it needs to change. Educational failure may, in fact, stem more from limited job opportunities that sap motivation than from badly run schools. As long as school managers treat failure as an unspeakable subject, however, the need for systemic change will go unheeded.

Another major fiasco that resulted from an unwillingness to recognize failure was the escalation of the Vietnam War. Month after month, the generals claimed that victory was in sight. From the field level on up, descriptions of success were either inflated or fabricated, while examples of failure were not passed on. Secretary of Defense Robert McNamara and his "whiz kids" in the Pentagon were prisoners of misleading information. So instead of recognizing that the strategy of military escalation was a failure and that major political reform in South Vietnam was essential, McNamara ordered more of the same. He presided over a debacle because he sat at the top of a giant organization that did not allow him to know the true consequences of his actions.

Denial of failure is neither partisan nor ideologically one sided. Conservatives cannot admit that unfettered property rights might cause unnecessary pain, and liberals are loath to recognize the harm caused by well-intentioned social programs. The fear of admitting failure permeates society, leading to chronic dysfunction and systemic injustice. Optimism is given more respect than the wisdom of accepting limits, so deception and denial are rewarded. Yet the world cannot afford those misplaced values. More than a million people died in Vietnam. The costs of widespread illiteracy have not been reckoned.

BETTER PAIN RECEPTORS

Like pain in the body, widespread suffering in a society should be viewed as a warning sign. Just as athletes court danger by masking pain with analgesics, covering up failure in social systems creates a deceptive atmosphere and false optimism. Organizations and entire societies need to develop better pain receptors so they can identify mistakes quickly and act to correct them.

A society has no organic pain receptors of the sort found in the body. For most of human history, direct observation provided people enough information about the condition of those around them. In a complex, urban society, however, direct observation is not possible. Diseases and injuries are cared for away from public view. Housing segregation makes poverty invisible. Social injustice is mediated through impersonal markets and legal systems. Anecdotal information is not adequate to discern social misery on the scale of modern life.

During the past century, industrial societies have established second-order pain receptors: economic and social indicators to provide information about the condition of society in condensed form. Indicators might be thought of as numbers used as metaphors or metonyms. That is to say, indicators are statistics that are collected or used with a purpose and imbued with meaning. At their worst, the advocates of economic and social indicators have shared in the numbers fetishism that marks our age. At their best, however, those who have sought to clarify social conditions with indicators have recognized that significance lies not in the numbers themselves, but in the larger reality to which they point.

In the seventeenth century, statistics were gathered that roughly indicated the power of the state. Many of the statistics still used by modern states serve the same purpose. In the nineteenth century, social workers began compiling information on the spending patterns, nutrition, and health of working-class households (Lamale, 1958). Those statistics not only were instrumental in gaining support for laws to help the poor, but also were metaphors for society becoming aware of its interrelatedness.

Although indicators can be used to identify social pain, they can also be designed to deny failure. For example, some economists have recommended reporting the employment rate in place of the unemployment rate. "Let's brag about our national success at creating jobs," they say, "instead of bemoaning the fact that some people are not working." Indicators can thus be used as narcotics, dulling the senses and creating a false sense of euphoria.

In a similar vein, I was told in 1995 by a staff member of the European Commission that the unemployment rate in Europe is not such a large problem because Europeans are now using a "new definition" of work. The new definition enables officials to deny the failure of the economic system to provide adequate job opportunities. If only reality could be so easily manipulated. One of the best indicators that unemployment remains a serious problem in Europe is the increasing strength of fascist parties across the continent. Those who would use indicators to mask pain are suggesting that statisticians should devise measures of well-being that make us feel good about ourselves, when what is clearly needed are indicators that identify where we are failing.

DESCENT INTO THE UNDERWORLD OF INDICATORS

Many people would agree that governments and other groups need better indicators of where they stand and where they are going. But the development of socially useful indicators is not as simple and straightforward as it might at first seem. It is seldom possible to measure directly what one wants to know. In addition, the design of an indicator may reveal more about the observer than the observed.

To explore the world of indicators, I have chosen to use an adaptation of Dante's tour of hell, which may say more about me than about indicators. Unlike Dante, we will begin with the lowest and coldest point in hell. In contrast to the biblical image of hell as a fiery lake, Dante's allegory is more psychologically accurate. He understood its lowest circle to be the coldest because it represented the point at which all human feeling was frozen.

First Circle

In the lowest circle of the inferno, we might find those who would deny the validity of indicators altogether. These poor souls have given up trying to make any value judgments because they have been intellectually frozen. In this century, social scientists and philosophers have banished all talk of values, purposes, and goals. They speak only of what is, never of what ought to be. Most of what passes for profound thought in universities is predicated on the idea that values are purely subjective, arbitrary, and individual. From this perspective, judgment of value is a private activity, and no direction for society can be deemed better than any other in the public sphere. This positivist orientation, which splits off purposes from facts, has made universities sterile learning environments and has damaged modern societies.

The idea that facts and values have to be kept in separate compartments has also hobbled efforts to devise better indicators of social and economic progress. If someone proposes a measure of social progress that includes components dealing with literacy or ecological diversity, intellectuals jump on it as a fraud. They demand: "How do you know it is better to live in a literate society or one with diversity of life forms?" The only answers the positivist will accept are market data (showing how consumers reveal their values by spending money) and poll data (showing how residents reveal values by answering questions). Reference to the implicit values in a culture, as revealed in art or literature, is declared out of bounds.

By avoiding all concerns with values, the positivist is insulated from the suffering that is everywhere visible. Without any measure of what is better or worse, the inhabitants of this circle of hell never have to face failure. But, as Dante understood, this detached observation of other people and separation from them is the worst form of suffering.

Second Circle

In the second circle are economists with a penchant for policy making. They need numbers to set policy. As policies are inevitably value laden, so are the numbers that guide them. Economists are willing to compromise their positivist principles for practical purposes, but they will not admit they are doing so. The prime example is the process by which economists defend the use of the gross domestic product (GDP) as a measure of national economic health. In the context of pure theory, economists will claim that GDP is a value-free measure of total market-based production each year and that it does not measure well-being. But, in the next breath, if the discussion shifts to policy, the same economist will treat growth of GDP as a norm or standard because an increase in total output supposedly makes everyone better off. Bringing this implicit value judgment in through the back door is akin to what Freud called "the return of the repressed." In practice, society cannot do without some indicators that evaluate its condition, so the people in the second circle are responsible for sneaking some in.

The doublespeak to which economists resort when speaking of GDP is common when people have to deceive themselves in order to accomplish something. Unfortunately, doublespeak leads to confusion of both listeners and speakers. The problem could easily be solved by stating honestly what values underlie economic policy. But that would be embarrassing because it would contradict positivist principles and because it would lay bare the real motives of national policy.

As in the seventeenth century, the power of the nation-state, not the health and well-being of citizens, is the moral principle behind most national indicators. GDP is a fairly good measure of national power. So are other measures that are frequently cited. For example, we hear a lot about productivity and the balance of trade when the competitive strength of the nation is uncertain. One might imagine that the constant drumbeat about the decline of private saving is based on concern about whether citizens will have enough money for retirement. In fact, this issue concerns economists primarily because a decline in domestic saving means the nation is more dependent on foreign borrowing and thus more vulnerable. The unwritten rule of national indicators seems to be that those indicators dealing directly or indirectly with national power will be allowed to bypass the guardians of intellectual propriety.

Third Circle

In the third circle from the bottom are those who speak publicly about the standard indicators of national life that are not related to power but that are still based on "hard numbers" because they can be readily measured. Figures for income distribution, unemployment, home ownership, life expectancy, infant mortality, literacy, and disposable income fit into this category. These simple measures of social well-being are ones traditionally used by Democrats running for office. In doing so, they come under attack from the Republicans, who dominate the second circle.

As Mihalec (1984) put it in an analysis of the 1984 presidential race, the Democratic Party is viewed as the "female" of the two major parties because of its "feminine ideology" of "compassion, tolerance, and social and economic equality." The feminine image handicaps Democratic candidates in presidential elections. "Voters consider the presidency, unlike the Congress, to be a masculine responsibility. This is why the Republicans with their more masculine (i.e., Darwinian, production-oriented, peace-through-strength) ideology always have a reasonable shot at the Oval Office, no matter how small a minority of the electorate they constitute." The "New Democrats," such as Bill Clinton, have taken that message to heart. They have shifted from indicators of compassion to indicators of power and control.

The point here is not simply that indicators play a role in partisan politics. What is most interesting about political culture in the United States is the extent to which we implicitly endow indicators with a gender and give more credibility to those that have a traditionally masculine image. It is also of note that the more masculine indicators (in the second circle) are often regarded as value-free because their implicit values are simply taken for granted.

Fourth Circle

As we move to the fourth circle from the bottom, the thaw becomes noticeable and the values explicit. Most indicators of well-being found at this level can no longer claim to be based on hard numbers or, if they are, the method of assigning values is more subjective. Rather than being tied to the positivist principles of neutrality and objectivity, the inhabitants of this circle are concerned primarily with efforts to bring suffering into awareness. Whereas the lowest circle of hell is filled with intellectuals who are obsessed with intrinsically interesting models that pose no threat to the status quo, the fourth circle is dominated by activists who use indicators to call attention to social problems. In contrast to those who rely on the single-dimension indicators of the third circle, this circle promotes experimentation with multidimensional indicators.

The desire to generate indicators that would aid in social transformation is not new. In earlier decades, a variety of efforts were made to introduce social indicators and alternative economic indicators into common use. I mentioned earlier the nineteenth-century programs to measure the living conditions of the working class. The construction in 1963 by Orshansky of the "poverty line," a standardized measure of income poverty, was an extension of that tradition (Harrington, 1984, pp. 69–70). During that decade, the poverty of other countries also gained attention, and some activists questioned whether the Western model of development was ideal. For example, the Overseas Development Council published a Physical Quality of Life Index, or PQLI, that combined literacy, infant mortality, and life expectancy at age one into an index number for each country (Morris, 1979). PQLI undermined the confidence many had placed in standard economic measures. For example, it showed that Sri Lankans were better off than Iranians, even though gross national product per capita showed Iranians to be several times richer.

In the United States, the question of larger purposes of economic development emerged on the national scene. In his State of the Union address in 1965, President Lyndon Johnson set the tone: "The Great Society asks not only how much, but how good; not only how to create wealth, but how to use it; not only how fast we are going, but where we are headed" (cited in Gross, 1966). Once affluence could be taken for granted, two issues had arisen: "What is affluence for?" and "Can social opportunity be made available for all Americans?" Efforts were then made to collect the information that would enable them to be answered.

In the 1970s, work continued on those themes. A series of three volumes, *Social Indicators I, II, and III* (U.S. Office of Management and Budget, 1973, 1976; U.S. Bureau of the Census, 1981), was published by the federal government. Each volume brought together a number of data series relating to social conditions. The data sets were ordered into categories, but because of political sensitivities, there was no attempt to offer theories about how they were related to well-being. Nevertheless, the series offers the most comprehensive set of social measures published to date.

During the 1970s, growth of the environmental movement introduced a new set of indicators. It was no longer enough to consider the condition of human societies. New measures were required to reflect the health of the environmental as well. The idea that economic growth might be limited by physical constraints, such as climate change or soil loss, was taken seriously for the first time in decades. *The Limits to Growth* (Meadows, Meadows, Randers, & Behrens, 1972), a computer model showing the interactions of population, resources, pollution, and environmental limits, was attacked by economists for failing to consider the capacity of the price system to avoid disaster by shifting from scarce resources to other, more plentiful ones. Although *Limits* was simplistic in that respect, economists' criticisms should not be regarded as conclusive: the price system is a poor indicator of long-range threats, and it does not reveal scarcity of common assets such as the atmosphere.

A few economists took some halting steps toward incorporating short-term environmental factors into national income accounts. At a 1971 conference entitled "Research on Income and Wealth," many economists agreed "that additional information was required on nonmarket activity," including "environmental costs and benefits" (Ruggles, 1983, p. 32). The U.S. Bureau of Economic Analysis (1982) did some research along those lines in the 1970s, but was forced to cut back because of budget constraints. Zolotas (1981) published a revised system of national accounts for the United States that included air and water pollution costs. The World Resources Institute estimated that when resource depletion and soil erosion were factored into Indonesia's national accounts, the adjusted growth rate of the economy was only half what the official figures showed (Repetto, Beer, Magrath, Rossini, & Wells, 1989).

Outside the domain of economic analysis, several indicators emerged in the 1980s that focused on nonmonetary aspects of development. The Human Development Index combined the elements of PQLI and GDP into a composite measure (United Nations Development Program, 1993, pp. 133–135). Lutz of the University of Maine amalgamated PQLI with the Human Rights Index developed by *The Economist* and called it the Authentic Socio-Economic Development Index (Ekins & Max-Neef, 1992, pp. 234–239). Various other composite indicators have been devised in recent years. Miringoff (1995) produced an Index of Social Health, combining elements such as illiteracy, suicides, teen pregnancy, poverty among the elderly, the real wage rate, and unemployment. This index shows the United States in decline during the 1980s and falling behind Western Europe. The National Center for Economic Alternatives developed the Index of Environmental Trends that also shows the United States faring worse than Europe (Alperovitz, Howard, Scharf, & Williamson, 1995). Analysts at Statistics Canada, using a model developed at the Center for Health Economics and Policy Analysis at McMaster University (Hamilton, Ontario), have formulated a provisional health status index (Health-Adjusted Life Expectancy) that combines life expectancy with eight health attributes (Wolfson, 1996).

Each of the preceding indicators is an array of variables united by an arbitrary weighting system. If sufficient commonality exists among the elements (if all are related to health, for example), this method is useful. If one wishes to combine economic, social, and environmental components into a comprehensive index, however, a common unit of measure is required. The standard way to combine diverse factors is to use monetary valuation as the measuring rod. This has the advantage of allowing unity of diverse elements, but it has the drawback of forcing all values into a procrustean bed framed by economic theory.

When we set out two years ago at Redefining Progress to devise a comprehensive measure called the Genuine Progress Indicator, or GPI, we chose to calculate it in monetary terms (Cobb, Halstead, & Rowe, 1995). Our measure is based in part on the Index of Sustainable Economic Welfare (ISEW), which was calculated in dollars (Daly & Cobb, 1992). Like ISEW, GPI is denominated in money terms so it can be compared directly with GDP, the leading (and mis-leading) measure of the economic health of a nation. GPI redefines the economy by including nonmarket elements that add to or detract from social well being. It encompasses personal consumption, income distribution, the value of house-work and volunteerism, changes in capital investment, pollution, resource deple-tion, crime, leisure, family breakdown, and several other factors. In the 1950s and 1960s, GPI rose almost as rapidly as GDP, but it declined during the 1970s, 1980s, and 1990s.

From the perspective of the guardians of objectivity in circles one through three, the basic problem with all of the indicators in circle four is their subjec-tivity and value-oriented character. All of these measures have abandoned the pretense of being value neutral. They ask readers to reflect on their own values and judge whether the proposed indicator measures problems that concern them. These indicators highlight problems that the guardians of objectivity ignore. The numbers do not simply describe what is; they reflect a set of values about what should be.

The lack of objectivity is scorned by those in the lower circles. Those who have worked on value-oriented indicators are aware that the roughness and arbitrariness of these measures make others uneasy. As Desai (1994), the pri-mary architect of the Human Development Index, has said, "Anything worth doing is worth doing crudely." That sentiment is echoed by Daly who has done pioneering work in environmental economics. He wryly suggests, "It is more important to be generally right than precisely wrong" (Daly & Cobb, 1992). Both are proposing that we should be more concerned that indicators and mod-els capture the relevant features of our experience than that they be mathemati-cally elegant or conform to a predetermined methodology.

Inexactness and crudeness should not, however, be used as an excuse for sloppy thinking in the development of indicators. A good indicator can clarify conceptual relationships even if precision is not possible. It can enable citizens to better understand what trade-offs are involved in choosing one policy rather than another. In order to serve that purpose, designers of indicators should try to provide sufficient information to allow users to judge both the quality of the data and the arbitrariness of the weighting schemes by which various factors are incorporated.

Fifth Circle

Eventually, a door into a fifth circle may open that will entirely change the way experts think of indicators and shift them into an arena that is more broadly accessible. Perhaps, however, that next level is not in hell but in paradise. In other words, reaching the new level may depend on a harmony of understanding and of interests that will never occur in human society as we know it.

Perhaps the passageway to the fifth circle lies in becoming more comfortable with the idea of indicators as metaphors. Rather than pretending to see our condition directly, we might affirm that we are like the figure in Plato's cave, looking at the shadows on the back wall. Human societies invariably use stories and images to talk about the cultural characteristics that we most care about. The use of quantitative indicators is our way of telling a story that communicates truths beyond direct experience, although numbers lack the same connotative power of words. Still, indicators—numbers that point beyond themselves—remain some of the foremost symbols of our cultural identity.

CONCLUSION: FORMULATING A RESEARCH STRATEGY

I began by talking about failure and what it has to teach those who will listen. I then suggested that indicators offer a way to measure success and failure and thus to guide policy. The promise of indicators is limited, however, by the fact that what a society most values is beyond measure. Indicators are metonyms or metaphors of larger issues that cannot be grasped whole. The value of indicators is thus both instrumental and expressive.

A number of organizations and agencies have begun to construct indices to measure trends in society or the natural environment. If that work is to bear fruit, it will help if those institutions go beyond their immediate concerns and ask larger questions about the purposes of indicators and how they function in a modern society. A research strategy should include not only the development of particular indicators, but also a component that will enable all work on indicators to become more sophisticated.

One important research need on which Redefining Progress has recently begun to focus is the history of indicators. Gaining clarity about the sources of conflict during the 1960s and 1970s would be of particular relevance in thinking about the future of research on indicators. Even with the aid of hindsight, debates about the meaning and significance of indicators are likely to be repetitious. Yet, knowing what issues were at stake in the past and who was on which side might help sharpen thinking in the present. It would also be helpful to know how different political and academic interests perceived the relevance of indicators to their work. If nothing else, discovering why the social indicators movement virtually collapsed in the early 1980s might shed light on what course not to follow. Learning from failure could prevent a lot of frustration.

An investigation of the forces in society that prevent the dissemination of socially relevant information should constitute a second item in the research agenda. It is naive to imagine that everyone in a society wants all types of information to be readily available. If that were true, humans never would have developed the capacity to lie, and ideologies never would have been developed to protect privilege. Those who hope to "speak truth to power" will inevitably find that information revealing the true nature of power will be hard to find, intentionally blended with irrelevant statistics, or simply not gathered. These days, information is increasingly privatized, and ideas are being excluded from public debate by the threat of lawsuits. Research on the growing financial and legal pressures that block public access to ideas and information could be of great value in keeping democracy alive.

Third, research could help identify the best way to present indicators and other information to clarify the value conflicts in American society today. At present, various political factions on an issue (such as health care reform) present indicators that reflect the particular value promoted by that group. One group might focus on costs, another on underserved populations, and another on declining individual freedom. Every group tends to treat its values as absolute and seldom in relation to other values that most Americans hold. All of this is very confusing. There is no systematic process for helping citizens think clearly about how to balance conflicting values. Research on institutional methods to make indicators relevant to this process could help citizens learn to think more clearly about which values they will give up for others.

Finally, it would be foolish to expect a transformation of society simply by increasing the flow of information or by improving the way it is presented. Citizens are already glutted with information that is packaged in sound bites. Much of the information that currently flows through the media, however, seems designed to put the public to sleep rather than alert it to important shifts taking place in American society and the rest of the world. One of the most important roles the nonprofit sector can continue to play is to provide thousands of channels of information, through internal publications, that can keep our society aware of itself and challenge those who would prefer quiet failure to risky success.

REFERENCES

Alperovitz, G., Howard, T., Scharf, A., & Williamson, T. (1995). *Index of environmental trends.* Washington, DC: National Center for Economic Alternatives.

Cobb, C., Halstead, T., & Rowe, J. (1995). *The genuine progress indicator: Summary of data and methodology.* San Francisco: Redefining Progress.

Daly, H., & Cobb, J. B., Jr. (1992). *For the common good.* Boston: Beacon Press.

Desai, M. (1994). Greening of the HDI. Remarks made at seminar, *Accounting for Change*, Toynbee Hall, London, England.

Ekins, P., & Max-Neef, M. (1992). *Real-life economics: Understanding wealth creation*. New York: Routledge & Kegan Paul.

Gross, B. (1966). The state of the nation: Social systems accounting. In R. Bauer (Ed.), *Social indicators* (p. 228). Cambridge, MA: MIT Press.

Harrington, M. (1984). *The new American poverty*. New York: Penguin Books.

Lamale, H. (1958). Changes in concepts of income adequacy over the last century. *American Economic Review, 48*, 291–299.

Meadows, D. H., Meadows, D. L., Randers, J., & Behrens, W. W., III. (1972). *The limits to growth*. New York: Universe Books.

Mihalec, J. (1984). Hair on the president's chest. *Wall Street Journal*, May 11, 1984, p. 30.

Miringoff, M. (1995). *Index of social health*. Tarrytown, NY: Fordham Institute for Innovation in Social Policy.

Morris, M. D. (1979). *Measuring the condition of the world's poor: The Physical Quality of Life Index*. New York: Pergamon Press for the Overseas Development Council.

National Center for Education Statistics. (1989/1990). *Digest of education statistics*. Washington, DC: U.S. Department of Education.

Repetto, R., Beer, C., Magrath, W., Rossini, F., & Wells, M. (1989). *Wasting assets: Natural resources in the National Income Accounts*. Washington, DC: World Resources Institute.

Ruggles, R. (1983). The United States National Income Accounts, 1947–1977: Their conceptual basis and evolution. In M. F. Foss (Ed.), *The U.S. National Income and Product Accounts* (p. 32). Chicago: University of Chicago Press.

United Nations Development Program. (1993). *Human development report* (pp. 133–135). New York: Oxford University Press.

U.S. Bureau of the Census. (1981). *Social indicators III*. Washington, DC: U.S. Government Printing Office.

U.S. Bureau of Economic Analysis. (1982). *Measuring nonmarket economic activity* (BEA Working Paper No. 2). Washington, DC: U.S. Department of Commerce.

U.S. Office of Management and Budget. (1973). *Social indicators I*. Washington, DC: U.S. Government Printing Office.

U.S. Office of Management and Budget. (1976). *Social indicators II*. Washington, DC: U.S. Government Printing Office.

Wolfson, M.C. (1996). Health-adjusted life expectancy. *Health Reports, 8* (1), 41–46.

Zolotas, X. (1981). *Economic growth and declining social welfare*. New York: New York University Press.

Chapter **3**

Challenges of Measuring Performance in Nonprofit Organizations

MELISSA M. STONE AND SUSAN CUTCHER-GERSHENFELD

In some ways, the title of this chapter is misleading, for we are well aware of the challenges inherent in measuring performance in nonprofit organizations. It is time to deal with the challenges directly. Young, Bania, and Bailey succinctly summarized the reasons for the task before us: "Having inherited from the 1980s a legacy of a full and growing agenda of social problems, and a stringent fiscal environment of restricted government funding and fierce competition for private contributions, nonprofits have now been challenged where it hurts most—their very integrity has been called into question" (1996, p. 347). Funders are under increasing pressure to demonstrate results from their resource allocation decisions; the public wants to know what outcomes justify inflated nonprofit executive salaries and fund-raising costs; and those who run nonprofits are beginning to realize that "doing good" must be measurable.

Organizational effectiveness has been a contested and complex academic arena with as many models as there are types of organizations (Cameron &

MELISSA M. STONE • Associate Professor, Hubert H. Humphrey Institute of Public Affairs, University of Minnesota, Minneapolis, Minnesota 55455.   SUSAN CUTCHER-GERSHENFELD • Quality Consultant, Executive Office of Elder Affairs, Commonwealth of Massachusetts, Boston, Massachusetts 02108.

Measuring the Impact of the Nonprofit Sector, edited by Patrice Flynn and Virginia A. Hodgkinson, New York, Kluwer Academic/Plenum Publishers, 2002.

Whetten, 1983; Scott, 1987). Even in the field of strategic management, which defines itself by its focus on performance, many are critical of how performance has been conceptualized as well as measured (Daft & Buenger, 1990; Meyer, 1991). Nonetheless, " . . . the option to move away from defining (and measuring) performance or effectiveness is not a viable one" (Venkatraman & Ramanujam, 1986, p. 801). Performance is of theoretical, empirical, and practical significance.[1]

In this chapter, we will examine performance or effectiveness from theoretical, empirical, and practical points of view. We begin by reviewing literature on effectiveness, focusing on major complicating issues, especially for nonprofit organizations, and describing three dominant models of organizational effectiveness. In the chapter's second section, we examine the empirical work on effectiveness in nonprofit organizations. In the third section, we draw on field interviews with various kinds of funders and nonprofit executives to present views of performance from practitioners and the major stumbling blocks they encounter in implementing outcome measurement systems. We conclude the chapter with a set of research questions.

THEORETICAL PERSPECTIVES ON ORGANIZATIONAL EFFECTIVENESS

There are many reasons why understanding and studying organizational effectiveness is complex. In addition to the many models of effectiveness (Cameron & Whetten, 1983; Scott, 1987), the concept is inherently subjective and value laden (Cameron & Whetten, 1983; Seashore, 1983), expressing the self-interested preferences of individuals, groups, organizations, or society. Preferences, of course, are problematic because they may not be easily known, they may change over time, they may conflict with each other, and so forth (Scott, 1987). Effectiveness is also a relational construct (Seashore, 1983); assertions about the construct must specify the indicators used, the value systems that underlie the choice of indicators, and the constituency or constituencies making those choices. For the researcher, identifying any of the three (indicators, value systems, or all relevant constituencies) is a difficult task.

In addition to these general complications, four specific ones arise consistently in the literature. First, multiple definitions and terminology are used. For example, the terms "organizational effectiveness," "organizational performance," "performance measurables," "efficiency," and others are used by scholars and practitioners. The terms may refer to general assessments of organizational climate, specific assessments of program outcomes, or comparisons between budget allocations and actual expenditures. Confusion about these terms can be seen in the early literature, where "effectiveness" is defined as achieving organizational purpose and "efficiency" as an organization's ability to satisfy individuals' motives (Barnard, 1938). On the other hand, effectiveness is viewed as an external standard of assessment made by critical resource suppliers regarding the usefulness of what is being done by the firm (Pfeffer & Salancik, 1978). Efficiency is an internal standard, a ratio of resource inputs to resource outputs.

Differences in terminology are not trivial. The often-quoted phrase, "Efficiency is concerned with doing things right; effectiveness is doing the right things" (Drucker, 1974, p. 45) has been reinterpreted (Scott, 1987). Much research on effectiveness has emphasized its microquality (doing things right) and not its macroquality (doing the right things). From society's perspective, it is critical to address the macroqualities of effectiveness—what the organization should be doing and for whom (Nord, 1983).

Second, there are contrasting conceptual frameworks often based on academic discipline. Effectiveness or performance may be examined from the fields of psychology (industrial organization, social, or cognitive), sociology, economics, operations research, organizational behavior, and business strategy. Each highlights different aspects of effectiveness. For example, a strategy researcher may operationalize performance as return on assets or sales growth while a psychologist might focus on individual attitudinal and behavioral outcomes. Similarly, research on effectiveness focuses on different levels of analysis—individual, group, organizational, or societal. In practice, a social services agency may be evaluated as part of an overall attempt to reform the state's welfare system, as a specific organization, or in terms of the leadership of key individuals in the organization.

These first two complications address questions concerning what indicators of effectiveness should be used and who does the measuring. The next two address questions of how effectiveness is measured and how indicators are selected.

There are multiple types of measurement (the third complication). Performance can be measured with quantitative or qualitative indicators, absolute or relative standards of comparison, direct or indirect measures, and other alternatives (Brewer, 1983). Data can also be cross-sectional or analyzed over time. Performance measures may utilize daily, weekly, annual, or multiyear data. The problem of choosing the best indicators has received a great deal of attention in the literature on performance in for-profit corporations. For example, scores of studies over the past 20 years have examined the relationship between planning and performance. As several reviews of this literature conclude, however, generalizing across studies is difficult because of the variety of financial *and* operational measures used, differences in time horizon, and lack of attention to industry effects (see Rhyne, 1986, and Venkatraman & Ramanujam, 1986, for useful reviews).

Fourth, while focusing on outcome indicators is critical to understanding performance, it is problematic for many types of organizations in which links between means and ends are not clear. In these situations, often the case with nonprofit organizations operating in institutional environments, the use of process and structural "proxy" measures dominates (Scott, 1987). This complication is addressed more fully below.

Added Complications in Nonprofit Organizations

Even though the lines dividing for-profit and nonprofit organizations are blurring with regard to performance measures (Kanter & Summers, 1987), measuring the performance of nonprofit organizations is more difficult because of their nonmarket quality and mission-driven services. Outputs are also often intangible, as is the case with many prevention and educational programs. There are, therefore, few bottom-line indicators of performance that are generally accepted. For example, a nursing home may have as its mission providing high-quality shelter and social and medical care for older adults who are physically challenged. The home may also be driven by religious values. Although nursing homes are assessed on countless measurables, such as bed occupancy or staff-to-patient ratios, no single indicator serves as a bottom-line measure of whether the nursing home is accomplishing its mission or is operating in a manner consistent with its core values.

As has been well documented, nonprofits often have vague goals that allow them to appeal to the multiple and often competing demands of constituencies (Fottler, 1981; Hatten, 1982; Kanter & Summers, 1987; Newman & Wallender, 1978; Nutt, 1984). A problem of goal displacement arises, however, when these organizations adopt specific input, throughput, or output performance measures, perhaps responding to demands from certain constituencies: The attention of organization members is then on the measurables and is diverted away from the organization's goals (Scott, 1987).

Another complication results from what some refer to as "loose coupling" between donors of resources and beneficiaries of services (Kanter & Brinkerhoff, 1981). For example, a mental health facility may be funded by government and private insurers who have priorities that do not necessarily match the priorities of people receiving the services. Funders emphasize performance indicators such as increased caseloads and staff productivity rather than individual gains for clients or overall client satisfaction. Furthermore, there may be no connection between a nonprofit's ability to raise funds and to effectively use those resources (Provan & Stewart, 1982).

MODELS OF ORGANIZATIONAL EFFECTIVENESS

Broadly speaking, there are at least three different conceptual models that underlie most approaches to assessing organizational effectiveness: the natural systems model, the goal model, and the decision-process model. Each approach highlights different types of measures and rests on different assumptions about the nature of organizations (Seashore, 1983).

The Natural Systems Model

The natural systems model conceptualizes an organization as "an intact behaving entity, autonomous except for interdependence with an environment in the form of information and energy exchanges" (Seashore, 1983, p.57). The model highlights the following aspects of organizational effectiveness:

- Attributes of the system have some significant function in the organization's adaptation, maintenance, and transformation process. The model focuses on organizational survival, adjustments in mission, shifts in services, and other indicators of viability and innovation.
- Indicators are intact sets, not independent values; thus, no single measure is viewed in isolation. Performance is seen as multidimensional; pursuing excellence in any one dimension may compromise performance in others.
- Indicators are seen in context. For example, a measurement of placement rates for job training programs will have different meanings in the context of two different organizations, one dealing with highly skilled but dislocated workers and another dealing with impaired individuals. A 50 percent placement rate for the first may be considered exceptional for the second.
- Linkages between indicators that may be causal in both directions are considered, enabling scholars to move beyond simple causal models for analyzing organizational performance.

In recent years, a systems approach has received broader public recognition through the work of system dynamics scholars such as Peter Senge. This perspective considers four elements of a system: inputs, throughputs, outputs, and feedback. The importance of feedback is a key insight. To the extent that an organization fails to utilize feedback in assessing its performance, it may be making decisions based on unchecked assumptions.

The Goal Model

In the goal model, the organization is seen as an entity "contrived and controlled to serve the purposes of the key influentials, including owner, managers, and others, whether 'inside' or 'outside' the organization, who have some controlling power in defining the operative purposes of the organization" (Seashore, 1983, p.59). The model refers not to goals inherent in the organizational system itself but to goals people have *for* the organization. It draws attention to the following:

- Perspectives and assumptions that lead to the dominance of some goals over others.
- Linkages between organizations and their value-laden environments. Standards for performance do not emerge from thin air, but are rather products of social norms and cultural assumptions.

Some argue that social constructionist and multiple stakeholder views of effectiveness are consistent with the goal model (Herman & Heimovics, 1994). Organizational outcomes are not seen as deterministic but as emerging from complex negotiations and social interactions. An important question to ask regarding why one indicator is used over another is "Whose interests are being served by that decision?" Measures of performance can be understood as reinforcing and legitimizing stakeholders who have power.

The Decision-Process Model

Focusing on organizations from a decision-process perspective highlights the relationship between *how* things happen in organizations and what occurs as a result. This model's assumption is that the quality of decision making is the central factor influencing performance. The quality of decision making, in turn, is the product of organizational structure, processes, and mechanisms for participant involvement. The model focuses attention on the following:

- How organizations optimize processes for getting, storing, retrieving, allocating, manipulating, interpreting, and discarding information.
- What capability an organization has for accommodating a wide range of types of information.

Focusing on decision processes is useful in highlighting ways to improve effectiveness as it can identify gaps or disconnects in the processing of information.

Taken together, the three models help explain why there is no easy consensus on what is meant by effectiveness. Each yields important insights but also further complicates the already untidy aspects of effectiveness discussed earlier. In the next two sections, these general points become more specific as we examine both the empirical research on performance in nonprofits and the comments practicing managers have made about performance measurement.

STATE OF RESEARCH ON EFFECTIVENESS AND PERFORMANCE IN NONPROFIT ORGANIZATIONS

Very little research has directly addressed questions of organizational effectiveness in the nonprofit arena. A recent review of empirical work on the strategic management of nonprofit organizations found only 5 of 53 journal articles published from 1977 through 1992 that explicitly studied performance or effectiveness variables in relation to strategic management activities (Stone, Bigelow, & Crittenden, 1996).

Table 1 summarizes selected empirical research on effectiveness in nonprofit organizations, identifies the implicit or explicit effectiveness model guiding the research, gives definitions of effectiveness, describes how effectiveness was measured and by whom, and lists the study's major findings.

Several observations can be made from these selected empirical studies. First, while there is considerable variability in the research questions asked, nearly half were concerned with the relationship between board effectiveness and organizational effectiveness, and 3 of the 10 studies examined how formal planning processes affect performance or effectiveness. As stated earlier, the for-profit literature abounds with studies trying to understand the link between planning and performance, with inconclusive results, but has not focused on governance activities as potential independent variables. The interest in governance in these nonprofit studies points to the growing recognition that board functioning and nonprofit health are interrelated.

Second, many studies either implicitly or explicitly used a combination of classical models of organizational effectiveness to frame the research, most often the natural systems and goal models. Many shared the perspective that effectiveness or performance had to be understood from a multiple stakeholder framework. This justified using language from the natural system model concerning adaptability of organizations to their environments and language from the goal model concerning multiple goals. The multiple stakeholder perspective carried through to how indicators of performance were defined and how they were assessed: Different groups of practitioners were often used to define

Table 1. Selected Empirical Research on Organizational Effectiveness in Nonprofit Organizations

Study	Research questions and database	Explicit or implicit effectiveness model	Definition of effectiveness	How measured	Findings
Crittenden, Crittenden, & Hunt, 1988	What was the relationship between planning and satisfaction of key stakeholders? Survey of 28 religious organizations.	Goal model and decision-process model.	Effectiveness = satisfaction of key resource contributors.	Increase (or decrease) in volunteer membership growth, amount of funds, satisfaction of administrator, program growth.	Select use of individual planning elements rather than a comprehensive planning process is sufficient to obtain needed resources.
Fisher & Dickey, 1995	How much and in what ways are key informant perceptions of performance of community health services affected by differences in structure and resource allocation?	Decision-process model and goal model.	Effectiveness = service adequacy; coordination and quality; administrative, clinical, and fiscal authority.	Survey instrument	Despite major organizational differences, key stakeholder perceptions of performance did not vary substantially.
Fried & Worthington, 1995	What are the perceived roles and performance of Canadian general psychiatric hospital units (GPHU) and provincial psychiatric hospitals (PPH) from viewpoints of multiple constituencies?	Goal model.	Effectiveness = perceptions of five different constituencies along three dimensions.	Use of open-ended questions to identify the three most important roles for both types of hospitals and, for each role, rated the organization's performance.	Constituency groups had different perceptions of both hospital types on all three roles.

Green & Griesinger, 1996	What is the relationship between board performance and organizational effectiveness? External ratings and survey of 16 nonprofits serving the developmentally disabled.	Natural system and goal models for organizational effectiveness. Decision process for board performance.	Organizational effectiveness = quality and sustainability of needed services to client. Board performance = nine areas from practitioner literature, including mission- and policy-setting, strategic planning, and program evaluation.	organizational effectiveness composite of rankings by experts using accreditation reports, rankings by regional official, and rankings by the researcher. Board performance: self-assessment by board members and CEOs on the 9 items.	Effective organizations were significantly correlated with board involvement for 7 of the 9 items, including board involvement in policy formulation, strategic planning, and financial planning and control.
Herman & Heimovics, 1990	What skills differentiate effective nonprofit leaders from less effective ones? Emphasis placed on board–executive relationship. Interviews with 51 nonprofit CEOs from a range of nonprofits.	Board–executive relationships help mediate organization–environment interaction and help with organizational adaptability.	Leadership skill items with critical incident methodology.	Raters' judgment of whether leadership behavior is exhibited in incidents.	Leaders with effective reputations provide more leadership for their boards than comparison group of CEOs.

Continued

Table 1. Continued

Study	Research questions and database	Explicit or implicit effectiveness model	Definition of effectiveness	How measured	Findings
Herman & Heimovics, 1994	What criteria are used to determine effectiveness in nonprofits? Comparison study of United States and United Kingdom using 20 graduate students in each country to rate vignettes.	Social constructionist view that authors argue incorporates goal, natural systems, and decision-process models.	Effectiveness = performance on 11 indicators, including change in revenues, surplus/deficits/% of budget spent on fund-raising.	Student-respondent ratings of each organization on the indicators.	Most important criteria determining effectiveness were percentage of budget on fund-raising; advocacy emphasis in programs; program unit costs; and change in surplus. Use of volunteers was more important for U.S. respondents and advocacy emphasis more important for United Kingdom respondents.
Herman & Renz, 1997	How do different stakeholders assess effectiveness? Interviews with 59 practitioner–experts in social service field and a survey of 250 stakeholders of 64 social service nonprofits.	Social constructionist view (modification of goal model).	Effectiveness = stakeholder judgments formed in an ongoing process of sense-making and implicit negotiations. Objective measures = efficient staff structure, planning document, bylaws, etc. Board effectiveness included review of mission and program, marketing, financial management.	Objective measures: those selected by the practitioner-experts. Board effectiveness items: drawn from the National Center on Nonprofit Boards guide.	Practitioner-experts define effectiveness as following correct procedures. Stakeholders use different judgments of what constitutes effectiveness. However, there is general agreement that board effectiveness is related to better-performing organizations.

Odom & Boxx, 1988	What are the relationships among church size and growth to perceptions of the environment and to the use of formal planning? Survey of 179 churches.	Goal model?	Performance = rate of growth	Performance measured as growth in Sunday school attendance, plate offerings, total membership, and baptisms.	Larger and growing churches tend to be formal planners. Causal direction between planning and growth is unclear.
Provan & Stewart 1982	What is the relationship between resource acquisition and resource use in studying the organizational effectiveness of nonprofits? Forty-one United Way member agencies.	Natural systems, goal model, and decision model.	Effectiveness = input, throughput, and output measures. Resource acquisition = acquiring funding, professional employees, and clients. Resource use = number of clients/expenditures and subjective assessments.	United Way data on members and subjective assessments by United Way staff and other nonprofit CEOs.	Effectiveness measures based on resource use are strongly tied to some measures of resource acquisition.
Siciliano & Floyd, 1992	What is the relationship between board characteristics, strategic management activities, and organizational performance? Survey of 240 YMCAs.	Goal model?	Performance = productivity, social performance, and percentage of contributed income.	Published YMCA statistics and annual performance reviews conducted by consultants.	Better performance related to board involvement in strategic planning. Board size not related to performance and having business people on the board associated with lower performance on all three measures.

indicators, and multiple "raters" were used to assess nonprofits on those indicators.

Third, while the natural systems and goal models dominated how these studies were conceptualized, indicators of effectiveness emphasized process and structural characteristics (decision-process model) as often as resource acquisition. Outcome variables were used in only four studies. This emphasis on process and structural indicators may be due to the fact that several studies relied on practitioner views of effectiveness, either through interviews or the use of indicators developed in the practitioner literature. As Herman and Renz (1997) found, practitioners were more likely to emphasize "correct procedures" as performance indicators. The lack of attention to outcome indicators probably reflects the fact that practitioners and researchers alike find it difficult to arrive at quantitative assessments of outcomes.

Fourth, while the small number of studies and the diversity of research foci make drawing conclusions from the findings difficult, two observations can be made: Board effectiveness appears to be related to organizational effectiveness, although causal direction is unclear; and different stakeholders hold different and sometimes conflicting views about effectiveness indicators. Despite this latter finding, few studies drew conclusions about the political nature of performance indicators or tried to relate findings to broader conceptualizations of organization–environment relations, using, for example, resource dependence or institutional theory.

The next section draws on our observations from interviews with a number of practitioners in the Boston area. Interviewees included state government officials deeply involved in developing performance-based contracting with nonprofit providers, private and corporate foundation staff, staff from the local United Way, and executive directors from nonprofit social service organizations.

EXAMPLES FROM THE FIELD

Government

The Government Performance and Results Act of 1993 (P.L. 103-62), taking full effect in the year 2000, places a renewed emphasis on accountability in federal agencies and nonprofit organizations receiving federal support. The federal government is not alone in its efforts to move toward performance-based outcomes; states such as Oregon, Minnesota, Texas, and Utah lead other states in developing benchmarks, clear language, and standard performance outcomes for contractors receiving state funds. For example, the Minnesota Human Services Department, which administers more than 50 programs and services in diverse areas, developed performance measures for all of their services in little over a year's time. The department faced this challenge as a result of legislative action that required 20 state agencies to submit annual performance reports. In its first annual report, the department included more than 350 performance objectives and measures for its various programs. While most were output measures (for example, the number of children of migrant farm workers receiving child care), many program outcomes were also included (for example, the percentage of individuals employed for six months after receiving job training and placement assistance).

Shifting procurement contracts from input to output or, especially, outcome measures occurs with some peril. In Massachusetts, the state spends $1.5 billion through its procurement system, contracting with mostly nonprofit organizations to provide social services previously delivered directly by the state. Massachusetts has a three-year conversion cycle; by the year 2000, all contracts are expected to have performance measures. The process being used to determine measures includes training and technical assistance regarding performance measures for the program staff of state agencies and negotiations between state agency staff and nonprofit providers to develop a plan for performance measurement. The resulting plan is then reviewed by the Division of Procurement and Purchased Services. According to state officials, they have encountered four major stumbling blocks in this process:

- *Relationship changes.* Performance outcomes change the nature of relationships with providers. Many nonprofits were created by state agencies desperate for community services. In the past, the relationship has been a close partnership. Under performance contracting, however, all players need to be held accountable to measurable standards. This changes the relationship to more of a business and economic exchange arrangement.
- *Trust and power.* Stakeholders, including state purchasers and nonprofit providers, are concerned with who is gong to see the information and how it is going to be used. With both budget and performance data available to interested parties, "it casts a whole different level of power in the system," according to one state official. The intent is for negotiations to be improved between purchasers and providers, which assumes stakeholders shift from the partnership to a buyer–seller model.
- *Costs.* Initially, resources need to be spent for data collection, evaluation, dissemination, and use. However, no new money has been identified for performance-based contracting, which is an issue for both state agencies and providers.

- *Incentives.* Determining appropriate incentives is critical because unintended consequences are possible, including organizations diverting resources from direct services to generate performance measurables, and organizations utilizing measurables to drive managerial and employee behavior in ways that maximize what is being measured, regardless of the effect on organizational goals.

The renewed effort in government to hold nonprofits systematically accountable for achieving program results follows a natural systems model approach to organizational effectiveness in that it distinguishes between inputs, throughputs, outputs, and feedback elements. In addition, the process is sensitive to some stakeholders; note, however, that other stakeholders, such as employees, clients, and community members, may not be represented in this process. The stumbling blocks draw attention to several key properties of effectiveness, described earlier, which make it such a complex construct. These include its relational and evaluative properties, measurement difficulties, and potential for goal displacement.

Foundations

Interviews with top managers from two types of medium-sized foundations, family and corporate, are included here. The family foundation, located in Boston, has an annual budget of approximately $3.4 million and funds nearly 200 projects per year. The corporate foundation, Shawmut Bank, prior to a merger, had an annual budget of $4 million and provided nearly 700 small grants for community initiatives, including operating grants, program support, and capital funding. For these foundations, performance assessment emphasizes a decision-process model in which attention is paid at the outset to assessing the fit between a grantee's budget and its proposed program plan.

Those interviewed noted that these foundations do not face the same external pressures that are driving government's concern for performance. When informed about the recent state initiatives focusing on outcome measurables, one foundation official expressed disbelief. Another foundation staffer reported that "we don't struggle with performance measurables." For the corporate foundation, the primary goal of grant making is to support community initiatives in areas where the corporation provides its services. In this context, program evaluation is less important; ensuring ongoing relations with community institutions is the main goal. Furthermore, the corporate foundation lacked the necessary work force to conduct evaluations. Funding decisions were based on their ongoing relationships with grantees and on a grantee's reputation in the community.

Evaluations involving the collaborative efforts of government agencies, corporations, foundations, and nonprofit organizations do occur. It took one collaborative a year and a half to build trust and internal agreement on the project's goals. Agreement on goals was necessary before collaborators could begin joint conversations about what constituted success. These discussions were complicated by the fact that the different types of organizations were subject to different kinds of public scrutiny; thus, what constituted "success" varied considerably.

Special fund initiatives are another type of collaborative effort that result from several funders pooling resources. In these cases, an outside evaluator is often hired. However, costs drive such evaluations; as one foundation official reported, if a math and science program in black churches had been evaluated rigorously, it would have cost more than the program itself.

Foundation officials cite the following obstacles to developing effectiveness measures:

- *Measurement.* Foundations face a special challenge in measuring performance when grants are given to support the general operations of a nonprofit. In these cases, it is hard to disentangle the degree to which program outcomes are different as a result of the grant or of an infusion of foundation operating funds. Pilot programs testing a new program model are a bit easier to evaluate.
- *Quality of the data.* Foundations may have to rely on public statistics, such as crime or poverty rates, that are generated from external sources for reasons that may not match the purpose of the project being funded. As a result, data may serve some audiences well but be inadequate from the point of view of the foundation.
- *Costs.* The cost of evaluation, including tracking performance, competes with direct program funding. There is always a tension between the importance of expanding the use of funds versus assessing what is accomplished with the money that is spent. This pressure has increased for foundations that have often been asked to pick up the slack from declining government support of nonprofits.
- *Collaboration.* Representatives from different funding sources will not always have the authority to make final decisions regarding overall project goals or specific measurables. And, once multiple funders agree on a common set of goals, they can then lock into this agreement and remain steadfast to it despite changing circumstances.

Compared to state government, the lack of external pressures on these foundations is surprising. Since many foundations are entering into multiparty partnerships, however, it is likely that they too will have to cope with changes similar to those facing their public sector partners.

United Way

The activities around performance measures at the United Way of America (UWA) resemble what is occurring in government more than what is occurring in small and medium-sized foundations. Driven by competition for scarce resources and by donors' (including corporations') desires to know how their contributions make a difference, this organization began a sustained effort to develop outcome measurement throughout the United Way system. UWA has taken the lead in working with a task force representing academia, evaluation firms, corporations, government, foundations, and national human services organizations to discuss outcome measurement. UWA has also developed training materials and conducted training sessions for local United Ways and their member agencies. Subsequently, a database will be developed to record effective outcome measures for different types of programs.

The move toward performance-based outcomes is seen as a fundamental change that needs to be incorporated into an organization's culture. Those local United Ways and affiliates that are at the forefront of this initiative indicate that it takes approximately three years to develop and train staff and another two years to incorporate the process into funding decisions. While outcome measures have been a component of the review process, the emphasis has been on managerial systems and process (such as use of strategic planning), *not* on program outcomes. At the United Way of Massachusetts Bay (UWMB), results and outcome data have been collected from affiliates for several years. UWMB is now undertaking a more intensive training and development program with its affiliates to institutionalize the performance-based measurements process.

The stumbling blocks UWMB has faced resemble many of the barriers experienced by government, but the nature of the change in relationships differs. While government has moved toward measures of greater accountability, UWMB has shifted its relationship with member agencies from a business arrangement that focused on accountability measures to a partnership in which all work together to better understand program goals, activities, and performance outcomes, as well as how these outcomes precipitate community change. This emphasis on community change is a rare example of an organization weighing the macroquality, or societal impact dimension, of performance.

Nonprofit Organizations

The extent to which nonprofits incorporate performance measures into their operations varies considerably. According to one executive director, on one end of the continuum are nonprofits that make full use of performance measures and data to drive decisions. These nonprofits welcome efforts by government to focus on outcomes and have been advocates for negotiating price-unit standards for funding. At the other end of the continuum are nonprofits that struggle to meet their monthly payroll. They understand the importance of performance measures but are too preoccupied with daily crises to incorporate such measures into their operations.

The Massachusetts Council of Human Service Providers, a trade association of large nonprofits that receive substantial amounts of state contracting dollars, describes two nonprofits as "ahead of the curve": Communities for People and Vinfen Corporation. Both contract with several state agencies for general management and direct services. Communities for People specializes in working with teenagers who have behavior problems; Vinfen provides assisted living services to developmentally disabled adults and children. While both face external pressures for accountability, they were also motivated internally to move toward performance-based outcomes.

Several years ago, Vinfen's interests in outcome data emerged from an accreditation process. Since then, data interests have been critical in determining their evolving information technology needs. Two years ago, Vinfen committed to an on-line child welfare case management system, known as FACTORS, that will deliver qualitative data and provide aggregate data across groups of programs for decision-making purposes.

Efforts to understand performance outcomes at Communities for People are more recent. Working with a local university, other nonprofits, and the Department of Social Services for more than a year and a half, the organization has developed an outcome tool to understand which teens with certain traits can do well in certain types of programs. According to the executive director, "in this age of managed care, the child welfare experts need to be the ones defining treatment models." He added that getting other nonprofit managers attuned to this need was not easy.

Several stumbling blocks to implementing performance-based outcome measures were identified by these nonprofit managers, as follows:

- *Developing broad consensus.* Developing a broad enough consensus for both internal and external use is difficult. While nonprofits might develop a long list of measurement possibilities, they found it more difficult to narrow down the list to the most appropriate choices.
- *Logistics and cost.* In a large, decentralized system with thin operating margins, information technology is difficult and costly to implement. Yet, it is essential.
- *Time.* It is important to get everyone committed to the effort, which takes enormous amounts of time for meeting and reaching consensus.

- *Training.* Even though human services professionals use similar terminology, such as "family work," there is great variation in meaning. Assumptions, therefore, need to be checked all along the way in the training process.
- *Concern for survival.* Some nonprofits may realize it is best for a client to
  be discharged, but they do not want to be stuck with an empty bed.
  However, if they keep the client longer than necessary, they will have a
  record of poorer performance. Communities for People addressed this
  problem by educating service providers in its network about the importance of outcome measures. In particular, it emphasizes that those who
  perform well will have steady referrals.

These two nonprofits have used a combination of models in moving toward performance-based outcomes. For example, a systems approach is implicit because both make distinctions between inputs, throughputs, and outputs. The data are intended to serve as feedback.

A decision-process approach is also evident at Vinfen in its use of information technology. The goal approach is apparent in the fact that many constituencies have come together to reach consensus on the framework for performance measurements.

Table 2 compares the impetus to develop performance measures and the
obstacles encountered to the process as experienced by government, foundation, United Way, and nonprofit service providers.

As all four types of organizations develop performance measures to improve their internal decision-making capabilities, they are responding to the
external pressures for accountability that have mounted in recent years. Funding sources, especially government agencies and the United Way, face numerous external pressures from their stakeholders, and nonprofits will likely feel
the effects of these pressures in the form of funding requirements that are more
closely tied to performance measurements. While some nonprofits are "ahead
of the curve" in developing their own measures, they will probably also have to
use measures determined by funders seeking to satisfy their own needs. Complexity aside, developing and maintaining multiple performance tracking systems is costly and time consuming. It is doubtful that additional resources will
be provided for these systems, and, thus, nonprofits will be faced with making
the dangerous trade-off mentioned earlier—that of diverting funds from programs in order to develop systems of assessment.

While costs and measurement issues were mentioned most frequently in
interviews, relationship issues were also dominant. *A move toward performance-
based measurement changes the nature of the relationship between funder and
grantee.* Government officials saw that change as moving away from a partner-

Table 2: Comparison of Field Responses to Questions on Performance Measurement

	Impetus to do performance measurement				Key stumbling blocks					
	Competition for scarce resources	Legislation or other directives	Accountability	Improve decision making	Costs	Measurement	Trust over how data will be used	Time	Relationship issues	Other
Government	X	X	X	X	X	X	X		X	X
Foundations				X	X	X			X	X
United Way	X		X			X	X	X	X	X
Nonprofit providers		X		X	X	X		X	X	X

ship model to more of a buyer-seller model (probably because of the push by Massachusetts state government toward privatization), while the United Way saw the shift in the relationship as moving away from a business model and toward a partnership. Issues of trust and power surface quickly and are complicated. How will data on outcomes be used and by whom? And, while power seems to shift toward funders because nonprofits will have to comply with funder requirements in order to gain resources, funders also need nonprofits to comply in order to justify their funding decisions to their stakeholders. As reported by several interviewees, the *process* used to develop performance measurements is critical to successful implementation where all relevant parties must be involved. This does not eliminate trust and power issues, but makes them more explicit and potentially discussible.

RESEARCH IMPLICATIONS

Drawing on material from the empirical literature and from interviews with funders and nonprofit executives cited earlier, this section presents three broad areas of future research opportunities. The first of these focuses on determinants of performance measures, paying particular attention to political factors. The second area of research is on the organizational consequences of implementing performance measures. The third is the influence of partnerships and collaborations on organizational performance.

Political Factors as Determinants of Performance Measures

This area calls for research that examines political factors associated with performance measurements, in particular, the political quality of the types of measures used and the political nature of the process used to determine measures. We are using the term "political" not in the sense of dishonesty to promote self-interest, but rather as negotiating and bargaining activities that are part of decision making.

The importance of examining political factors associated with performance measures was highlighted in both the empirical literature and the interviews. For example, the empirical literature draws attention to the fact that important stakeholders hold different and often conflicting perceptions of organizational effectiveness or performance. And, interviewees frequently described how power balances shifted between funders and nonprofits when funding became tied to performance measurement. Both of these examples suggest that determining performance measures is a contested terrain.

The political quality of the measures themselves deserves more research attention. The subjective properties of performance measures has long been understood, as described earlier in this chapter. Because much of what nonprofit organizations do is difficult to measure, these subjective properties are likely to be particularly strong. What we need to understand further is what *values,* implicit as well as explicit, undergird these subjective judgments of proper performance measures. And, whose values are being expressed? Do measures primarily express values related to the microqualities of effectiveness (doing things right) such as cost efficiency, managerial professionalism, attending to correct procedures and rules? Or do measures express macroqualities (doing the right things) associated with changed lives, changed communities, and so forth?

Related to questions of values are questions that focus on the political nature of the process used to determine measures. Many of the interviewees, for example, described how important and difficult is the development of trust among parties engaged in determining performance measures. Some work has been started here (see, for example, Tassie, Murray, Cutt, and Bragg, 1996, and Forbes's argument about organizational effectiveness as an "emergent" process, 1998). More needs to be done, however, to examine the bargaining and negotiating that takes place as a performance measurement system is being designed. As many interviewees described, putting into place a performance measurement system changed the nature of the relationship between funders and nonprofits. In some cases where accountability measures dominated, the relationship became more characterized as an instrumental exchange or business one. In the case of the United Way, however, relationships between it and its member agencies became more of a partnership as they searched together for outcome measures that captured community change. How can we better understand these processes and the change in relationships among parties that results?

Further, research is needed not only on processes between different organizations (such as funders and nonprofits) but also on processes within organizations. Because performance measures implicitly or explicitly express certain values, it is likely that these values will be contested within as well as between organizations.

In examining political factors as determinants of performance measures, it is critical that research explore the broader environmental context in which measures are being defined. Concepts such as organizational field (DiMaggio & Powell, 1991) or societal sector (Scott & Meyer, 1991) are useful because these concepts draw attention to the hierarchical arrangements between organizations and to the diffusion of prevalent norms and beliefs within a field. Determining the central characteristics of the environment will illuminate research on the political quality of the measures and of the negotiating process. For example, if the field is structured hierarchically around a central funding source and has members from the same profession, then it may be likely that there are dominant and commonly agreed upon values that will be expressed in performance measures. If the field is fragmented without a dominant coalition of organizations and with few congruent professional norms, then it is likely that there will be diverse sets of values in the field and hotly contested debates over which performance measures are most appropriate.

Organizational Consequences of Implementing Performance Measures

The empirical literature and material from interviewees present several potential consequences of performance measurement systems for organizations. For example, interviewees described how costly measuring performance can be, in terms of both time and money. Several also raised the fear that money spent on evaluating performance was money that would have to be taken away from program delivery. Research is needed that documents the actual costs involved, much in the same way that Grønbjerg (1991) documented how different types of funding environments imposed different types of costs on nonprofits.

The possibility of goal displacement when organizations focus on meeting measurement standards that do not reflect their mission was also raised in the literature and by interviewees. Does goal displacement actually occur or do organizations find ways of manipulating measures to protect the core work of the organization? Under what circumstances is goal displacement more or less likely? Similar questions were asked regarding the impact of government funding on nonprofit organizations. Early studies found that goal displacement in nonprofits was not likely to occur with the onset of government monies (Kramer, 1981) while more recent studies suggest that subtle but significant shifts in mission do occur (see, for example, Smith & Lipsky, 1993). Comparable research is needed on the effects of performance measurements on the mission and goals of nonprofit organizations.

Other research is needed on the extent to which organizational learning is a likely consequence of implementing a performance measurement system. The best measurement systems should provide accurate and current feedback to organizations about how they are doing. This kind of information is particularly important to nonprofit organizations because they lack feedback from the market. Furthermore, the process of developing measures, described by one interviewee as a process of developing "broad consensus" within his nonprofit, may have additional benefits in terms of greater commitment of members to a clearer organizational vision. With what types of measurement systems and under what conditions is organizational learning most likely to take place?

The Effects of Collaborations on Organizational Performance

A final set of research questions concerns performance measures in the context of collaborations or partnerships. As more and more nonprofits move into collective decision-making settings, through the types of collaborations described by foundation staff, how does the work of the partnership affect the performance of individual organization members? Setting aside the question of how one measures the performance of the collaboration, it is important to understand the effects of collective decision making on individual organizational performance. Just as many corporations are finding it necessary to evaluate the performance of teams rather than individuals, nonprofits (and funders) are likely to see much of their work and performance dependent on what other partners do. In other words, how do dense interconnections among organizations affect the performance of individual entities?

This set of questions, hardly an exhaustive list, reinforces the untidy nature of performance measures. Research into this area, however, also provides rich opportunities to explore other, critically important issues for the sector. Research on performance measures can give us a window from which to view dominant and contested values within the sector and between sectors. It can highlight the broader political, social, and economic contexts within which nonprofits are embedded. It can add to our understanding of goal displacement and organizational learning. And, it can draw attention to the growing importance of collective decision making and problem solving through the work of collaborations and partnerships. Organizational performance is of theoretical, empirical, and practical significance.

NOTES

1. We use the terms "effectiveness" and "performance" interchangeably, although some would argue that effectiveness is a more abstract construct than organizational performance. To the extent that specific authors or studies use one term and not the other, we will follow their terminology.

REFERENCES

Barnard, C. I. (1938). *The functions of the executive.* Cambridge, MA: Harvard University Press.
Brewer, G. D. (1983). Assessing outcomes and effects. In K. S. Cameron & D. A. Whetten (Eds.), *Organizational effectiveness: A comparison of multiple models.* New York: Academic Press.
Cameron, K. S., & Whetten, D. A. (1983). Organizational effectiveness: One model or several?

In K. S. Cameron & D. A. Whetten (Eds.), *Organizational effectiveness: A comparison of multiple models*. New York: Academic Press.

Crittenden, W. F., Crittenden, V. L., & Hunt, T. G. (1988). Planning and stakeholder satisfaction in religious organizations. *Journal of Voluntary Action Research, 17*(2), 60–73.

Daft, R. L., & Buenger, V. (1990). Hitching a ride on a fast train to nowhere. In J. Frederickson (Ed.), *Perspective on strategic management*. New York: Harper & Row.

DiMaggio, P. J. and Powell, W. W. (1991). The iron cage revisited: Institutional isomorphism and collective rationality in organizational fields. In W. W. Powell and P. J. DiMaggio (Eds.), *The new institutionalism in organizational analysis*. Chicago: University of Chicago Press.

Drucker, P. F. (1974). *Management: Tasks, responsibilities, practices*. New York: Harper Collins.

Fisher, W. H., & Dickey, B. (1995). Regional variation in service system performance: Comparing the perceptions of key stakeholders. *Journal of Mental Health Administration, 22*(1), 68–76.

Forbes, Daniel P. (1998). Measuring the unmeasurable: Empirical shading of nonprofit organization effectiveness from 1977 to 1997. *Nonprofit and Voluntary Sector Quarterly, 27*(2), 183–202.

Fottler, M. (1981). Is management really generic? *Academy of Management Review, 3*, 1–12.

Fried, B. J., & Worthington, C. (1995). The multiconstituency approach to organizational performance assessment: A Canadian mental health system application. *Community Mental Health Journal, 31*(1), 11–24.

Green, J. C., & Griesinger, D. W. (1996). Board performance and organizational effectiveness in nonprofit social service organizations. *Nonprofit Management and Leadership, 6*(4), 381–402.

Grønbjerg, K. A. (1991). How nonprofit human service organizations manage their funding sources: Key findings and policy implications. *Nonprofit Management and Leadership, 2*(2), 159–175.

Hatten, M. L. (1982). Strategic management in not-for-profit organizations. *Strategic Management Journal, 3*, 89–104.

Herman, R. D., & Heimovics, R. D. (1990). The effective nonprofit executive: Leader of the board. *Nonprofit Management and Leadership, 1*(2), 167–180.

Herman, R. D., & Heimovics, R. D. (1994). A cross-national study of a method for researching non-profit organisational effectiveness. *Voluntas, 5*(1), 86–100.

Herman, R. D., & Renz, D. O. (1997). Multiple constituencies and the social construction of nonprofit organization effectiveness. *Nonprofit and Voluntary Sector Quarterly, 26*(2), 185–206.

Kanter, R. M., & Brinkerhoff, D. (1981). Organizational performance: Recent developments in measurement. *Annual Review in Sociology, 7*, 321–349.

Kanter, R. M., & Summers, D. (1987). Doing well while doing good. In W. W. Powell (Ed.), *The nonprofit sector: A research handbook*. New Haven, CT: Yale University Press.

Kramer, R. M. (1981). *Voluntary agencies in the welfare state*. Berkeley, CA: University of California Press.

Meyer, A. D. (1991). What is strategy's distinctive competence? *Journal of Management, 17*(4), 821–833.

Newman, W. H., & Wallender, H. W., III. (1978). Managing not-for-profit enterprises. *Academy of Management Review, 3*, 24–31

Nord, W. R. (1983). A political-economic perspective on organizational effectiveness. In K. S. Cameron & D. A. Whetten (Eds.), *Organizational effectiveness: A comparison of multiple methods*. New York: Academic Press.

Nutt, P. C. (1984). A strategic planning network for nonprofit organizations. *Strategic Management Journal*, 5, 57–75.

Odom, R. Y., & Boxx, W. R. (1988). Environment, planning processes, and organizational performance of churches. *Strategic Management Journal*, 9, 197–205.

Pfeffer, J., & Salancik, G. (1978). *The external control of organizations*. New York: Harper & Row.

Provan, K. G., & Stewart, D. W. (1982). Measuring organizational effectiveness in the not-for-profit sector. Academy of Management Proceedings. Paper presented at annual meeting of Academy of Management, August 15–18, 1982, New York City.

Rhyne, L. C. (1986). The relationship of strategic planning to financial performance. *Strategic Management Journal*, 7, 423–436.

Scott, W. R. (1987). *Organizations: Rational, natural, and open systems*. New York: Prentice-Hall.

Scott, W. R., & Meyer, J. W. (1991). The organization of societal sectors: Propositions and early evidence. In W. W. Powell and P. J DiMaggio (Eds.), *The New institutionalism in organizational analysis*. Chicago: The University of Chicago Press.

Seashore, S. E. (1983). A framework for an integrated model of organizational effectiveness. In K. S. Cameron & D. A. Whetten (Eds.), *Organizational effectiveness: A comparison of multiple models*. New York: Academic Press.

Siciliano, J., & Floyd, S. (1993). Nonprofit boards, strategic management and organizational performance: An empirical study of YMCA organizations (Working Paper No. 182). New Haven, CT: Yale University Program on Non-Profit Organizations.

Smith, S. R., & Lipsky, M. (1993). *Nonprofits for hire: The welfare state in the age of contracting*. Cambridge, MA: Harvard University Press.

Stone, M. M., Bigelow, B., & Crittenden, W. F. (1996). Strategic management in nonprofit organizations: A review and synthesis of research. Unpublished manuscript, Boston University School of Management.

Tassie, B., Murray, V. Cutt, J., & Bragg, D. (1996). Rationality and politics: What really goes on when funders evaluate the performance of fundees? *Nonprofit and Voluntary Sector Quarterly*, 25(3), 347–363.

Venkatraman, N., & Ramanujam, V. (1986). Measurement of business performance. *Academy of Management Review*, 11(4), 801–814.

Young, D. R., Bania, N., & Bailey, D. (1996). Structure and accountability: A study of national nonprofit associations. *Nonprofit Management and Leadership*, 6(4), 347–365.

Chapter 4

Social Indicators for Assessing the Impact of the Independent, Not-for-Profit Sector of Society

KENNETH C. LAND

In discussing how to measure the impact of the independent, not-for-profit sector on society, researchers invoke notions of data systems and "social indicators" for impact measurement. Such discussions are also often couched in terms of the impacts of the independent sector on "quality of life." My objective in this chapter is to give specific meanings to these terms. I will review results of research that clarify the behavior of social indicators and cite some commonly used indicators and their limitations and potential as adequate measures. Finally, I will describe the data systems necessary to develop social indicators for measuring nonprofit sector performance.

The chapter is organized into two major sections. The first section briefly reviews the historical development of the field of social indicators and its current state. The second defines major categories of organizations in the not-for-profit sector and articulates some possible approaches to constructing social indicators that assess the impacts of these organizations on society.

KENNETH C. LAND • John Franklin Crowell Professor, Department of Sociology, and Senior Fellow, Center for Demographic Studies, Duke University, Durham, North Carolina 27708.

Measuring the Impact of the Nonprofit Sector, edited by Patrice Flynn and Virginia A. Hodgkinson, New York, Kluwer Academic/Plenum Publishers, 2002.

SOCIAL INDICATORS: HISTORICAL DEVELOPMENTS AND CURRENT STATE

The Classical Heritage

The identification of social indicators (SI) and quality of life (QOL) as terms and subjects for research dates back approximately three decades. During the past 30 years, a voluminous literature has grown, and certain contributions from the 1960s and 1970s now stand as "classics" in the literature on QOL measurement and SI.

Reviewers (see, e.g., Land, 1983, 1992; Noll & Zapf, 1994) trace the origin of SI research to a 1960s project of the American Academy of Arts and Sciences, sponsored by the National Aeronautics and Space Administration, that investigated the side effects of the space program on American society. Investigators came to the conclusion that there was almost a complete lack of adequate data *and* adequate methodology for measuring and anticipating such social consequences. Further scholarly collaboration resulted in the publication in 1966 of the book titled *Social Indicators,* edited by Raymond Bauer, the director of the Academy project. In Bauer's terms, social indicators were "statistics, statistical series, and all other forms of evidence that enable us to assess where we stand and are going with respect to our values and goals" (1966, p. 1). *Indicators of Social Change: Concepts and Measurements,* edited by Eleanor Bernert Sheldon and Wilbert E. Moore (1968), is a second SI classic from the 1960s. Noting the far-reaching change taking place in American society, this massive volume reported on changes in the demographic, structural, distributive, and aggregative features of American society and advocated that these trends be monitored. *Toward a Social Report* (U.S. Department of Health, Education, and Welfare, 1969), released by the U.S. Department of Health, Education, and Welfare on the last day of President Lyndon B. Johnson's administration, surely is a third SI classic from the 1960s. Conceived of as a prototypical counterpart to the annual economic reports of the president, it addressed major issues in important areas of social concern (health and illness; social mobility; the physical environment; income and poverty; public order and safety; learning, science, and art; and participation and alienation) and provided readers with an assessment of prevalent conditions.

Generally speaking, this sharp impulse of interest in social indicators in the 1960s sprang from the movement toward collection and organization of national social, economic, and demographic data that began in Western societies during the seventeenth and eighteenth centuries and accelerated in the twentieth century (Gross, 1966; Carley, 1981, pp. 14–15). The work of William F. Ogburn and his collaborators at the University of Chicago in the 1930s and

1940s on the theory and measurement of social change is more proximate and sociologically germane (Land, 1975b). As chairman of President Herbert Hoover's Research Committee on Social Trends, Ogburn supervised production of the two-volume *Recent Social Trends in the United States* (President's Research Committee on Social Trends, 1933), a ground-breaking contribution to social reporting. Ogburn's ideas about the measurement of social change influenced several of his students, notably Albert D. Biderman, Otis Dudley Duncan, Albert J. Reiss, Jr., and Eleanor B. Sheldon, who played major roles in the development of the SI field in the 1960s and 1970s.

It was observed early on in *The Human Meaning of Social Change* (Campbell & Converse, 1972) that most of the data available for analysis in the foregoing volumes were "objective" and one should not presume that the "subjective" meaning of social conditions would perfectly correlate with objective indicators. Efforts to explore subjective assessments of social conditions led to two additional classics in the SI/QOL literature: *The Quality of American Life: Perceptions, Evaluations, and Satisfactions* (Campbell, Converse, & Rodgers, 1976) and *Social Indicators of Well-Being: Americans' Perceptions of Life Quality* (Andrews & Withey, 1976). Using data from focus group and national surveys, these studies investigated perceptions of well-being and QOL, studied how these concepts are organized in the minds of different groups of American adults, developed valid and efficient ways of measuring these perceptions, suggested how the measurements could be implemented to yield a time series of subjective social indicators, and provided some initial readings of such indicators.

The construction of time series of social indicators and measurements of the quality of life led during the 1970s to the development of social modeling and social accounting systems and their application to national- and regional-level policy analyses within particular fields (i.e., health, education, crime, and science) (Land, 1992). Initial approaches to modeling variations in social indicators across social space and over time were sketched over 25 years ago in *Social Indicator Models* (Land & Spilerman, 1975), while demographic and time-use approaches to social accounting systems were studied in *Social Accounting Systems: Essays on the State of the Art* (Juster & Land, 1981).

Several key principles of SI and QOL research and social reporting emerged from these classics, as follows:

- *Normative social indicators*, which directly measure social well-being (social welfare), living conditions, or the QOL, and *descriptive social indicators*, which provide information relevant to understanding the directionality of changes in the normative indicators, are essential.
- Both types of indicators can be either objective or subjective. Normative social indicators contain statistics that represent social facts indepen-

dently of personal evaluations. Descriptive social indicators emphasize individuals' experiences and evaluations of social circumstances.
- *Major research tasks* are to monitor or describe social trends, explain these trends, identify relevant relationships between different developments, and investigate the consequences of those developments and likely future developments in time series of indicators (Land, 1983).
- The products of these efforts should be presented to the public via periodic social reports.

The construction of *objective SI* is based on the premise that a societal consensus exists about (a) the dimensions that are relevant for social well being, (b) good and bad conditions on these dimensions, and (c) the direction in which society should move to achieve described goals. While reasonably high levels of consensus exist in many societies about some social conditions (such as crime or environmental pollution), the increasing demographic, socioeconomic, and cultural diversity of many contemporary societies makes these presumptions of consensus about other social conditions problematic. This leads to a focus on *subjective SI*, measured in terms of individuals' subjective well-being and satisfaction or happiness with life as a whole and its various domains (e.g., self, family, home, leisure and leisure-time facilities, friends and associates, neighborhoods, education, job, services and facilities, community, general economic situation, local and national governments, the nation). The use of subjective SI is based on the premise that well-being, in the final instance, is perceived and best judged by individual citizens (Campbell & Converse, 1972). In fact, however, studies of subjective well-being and studies of objective SI can inform each other with domains from the latter used to define the objects for subjective ratings in the former, and measures of subjective salience from the former used to develop weights and scales for the latter.

The Social Indicators Movement and Beyond

The SI/QOL research stimulated by the classic literature was undertaken with a focused mission and strong sense of commitment that united all participants and thus was termed the "social indicators movement." In addition to social scientists, economists, and statisticians, the movement was supported by high-ranking civil servants and politicians, which is quite unusual for a research program. Noll and Zapf (1994, p. 10) note that the boom period of SI research took place in the 1970s. During this time, the center of activities for periodic official social reports shifted from the United States to Europe and especially to Scandinavia, the Netherlands, and Germany. Several European national social report series that continue to be produced periodically were established during these years.

By comparison, the period from the end of the 1970s to the mid-1980s was characterized by stagnation and decreasing interest in SI research: The number of publications declined, research projects ended, and the promotion of SI research was drastically reduced in the United States. In addition, international organizations greatly reduced their commitment to this program. These changes were caused by the economic crises of the early 1980s, the changed political climates under conservative governments, and the inability of the SI movement to communicate its successes and the usefulness of its products.

However, what some had regarded as crisis, disillusionment, and disappointment in the SI program is now seen as a process of consolidation and maturation (Noll & Zapf, 1994, p. 10). The central activities of social monitoring and social reporting have continued in many countries, and, since the mid-1980s, a revitalization in SI has occurred that has given rise to a new wave of social reporting efforts on subnational, national, and international levels; establishment of new institutions of social monitoring; and further elaboration of social science and statistical infrastructures. As Noll and Zapf (1994, p. 11) observed, it is now apparent that the success of SI research is located more in the area of *general societal enlightenment* than in the production of technical expertise or the provision of special planning intelligence for politics. Instead of an instrumental or technocratic model that demands from politics the scientific information to solve social policy problems (a model characteristic of the 1960s), a *model of enlightenment*, in which social reporting places social well-being/quality-of-life issues on the political agenda, supplies material to the media and the public debate, and thus indirectly affects the political apparatus, seems more realistic in the 1990s.

Recent developments in social reporting have emphasized the need for *prospective social reporting and forecasting* (Noll & Zapf, 1994). The basic idea here is to supplement the retrospective model of most SI/QOL work with a prospective model that anticipates the future implications of trends. Land and Schneider (1987) began exploring (a) the limits of forecasting accuracy in large-scale natural and social systems that resulted from data/model limitations and (b) the distorting effects of the social institutional context in which forecasts are constructed. These limits aside, it seems clear that the cautious application of projection techniques, scenario explorations, and simulations could provide insights into possible developments in social conditions and extend the time horizon of social reports from the recent past to the future. (See Ahlburg & Land, 1992, for examples of this application in the area of population forecasting.)

Extending indicators of social conditions into the future leads naturally to a related interest in using social indicator models and accounting systems in policy analysis. Policy analysts (see, e.g., MacRae, 1985) have always hoped that social indicators could be used to actively shape social policy and planning through the policy choice process. At a minimum, this move requires identification of key variables that determine policy criterion indicators and changes therein (i.e., causal knowledge). More generally, it requires the construction of elaborate causal models and forecasting equations (often in the form of a computer model) that can be used to simulate "what would happen if" under a number of scenarios about policies and actions. An example is the development of the National Cancer Institute model for the control and reduction of the incidence of cancer in the United States to the year 2000 (Greenwald & Sondik, 1986). Various policy and action scenarios involving prevention, education, screening, and treatment, and their implications for cancer mortality were simulated and estimated with this computer model. These simulations led to a decision to allocate additional funds to a prevention program. We can expect to see many more applications of social indicators to policy choice and evaluation, given the currently accepted model of enlightenment, in which policy applications of social indicators are used to place issues on the political agenda and provide information for public debate.

Quality of Life as a Unifying Concept

Also during the decade of the 1990s we have seen the concept of "quality of life" take on widespread political, popular, and theoretical appeal. This concept emerged in the late 1960s and early 1970s as highly developed Western industrial societies began to question the appropriateness of viewing economic growth as the major goal of societal progress (Noll & Zapf, 1994, pp. 1–2). The QOL concept that resulted from the debate gave social policy and politics a new and more complex, multidimensional goal. As a goal of social policy, QOL encompasses all domains of life and subsumes, in addition to individual material and immaterial well-being, social collective values such as freedom, justice, and the guarantee of natural conditions of life for the present and for future generations.

The political use of QOL is reflected in the widespread use and popularity of numerous rankings, based on weighted scales of multiple domains of well-being, of the "best" places to live, work, play, and so on, be they cities, states, regions, or countries. Efforts to construct summary indices have been associated with these various studies of rankings. Summary indices attempt to synthesize the various dimensions of well-being into one single measure of quality of life. Examples include (a) the Human Development Index constructed by the United Nations Human Development Program to rank nations according to their state of human development (United Nations Development Programme, 1994); (b) Diener's (1995) value-based index for measuring national quality of life; and (c) Kacapyr's (1996) *American Demographics* Index of Well-Being (which is intended to measure whether life in the United States is improving or deteriorating on a month-by-month basis).

As noted earlier, the theoretical appeal of the QOL concept as an integrating notion in the social sciences and related disciplines is caused, in part, by its focus on individuals' assessments of their satisfaction with various life domains and with life as a whole. Indeed, already in the mid-1970s, Campbell et al. (1976, p. 1) observed that "those who presume to define the national goals increasingly speak of QOL rather than of further material possessions" and that, while seldom precisely defined, the implication is that the focus should shift "from a concentration on being well-off to a concern with a sense of well-being."

During the two decades since publication of the initial methodological studies of the subjective QOL concept, this notion has become embedded within the theoretical apparatus of many disciplines. For instance, methods for assessing QOL have become a key part of clinical work and evaluations of medical procedures in behavioral medicine, medical psychology, medical sociology, and social gerontology. Albrecht and Fitzpatrick (1994) found that more than 1,000 articles on quality of life in health care are published each year. The concept also has become a construct that bridges the disciplines of marketing research and strategic business policy with social indicators. Marketing consumer and business products is an important social force that, by impacting consumer satisfaction, has far-reaching direct and indirect impacts on a society's prevailing QOL (Samli, 1987; Sirgy & Samli, 1995). Thus, there is research on how marketing affects QOL and on how this impact can be measured and improved so that society as a whole can benefit.

Numerous studies of the psychodynamics of the QOL defined as subjective well-being (which is defined, in turn, as happiness or satisfaction with life as a whole or with one of its specific domains) have improved understanding of this construct during the past two decades. For instance, we now know that subjective well-being has both *trait-like properties* (i.e., it is a durable psychological condition that differs among individuals and is relatively stable over time and consistent across situations for a given individual) and *state-like properties* (i.e., it is a condition that is, at least in part, reactive to situational differences and changes therein, especially in the relatively immediate aftermath of such changes) (see, e.g., Stones, Hadjistavropoulos, Tuuko, & Kozma, 1995; Veenhoven, 1994). This research also has identified some of the limitations of the use of overall happiness to monitor the effects of social or therapeutic interventions.

SOCIAL INDICATORS FOR ASSESSING
THE NONPROFIT SECTOR

A Classification of Nonprofit Organizations by Mission

The task now is to focus on how the accumulated literature on social indicators and lessons learned from that literature can be applied to the task of measuring the impact on society of the independent, not-for-profit sector. This is a large, open-ended question with many different aspects and many types of answers.

To begin, it is helpful to disaggregate the nonprofit sector somewhat according to various missions or organizational objectives. Wolpert (Chapter 8) introduces such a classification to aid assessment of the distributional impacts of nonprofits. His classification was based on a triangle whose corners are defined by missions of charity, philanthropy, and service. This threefold scheme misses a major category of nonprofit organizations, such as lodges, bowling teams, and other voluntary associations, whose mission revolves around fellowship, affiliation, and association with other members. Similarly, while churches, synagogues, temples, and related religious organizations typically have charitable and service missions, their formation is prompted by fellowship, affiliation, and association objectives. Thus, we will transform Wolpert's triangle into a rectangle by adding this fourth dimension (Figure 4.1).

The corners of our rectangle define "pure types" of nonprofit organizations according to the following primary objectives or missions of the organizations:

1. *The provision of services* (e.g., the American Red Cross, nonprofit health care organizations) to foster mutual benefit and pluralism, to serve "thin"

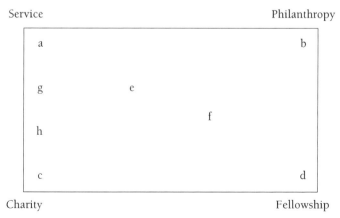

Figure 4.1. A classification of nonprofit organizations by organizational mission.

markets not served by private or public sectors, and to enhance quality, variety, compassion, and efficiency in service delivery.

2. *Philanthropy* (e.g., foundations, large donors) to establish and enhance civic institutions, such as hospitals, universities, museums, and community social capital.

3. *Charity* (e.g., the Salvation Army, Catholic Charities) to redistribute or transfer resources from the more fortunate to the needy.

4. *Fellowship* to provide affiliation and association with other members who share an activity or interest.

Some real-world nonprofit organizations might be located relatively near these pure types, such as represented by points a, b, c, and d in Figure 1. In reality, of course, many nonprofit organizations have missions that are some convex combination of the pure types. In the figure, for example, points e and f represent organizations that include both fellowship and the provision of services (perhaps to a local community), while points g and h represent organizations that combine charitable and service objectives.

Within each of these areas of nonprofit organizations, it is sometimes useful to further cross-classify by functional category. For instance, within the class of nonprofits whose primary mission is the delivery of services, it may be useful to distinguish the subsectors of health, education, culture and the arts, etc.[1] Similarly, within the class of nonprofits whose primary mission is philanthropy, various functional subcategories of foundations can be distinguished. Whether to impose such functional classifications depends entirely on the purposes to which the classification will be put.

The diagrammatic scheme for social indicator models introduced by Land (1975a) (Figure 4.2) is also helpful for measuring the impact of the nonprofit sector on society. This diagram identifies five types of descriptive indicators bound together in the context of a social system model (containing analytic indicators of its own) that connects all indicator variables. The model begins with the conventional distinction between *exogenous variables* (those determined outside the model) and *endogenous variables* (those determined within the model). Within the class of exogenous variables, the scheme further distinguishes between *input descriptive indicators* (exogenous variables that can be manipulated in a nonprofit organizational or institutional context) and *nonmanipulable exogenous descriptive indicators* (exogenous variables that are determined outside the system under consideration and cannot be manipulated). Similarly, within the class of endogenous variables, the scheme distinguishes between *output descriptive indicators* (indicators of the quantity and other characteristics of nonprofit organizational or institutional products, as they relate to the primary mission of the organization/institution), *end-product* or *outcome descriptive indicators* (indicators of the benefits of the nonprofit or-

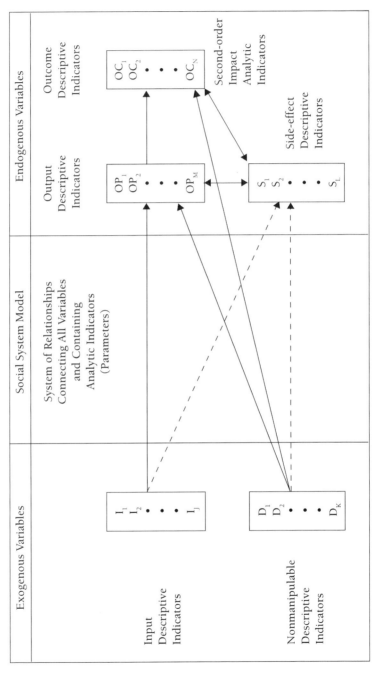

Figure 2. Relationships among indicator types.

ganizational/institutional outputs for those individuals or populations served by or otherwise involved with the organization or institution), and side-effect descriptive indicators (indicators of general social conditions influenced by the output and outcome indicators). Relating these five sets of indicators, the figure portrays a model or system of relationships that identify certain parameters or *analytic indicators* of the production and related processes represented in the model. The main relationships determining output and outcome indicators are shown with solid arrows; those determining side effects are shown with broken arrows. The arrows connecting the output and outcome indicators to the side-effect indicators are labeled *second-order impact analytic indicators* because they seem to be the type of indicator that Bauer (1966) and his collaborators were commissioned to assess in the original American Academy of Arts and Sciences project. Furthermore, this is a two-headed arrow, exemplifying that side effects can both influence and be influenced by the social conditions measured by the output–outcome indicators.

It should be emphasized that the situation illustrated in Figure 4.2 is more the ideal than an actual description of any particular SI research effort. Nonetheless, the configuration in the figure helps illuminate the measurement and analytical problems that underlie SI research efforts. In the Academy research (Bauer, 1966), the basic output indicators were a successful moon flight and the time necessary to complete the flight; the input indicators pertained to the monetary, physical, and manpower resources allocated to the program. Nonmanipulable descriptive indicators included such constraints as the state of physical science and technology in the 1960s and the availability of trained manpower. Finally, side effects of the space program included indicators of the concentration of space program employees and resources in particular occupations and geographical locales as well as technology spin-offs for civilian uses.

The question now is, can the scheme in Figure 4.2 be usefully applied to measure the impacts of the nonprofit sector on society? Let us consider the application of this modeling scheme to each of our major categories of nonprofit organizations and institutions. For each category, we will consider measuring the impacts of a particular organization's activities. We will consider whether it is possible to subsequently aggregate these assessments to an entire nonprofit sector.

The Impacts of Nonprofit Service Organizations

Consider measuring the impacts on society of nonprofit organizations whose primary mission is the provision of services. An obvious measurement focus could be on the production of outputs (services delivered) and the associated outcomes for clients or participants. But it also may be desirable to measure the side effects of the delivered services on the lives of clients and on the communities in which they live.

Suppose the service organization being assessed is a local Meals-on-Wheels operation whose primary mission is to deliver hot meals within some well-defined geographic area to elderly, disabled individuals. According to Figure 1, a large array of indicators can be defined in this case: *Input indicators* might include the dollar values of the foods and facilities used to produce the meals; the number of individual volunteers or paid workers involved in the production and delivery of the meals; and the time and transportation costs involved in this delivery. *Nonmanipulable exogenous indicators* might include measures of the geographic dispersion or density of locations to which meals are to be delivered. *Output indicators* might include the numbers of meals delivered and persons served (both as an absolute number and as a percentage of the total population of potential clients). *Outcome indicators* might focus on characteristics of the organization's clients and on client satisfaction with the meals delivered. *Side-effect indicators* could be defined in terms of the effects of the meal delivery on the nutritional or health status of the clients and the impact of meal delivery on client satisfaction and thus on their overall subjective well-being or quality of life. Finally, assuming that data for a reasonable array of such indicators could be compiled, *analytic indicators* relating, for example, input indicators to output, outcome, and side-effect indicators could be estimated.

Three comments are pertinent to this example. First, the data requirements necessary to operationalize such a scheme are clearly substantial. In most cases, a full assessment of impacts of nonprofit service organizations will require the compilation of operational data specific to the organization as well as sample survey data on the clients served. Nonetheless, though difficult, this goal can be achieved, at least in one aspect or another; some examples are described in Greenway (1996).

Second, we must note a key distinction among output, outcome, and side-effect indicators:[2] If the primary mission of nonprofit service organizations is the delivery of specific services, then output indicators typically can be defined as measures of the quantity and quality of products or services delivered or as measures of individuals served. In contrast, outcome indicators pertain to measures of the end product or final delivery or consumption of the services or products. These include measures of client characteristics and client satisfaction. Client characteristics typically include such basic demographic variables as age, income level, race/ethnicity, gender, and marital status. They might also include additional information pertaining to client status prior to delivery of outputs, referral source, and other relevant background information. The specific information collected on clients must be adapted to each service organization and be determined by its service methodology and its funding and licensing requirements. Client satisfaction as an outcome measure can draw from a vast research literature on consumer satisfaction in marketing research (see, e.g., Sirgy & Samli, 1995). It can include various dimensions of satisfaction with the service or product delivered as well as overall satisfaction with the service provider.[3] Side effects of the delivery of specific products or services and the satisfactions that result can include a variety of measures of the impacts of these on other aspects of the individual's life. These side effects usually can be measured in terms of changes in clients' values, attitudes, knowledge, skills, behavior, and conditions of life.

Third, in addition to output, outcome, and side-effects indicators that focus on the impacts of the services on individuals served, indicators could be defined to address relational, distributional, and community impacts in the manner indicated by Greenway (Chapter 13, this volume) and Wolpert (Chapter 7, this volume). For instance, questions could be posed regarding the relative efficiency with which nonprofit service organizations deliver services as compared with each other, or with government or market sector organizations. If a nonprofit's goals are charitable (i.e., the redistribution of resources to the needy), measures for charitable organizations could be constructed. Efforts to ensure representative boards, the use of sliding fee schedules, and similar indicators also could be defined. The impacts of human services programs at the client, program, and community levels might also be measured. A Meals-on-Wheels program may be very successful at improving the social conditions and quality of life of its clients and yet may not have substantial community-wide impact on these conditions for a community's elderly residents unless it reaches a large percentage of the eligible population. Community-level conditions are also affected by aspects of the community other than the outputs of individual, human services programs—such as local economic conditions and public policies, and other nonprofit and private social institutions such as civic groups, churches, neighbors, and families. Constraints on social conditions that are created by these structural features of a community can cancel out or reverse the positive impacts of a nonprofit service organization.

The Impacts of Charitable Organizations

As noted earlier, the primary mission of purely charitable organizations is to redistribute or transfer resources from the more fortunate to the needy. In practice, many charities seek to accomplish this mission by providing services to recipients. To measure the impacts of charitable activities, we can apply much of the same strategy as we have just outlined for measuring the impacts of nonprofit service organizations. In addition, as Wolpert (1996) has indicated, assessment of the redistributional impacts of charitable organizations requires a focus on the income difference between donors and recipients, on the percentage of the lowest income group that has been assisted, and on similar measures.

The Impacts of Philanthropic Organizations

The primary mission of nonprofit philanthropic organizations is to establish and enhance civic institutions. When these civic institutions provide services, we can measure their philanthropic impacts by building on the measurement of the impacts of service organizations described above. The focus of measurement now becomes an assessment of the extent to which philanthropic activities enhance the provision of services. It may also be feasible to measure philanthropy's contribution to the quality of life of individuals living in the communities served by the art museum or hospital that receives the philanthropy, for example. At the objective level, this assessment may involve measuring the diversity of institutions to which the philanthropy contributes as well as any increase in availability of services to members of the community. At the subjective level, it may require using sample survey data on contributions to satisfaction with appropriate life domains as well as indicators of satisfaction with life as a whole. In principle, all of these impacts can be measured, but such measurement is difficult to carry out in practice. Assessing the impacts of philanthropic activities that support artists, researchers, and public interest activist groups is even more difficult. In this case, quantities of input resources (e.g., number of grants and dollar amounts awarded) clearly can be measured, as can certain output indicators (e.g., number of individuals or groups supported, pieces of art or research reports produced, legislative measures enacted). Measures of outcome indicators (e.g., benefits to community members) are more difficult to identify, as are secondary impact indicators (e.g., distributional consequences).

The Impacts of Fellowship Organizations

Nonprofit fellowship organizations, whose primary mission is to provide affiliation and association for other members, fall into two types. A neighborhood bridge club is an example of a relatively pure type of nonprofit fellowship organization. Churches, Masonic lodges, neighborhood athletic associations, and bowling leagues represent a second type—those with a voluntary association component combined with fellowship, service, charitable, or philanthropic missions. To the extent that these organizations also provide service, charity, or philanthropy, they face the same problems in measuring their impact as do charitable or philanthropic organizations and can use the same measurement approaches as described for these groups.

In addition, nonprofit fellowship organizations provide their members with an opportunity for interaction with like-minded individuals and the social support that goes with it. In principle, it is possible to measure the impacts of this social support on members' health status. The impacts on physical well-being in general and mental health in particular are well established (see, e.g., House, Landis, & Umberson, 1988; Lin, Dean, & Ensel, 1986). Thus, any serious attempt to measure the impacts of nonprofit fellowship organizations should assess this health connection.

The Challenge of Aggregation

From the beginning, the SI/QOL literature has been filled with discussions of the extent to which aggregation into a single summary indicator, or at least a small number of summary indicators, is feasible and meaningful. But the objective of measuring the impact of the "nonprofit sector" on society is more ambitious and complicated than the original quest of SI, which was to measure the impact of the American space program on society in the 1960s. The space program had identifiable research, engineering, and management efforts, as well as geographic regions and professions. The nonprofit sector permeates virtually every aspect and area of the United States.

While daunting, some dimensions of the challenge are more readily achievable than others. Substantial measurements for national aggregations of trends and of dollar values of inputs to the nonprofit sector already exist in Hodgkinson and Weitzman's (1996) *Nonprofit Almanac*. This volume also contains similar information on employment levels, private sources of support, and the financial conditions of nonprofit organizations.

With few exceptions, however, little systematic information is available at the national level regarding output, outcome, and side-effects indicators. Indeed, it probably is not feasible to measure outputs and outcomes for most local service, charity, philanthropic, or fellowship nonprofit organizations in America. Some nonprofits do not have clearly defined missions and, hence, do not have well-defined outputs or outcomes. Even among those that do, some deliver products or services to anonymous participants; others have missions that are intangible, such as advocacy on behalf of issues or constituents. The impact of either is difficult to measure.

Clearly, we need national parameters and national sampling methodology. For example, if data were available on selected output and outcome (and possibly side-effect) indicators for a probability sample of local Meals-on-Wheels programs from around the country, it is in principle possible to estimate the corresponding national levels of such indicators. The availability of such data over successive time points would allow us to study trends, interrelationships, and so forth.

While such efforts undoubtedly would contribute to an understanding of some of the impacts of nonprofit organizations on society, the task remains huge and no claim for completeness will likely ever be made. Even if much effort is devoted to measurement along the lines sketched here, there no doubt will be dimensions of impact that are not represented or that are poorly measured. Whether this means that the measurement goal is probably impossible but possibly useful (DiMaggio, 1996) remains to be seen.

NOTES

1. A useful starting point for a functional classification of nonprofit organizations is "The National Taxonomy of Exempt Entities" in Appendix A of Hodgkinson and Weitzman (1996).
2. The distinctions here are similar to those made by Greenway (1996). However, in contrast to the classification used here, Greenway does not treat participant satisfaction and participant characteristics as outcome measures. Rather, she classifies these as output measures. Greenway's outcome measures category then refers to what are termed "side-effect indicators" here. Thus, in the Meals-on-Wheels example, Greenway would consider impacts of the meals on client nutrition or health as an outcome, whereas we consider it a side-effect indicator here. That is, outcome measures are here limited to those end-product or consumption indicators that pertain to the services or products that are the primary mission of the service organization to deliver. Thus, unless the Meals-on-Wheels organization defines an improvement in nutritional or health status of its clients as its primary mission, measures of this type would be considered side-effect indicators, not outcomes of service or product delivery.
3. We can use the research cited earlier on the psychodynamics of satisfaction measures of subjective well-being to conclude that queries about client satisfaction with products should be made relatively quickly after the product is delivered.

REFERENCES

Ahlburg, D. A., & Land, K. C. (Guest Eds.). (1992). Population forecasting [Special issue]. *International Journal of Forecasting, 8*, 289–542.

Albrecht, G. L., & Fitzpatrick, R. (Eds.). (1994). *Advances in medical sociology: Quality of life in health care*. Greenwich, CT: JAI Press.

Andrews, F. M., & Withey, S. B. (1976). *Social indicators of well-being: Americans' perceptions of life quality*. New York: Plenum.

Bauer, R. A. (Ed.). (1966). *Social indicators*. Boston, MA: MIT Press.

Campbell, A., & Converse, P. E. (Eds.). (1972). *The human meaning of social change*. New York: Russell Sage Foundation.

Campbell, A., Converse, P. E., & Rodgers, W. L. (1976). *The quality of American life: Perceptions, evaluations, and satisfactions*. New York: Russell Sage Foundation.

Carley, M. (1981). *Social measurement and social indicators: Issues of policy and theory*. London: George Allen and Unwin.

Diener, E. (1995). A value-based index for measuring national quality of life. *Social Indicators Research, 36*, 107–127.

DiMaggio, P. (1996, September). Measuring the impact of the nonprofit sector on society is probably impossible but possibly useful: A sociological perspective. Paper presented at the meeting of Independent Sector, "Measuring the impact of the independent, not-for-profit sector on society." Washington, DC.

Greenwald, P., & Sondik, E. J. (Eds.). (1986). *Cancer control objectives for the nation: 1985–2000* (NCI Monograph No. 2). Washington, DC: U.S. Government Printing Office.

Greenway, M. T. (1996). *The Status of Research and Indicators on Nonprofit Performance in Human Services*. Paper presented at the Independent Sector Conference on Measuring the Impact of the Independent Not-for-Profit Sector on Society, September 5–6, 1996, Carnegie Conference Center, Washington, DC.

Gross, B. A. (1966). The state of the nation: Social systems accounting. In R. A. Bauer (Ed.), *Social Indicators* (pp. 154–271). Boston, MA: MIT Press.

Hodgkinson, V. A., & Weitzman, M. S. (1996). *Nonprofit almanac: Dimensions of the independent sector 1996–1997*. San Francisco: Jossey-Bass.

House, J. S., Landis, K. R., & Umberson, D. (1988). Social relationships and health. *Science, 241*, S40–45.

Juster, F. T., & Land, K. C. (Eds.). (1981). *Social accounting systems: Essays on the state of the art*. New York: Academic Press.

Kacapyr, E. (1996). The well-being index. *American Demographics*, (February), vol. 18, 32–43.

Land, K. C. (1975a). Social indicator models: An overview. In K. C. Land & S. Spilerman (Eds.), *Social Indicator Models* (pp. 5–36). New York: Russell Sage Foundation.

Land, K. C. (1975b). Theories, models and indicators of social change. *International Social Science Journal, 27*, 7–37.

Land, K. C. (1983). Social Indicators. *Annual Review of Sociology, 9*, 1–26.

Land, K. C. (1992). Social indicators. In E. F. Borgatta, & M. L. Borgatta (Eds.), *Encyclopedia of sociology* (pp. 1844–1850). New York: Macmillan.

Land, K. C., & Schneider, S. H. (Eds.). (1987). *Forecasting in the social and natural sciences*. Boston, MA: D. Reidel.

Land, K. C., & Spilerman, S. (Eds.). (1975). *Social indicator models*. New York: Russell Sage Foundation.

Lin, N., Dean A., Ensel, W. M. (1986). *Social support, life events, and depression*. New York: Praeger.

MacRae, D., Jr. (1985). *Policy indicators: Links between social science and policy*. Chapel Hill: University of North Carolina Press.

Noll, H. H., & Zapf, W. (1994). Social indicators research: Societal monitoring and social reporting. In I. Borg & P. P. Mohler (Eds.), *Trends and prospects in empirical social research* (pp. 1–16). New York: Walter de Gruyter.

President's Research Committee on Social Trends. (1933). *Recent social trends in the United States*. New York: McGraw-Hill.

Samli, A. C. (Ed.). (1987). *Marketing and the quality-of-life interface*. Westport, CT: Quorum Books.

Sheldon, E. B., & Moore, W. E. (Eds.). (1968). *Indicators of social change: Concepts and measurements*. New York: Russell Sage Foundation.

Sirgy, M. J., & Samli, A. C. (Eds.). (1995). *New dimensions in marketing/quality-of-life research*. Westport, CT: Quorum Books.

Stones, M. J., Hadjistavropoulos, T., Tuuko, H., & Kozma, A. (1995). Happiness has trait-like and state-like properties: A reply to Veenhoven. *Social Indicators Research, 36*, 129–144.

United Nations Development Programme. (1994). The human development index revisited. In *Human development report: 1994* (pp. 90–110). New York: Oxford University Press.

U. S. Department of Health, Education, and Welfare. (1969). *Toward a social report*. Washington, DC: U.S. Government Printing Office.

Veenhoven, R. (1994). Is happiness a trait? Tests of the theory that a better society does not make people any happier. *Social Indicators Research, 33*, 101–160.

Wolpert, J. (1996). *The Distributional Impacts of Nonprofits and Philanthrophy*. Paper presented at the Independent Sector Conference on Measuring the Impact of the Independent Not-for-Profit Sector on Society, September 5–6, 1996. Carnegie Conference Center, Washington, DC.

Part III

Civil Society and Governance

Part III includes four chapters devoted to civil society and governance. Alexis de Tocqueville noted that associations of all types (e.g., political, special interest, moral, and religious) were the schools of democracy. In recent decades, scholars have revisited the role of associations and all sorts of voluntary organizations as essential ingredients of a democratic society. These intermediary organizations between the family, the private, and the large institutions of market and government include clubs, religious groups, schools, symphonies, choirs, and neighborhood associations among a host of other voluntary associations and organizations. In the post Cold War world, many eastern and central Europeans use the term "civil society" as an antidote to a strong state and market for preserving freedom for citizens. Defining civil society has become a subject of debate that provides a series of questions that lend themselves to measurement of various kinds.

The measurement of civil society and democracy is in its infancy. Attempts have been made to build a civic participation index to measure the strength of citizen involvement in their communities. Ongoing efforts have been made for many years to measure freedom within nations through the Freedom House Index. More recently, there have been efforts by the World Bank to measure the impact of civil liberties and democracy on the efficacy of World Bank–funded projects. A recent study by World Bank economists used a combination of indexes to develop such measures including Freedom House and Humana, a human rights index, and a number of governance indicators. The results are promising and indicate that countries in which citizens had civil liberties also had better government performance on World Bank–financed projects (World Bank, 1998). There seemed to be some evidence to suggest that developing nations with a higher number of nonprofit organizations per capita seemed to have greater levels of freedom or stronger civil societies.

Another theme that is important to the study of civil society is the role of government and leadership. Colin Campbell (Chapter 5) focuses on neoliberalism and its impact on social welfare in Anglo-American states. He argues that the neoliberal view that the role of state should be minimal in a *laissez-faire* economy has led to a crisis in leadership and a decline of the welfare state. With rising inflation and declining economies during the 1970s in Australia, New Zealand, Great Britain, Canada, and the United States, citizens became convinced that "interventionalist" government could not solve social problems. For Campbell, the measure becomes the ability of leaders and legislatures to define the appropriate role of the state. Public leaders "holding the microphone in public discourse" also will determine the future of the not-for-profit sector, which could face impossible burdens in a minimalist state. He posits that the role of the independent sector rests "not in a mad dash to catch bodies as they fall through safety nets, but rather to contribute to maintaining a vibrant civil society."

One of the most important roles of nonprofit organizations is to advocate causes in the public interest. It is this role that is most identified with the contribution of nonprofit organizations to democracy. John McCarthy and Jim Castelli (Chapter 6) argue that measuring policy advocacy of nonprofit organizations is the major goal of research, but much needs to be put in place before that goal is achieved. Policy advocacy must be measured across all nonprofit organizations, not simply the small group of organizations that are called advocacy organizations. Advocacy efforts need to be studied at local, state, and national levels for their various impacts. Furthermore, advocacy efforts need to be compared with those of business, government, and political organizations in order to measure the particular contributions that nonprofit organizations make in policy advocacy. The authors outline a broad research agenda for defining advocacy activities, studying both institutions and individuals, and identifying direct and indirect advocacy—that is, the mobilization of individual citizens by nonprofit organizations.

McCarthy and Castelli examine extant research to demonstrate that advocacy is widespread among all types of nonprofit organizations. They recommend that certain ongoing research efforts, such as the Independent Sector's *Giving and Volunteering* survey, include questions related to the extent and variety of citizen advocacy. Other kinds of studies examine advocacy campaigns to measure the specific impact of nonprofit organizations. Comparative studies of communities could also provide a fruitful analysis of civil societies.

From the role of public leadership, Julian Wolpert (Chapter 7) focuses on the question of measuring the impact of various types of nonprofit organizations. Wolpert takes a broad approach by examining distributional impacts, not just income redistribution. His emphasis is on the ability to measure the "incidence of benefit," that is, who benefits from different types of nonprofit organizations. Since the depression, government rather than not-for-profit organizations has had the primary role in income redistribution and the provision of safety nets for the poor. Nonprofit organizations play a supplementary role in this responsibility and at times are partners with government in providing services. In the little research that has been accomplished related to the beneficiaries of nonprofit organizations, there seems to be little redistribution. Wolpert argues that the measurement of inputs of nonprofit organizations has improved over the last decade. These inputs include such data as the sources of revenue, type of expenditures, and the number of employees and volunteers. However, data available for the measure of outputs, outcomes, and impact are very primitive, or nonexistent.

Even more challenging is the lack of measures related to who benefits and how. Some of the questions to be examined include the following. Who receives services and of what kind and quality? How do students of private schools, museum-goers, patients in hospitals, or church members benefit? Do some clients benefit more than others from nonprofit activities? While these are challenging questions, Wolpert argues that outcomes measurement will become even more important in an era of government devolution and cutbacks in funding. He proposes ways to approach research with particular attention to the redistributional effects and services of nonprofit organizations through national surveys, reputational surveys, and case studies. While acknowledging that serving clients in need is important for nonprofits, he argues for the importance of trying to measure the "distinctive and independent agenda" of nonprofit organizations in their distributory roles, including the enrichment of civic life, ensuring quality and variety in community services, and responding ethically to community needs.

The last chapter in this section brings the issue of democracy and citizen participation full circle. Reflecting upon nearly two decades of effort by the Kettering Foundation and others to understand public life, David Mathews (Chapter 8) wonders whether it is possible to "regenerate public life." Mathews presents a paradigm of what public life is in order perhaps to strengthen it. He asserts that no one knows if public life can be renewed, but possibly his set of assumptions built on learnings might eventually be "tested by experience."

Using the examples of cities with vibrant public lives such as Tupelo, Mississippi, Mathews distinguishes public life from the social lives of citizens who are joined through everchanging alliances in the practical business of addressing common problems. To do this, social capital is distinguished from political capital as the range of occasions "where people can get to know one another as citizens." People do not have to even like each other to work together as citizens, but they must be able to engage in conversations about the well-being of the community.

Mathews lays out a framework "for ordering what we are learning about public life" which could generate assumptions for strengthening or regenerating public life. He delineates the various categories that the Kettering Foundation found to be essential elements of public life. These include ways of relating governed by precepts, not by norms. Strong communities have a "civil infrastructure" or a group of networks, associations, and organizations that provide channels of communication in the community and a forum for public deliberation among citizens. Mathews argues that strong communities have "practices" in their public life that become habits including the ability of citizens to name problems, to make decisions together through public deliberation about how to act on these problems, to engage in public action, and to evaluate or judge the results of the public action.

Communities with a successful public life use power inclusively and laterally, rather than vertically. This includes the belief that all citizens, even those without official power, have assets to bring to community problem solving. Ultimately, the community makes decisions through public deliberation, public action, and assuming responsibility for the results of citizen action.

Chapter **5**

The Vicious Circle
of the Constricting State
as Viewed through the Failure
of Executive Leadership
in Anglo-American Democracies

Colin Campbell

INTRODUCTION

I have a dirty little secret to tell. On the night of February 4, 1997, when President Bill Clinton was to give his State of the Union address and the judge in the O.J. Simpson civil case was to read the jury's verdict, I surfed the channels to find a station that was covering the latter story rather than the speech.

This might come as a surprise. As a presidency scholar, I should have been hanging on Clinton's every word. But I, along with a lot of Americans, have been burned too often by presidents in the age of minimalist leadership. Even George Bush's surprisingly eloquent and disarmingly conciliatory 1989 inauguration address proved illusory. After Clinton's 1997 inauguration address,

Colin Campbell • University Professor in Public Policy, The Georgetown Public Policy Institute, Washington, DC 20007.

Measuring the Impact of the Nonprofit Sector, edited by Patrice Flynn and Virginia A. Hodgkinson, New York, Kluwer Academic/Plenum Publishers, 2002.

my wife counseled me to be kind to the president as I headed to CNN to offer my observations. I pulled my punches and later found myself one of the only commentators not to come right out with it. The speech had proved a huge disappointment. I had declined to make myself available for interviews about Clinton's State of the Union address and, therefore, lacked motivation to watch it. I guess that movie critics do not waste time on films by bad producers unless forced to by their editors.

We find in this volume compelling arguments in favor of the not-for-profit sector's role in fostering and sustaining civil society. Yet we would be remiss if we did not recognize that such efforts will not succeed, indeed, will produce little, if our leaders do not lift political discourse to a level that comports with the aspirations of a society genuinely committed to civic culture. Benjamin Barber puts it well in saying that the two principals in the ongoing spats over our future at the time, Newt Gingrich and Bill Clinton, failed us by proclaiming "the end of the era of big government without having identified clear alternatives to the solitariness and greed of the private sector" (1996, p. 17).

Indeed, we have to ask some fundamental questions about how long this nation can afford governance through distemper. In the 1960s, Americans probably ran the best "civic culture" in the world (Almond & Verba, 1963). To be sure, the deadlock of democracy accompanying the separation of powers frustrated social democrats (Burns, 1963). However, a resilient political psyche dealt relatively easily with the ambiguity inherent in a nation serving as a beacon for all other democracies while lagging behind others in structured provision for the less advantaged.

Of course, America found itself in the 1960s at the height of its economic hegemony in the free world. Wealth covered a multitude of lapses in state social provision. But now it has become highly questionable whether we run the most robust democracy in the world, especially when only 25 percent of eligible voters even bothered to register and cast a ballot in the 1996 election. And we have experienced the decline of our economic competitiveness, which we seem capable of arresting only by relying increasingly on the cheap labor of our burgeoning underclass.

Thus, those expecting the not-for-profit sector to play a critical role in the unknown world that will result from the decline of government in our lives have to pay a great deal of attention to the type of leadership offered by those who control the microphone in political discourse. If political leaders summon the persuasive wherewithal to persuade the public to support greater efforts to tackle what ails this nation, then the independent sector will find that fewer demands will land on its lap by default. It will also gain clearer parameters and a more supportive environment for achieving what society expects of it.

The future for the independent sector does not rest in a mad dash to catch bodies as they fall through safety nets. Rather, it depends on whether leaders will turn political discourse around to the deleterious consequences of a minimalist state and then point the way to governance that will once again take on the big issues whose resolution will determine whether we remain a vibrant civil society at all. Indeed, if we ever concluded that the independent sector could not so effect political discourse to contribute to such a reversal as urged here, then we would be writing an obituary for the American civil culture.

THE CRISIS OF EXECUTIVE LEADERSHIP IN A WIDER CONTEXT

At the outset, it is important for the analysis to place America's problems with executive leadership within the wider context of ambivalence toward the state, which pervades the Anglo-American world. Thus, this chapter focuses on the issue of executive leadership in the age of the constricted state. It posits a vicious circle whereby executive leaders respond to public skepticism about the role of the state by ratcheting down the objectives of governance. This strategy often functions as a self-denying ordinance because a scaled-down view of governance frequently falls short of what circumstances actually require, especially in contending with new or unforeseen dysfunctions in the state's interface with society. The resulting breakdowns further deepen public disenchantment with the state.

This process constitutes a major component of any assessment of the future role of the not-for-profit sector within the current frame of democracy throughout much of the world. The relentless building down of the state's role in myriad social sectors operates as a driving force behind the rapid increase of burdens on the nonprofit sector over the past decade. And, the perverse calculus of executive leadership in the ever-constricting state offers little evidence that the current pattern will soon ebb. Only the exceptionally skilled executive leaders will be able to motivate citizens to engage in a refashioning of the role of the state so that it might better meet the social challenges of our age.

Scanning the established democracies in the world, we would likely conclude that the oldest of these—the Anglo-American democracies: the United States, United Kingdom, Canada, Australia, and New Zealand—constitute some of the most challenged of troubled regimes. Part of the problem rests in a sea of change in public assent to the role of the state in their lives. And each of these countries has found itself in a less competitive economic situation in the last 20 years than it did in the immediate postwar era. Perhaps more fundamentally, the dynamics of the relationship between executive leaders and voters have changed almost entirely in the new electronic era of politics. Almost messianic expectations emerge around certain figures, often relatively unseasoned, who manage to obtain power. However, lynch law often sets in when these individuals seem to compromise principle for pragmatic considerations. The public also appears not to consider honest mistakes as forgivable. If Anglo-American voters instituted a three-strikes-and-you're-out policy, most hapless chief executives would heave a sigh of relief.

If the crisis of executive leadership in Anglo-American democracies were a linear phenomenon, then it might not be that interesting to examine in detail. In fact, it has served up a number of inconsistencies and ironies that make the topic inherently engaging. Even looking for a moment at the immediate landscape, imagine the richness of what presents itself. In the United States in 1994, voters rebuked Bill Clinton by turning Democrats out of power in the Senate and the House of Representatives. For a year, the action significantly marginalized the presidency while turning Newt Gingrich into a quasi–prime minister. Then the public turned on Gingrich. They reelected Bill Clinton as president but kept the Republicans in control of the Senate and the House. Now nobody knows who's on first base!

In the United Kingdom, John Major retained power in a 1992 election even though voters liked him much less that his predecessor, Margaret Thatcher, and he ran a poor campaign (Newton, 1993; Butler & Kavanagh, 1992, pp. 247–268). Voters shied from going back to the Labour Party. They immediately turned on Major—especially after the collapse of the pound in September 1992—making Major's second term a torment.

From 1984 to 1993, Canada experienced nine years of rule by a man, Brian Mulroney, who interpreted voter unhappiness with the Liberal Party as a mandate to redefine the Canadian state. In the 1993 election, two new parties emerged that brought Mulroneyism to its logical conclusions: the Reform, which embodied the rugged individualism of the western provinces, and Bloc Quebecois, which brought committed separatists to the federal Parliament. These two vehicles for those unhappy with the nature of the Canadian state struck voters as much slicker streetcars than the Progressive Conservatives. Canada's first party of government ended up with two seats in the House of Commons, fewer than required to be considered a party at all.

In the antipodes, Australia and New Zealand have attracted international attention for their pursuit of market-oriented economic policies. Interestingly, Labo(u)r governments pressed the core reforms in each case during the mid-1980s. Right-of-center parties currently govern in each country. However, one finds in both that the market-oriented, managerialist era seems now to have plateaued, prompting the question of whether governance can live solely on building down the state.

Anglo-American systems thus share the experience of passing through especially difficult times for executive leadership. This chapter isolates Anglo-American systems for four reasons. First, all share similar constitutional legacies, although, of course, the United States is presidential, not parliamentary, and the United Kingdom and New Zealand are unitary (the United Kingdom not even having a written constitution). The British constitutional tradition has, however, played a significant role in the development of the U.S., Canadian, Australian, and New Zealand systems. Second, elites in the five systems tend to refer to the practices of one another when adapting to change. Third, all five countries consider themselves "victors" of World War II. They went through two postwar decades of relative economic prosperity. The upbeat view of democracy and sense of well-being fueled unprecedented inventiveness and expansiveness in governance in all five systems. By the 1970s, all five countries—especially in the face of two energy shocks, disillusionment with democracy, and sharp declines in relative economic advantage—began to wake up to the fact that they had in some respects perhaps lost World War II.

Fourth, all systems maintain fairly sharp distinctions between the vocations of political leadership and permanent government officials. This does not suggest a greater salience in these countries' distinction between policy and administration—far from it. However, even in the United States—with the immense importance of political appointees—a line is drawn between what is proper for political executives and for career bureaucrats. Differences between the executive–bureaucratic cultures of the Anglo-American systems and those of other advanced democracies mean that the former make creative symbiosis between politicians and bureaucrats more difficult to attain. Neoliberal regimes have tried, indeed, to reenshrine the view that politicians make policy and bureaucrats administer it. This has meant that inventiveness increasingly must come from outside the permanent state apparatus, thereby placing yet another burden on the nonprofit sector.

The experience of executive leadership in the five countries since the late 1970s suggests a crisis situation for three reasons. All have made a sharp diversion to minimalist government, which has had wrenching effects on the functions and performance of the state. The resulting building down of government has borne serious consequences for infrastructure, the balance between regulation and markets in the operation of the economy, and the social well-being of citizenries. Finally, with the emphasis on minimalism and disengagement of leaders from the state apparatus, political executives have stressed style at the expense of substance. This emphasis has resulted in an overuse of direct appeals to the public with little regard to the standing political–bureaucratic complex—a practice that not only makes systems prone to error but, as noted above, also shifts much of the burden for inventiveness to the nonprofit sector.

ANGLO-AMERICAN SYSTEMS IN THE AGE
OF INTERVENTIONIST GOVERNANCE

Each of the Anglo-American nations played a role in pioneering liberal democracy in this century. In the first third of the century, attention focused on extending suffrage. Interestingly, Australia and New Zealand—not the United States—led the pack in this process. Australia's efforts were helped by the fact that it was writing on a clean slate as it took shape as a nation in the late nineteenth century. Reformers could implement liberal ideals espoused in nineteenth-century British political philosophy with relatively little entrenched resistance (Thompson, 1994, pp. 13–14).

In the middle third of the century, Anglo-American systems shifted their attention to how governance might attain a high degree of both democracy *and* social security. The collapse of the world economy in the late 1920s had spawned both the Great Depression and the rise of fascism and Nazism in Europe. The view emerged that governments must do more to protect individuals from economic downturns and to redistribute wealth (Hennessey, 1992). In the immediate postwar period, the increased attractiveness of communism in some Western states worried leaders of Anglo-American democracies. All five grappled with the need to provide workers with tangible signs of the benefits of the liberal tradition.

Unlike many of the recovering democracies in continental Europe, none of the Anglo-American systems had developed strong "statist" traditions, at least within the fields of domestic policy (King, 1986, pp. 38–39; Rockman, 1984, p. 49). That is, they all shared a high degree of skepticism about the role of the state in guiding the economy and safeguarding the well-being of citizens (Esping-Anderson, 1990, p. 31). For instance, the Germans under Bismarck had pioneered the concept of the welfare state (Pierson, 1991, pp. 104–105), albeit one that relied on societal stratification (Esping-Anderson, 1990, p. 24). And the French had, throughout the century, drawn upon a strong tradition of harmonization between state policy and private enterprise (Feigenbaum, 1985).

In so far as it had existed at all, statism in Anglo-American democracies tended to derive from the ability to mobilize civilian armies. Occurrences such as the American Civil War, the Boer War in South Africa, the Spanish-American War, and the two World Wars all tended to work strong rally effects. These stemmed from a mixture of imperial aspirations and indignation over the perceived lack of democracy among antagonists.

The extension of statism to the domestic arena involved a complicated process. Political leaders would have to hone skills that would take them beyond the relatively negative task of fanning contempt for "inferior" societies.

They would have to motivate citizens toward the construction and maintenance of state capacities for economic and social intervention.

In none of our systems did this prove an easy process. However, each greatly enhanced the role of the state in domestic affairs—especially in the late 1930s, in the immediate postwar period, and in the mid-1960s. The successive iterations in the process placed a high premium on the expansiveness and inventiveness of political leadership. In turn, the leaders of the time inspired many young, able, and idealistic men and women to choose careers in the public sector rather than the private sector.

To be sure, consolidators emerged in this period, and not every system achieved the same level of state intervention. But the epoch marked one of the most explosive phases of governmental adaptation yet experienced. The fact that it bucked a decidedly Anglo skepticism of the state made it all that more remarkable. On the other hand, the Anglo-American states reaped the benefits of one feature that distinguished them from many continental European nations: The Anglo-American countries enjoyed the relative absence of deep sectarian divisions over the roles of the state and church in social provision. This paved the way for the former to advance the welfare state with little or no religiously based opposition. That is, the classic struggle between Catholicism and socialism—which has dominated politics in much of Western Europe—played relatively small roles in the Anglo-American democracies (Castles & Mitchell, 1992, pp. 16–17). In fact, the Labor Party in Australia actually drew the bulk of its support in the first half of this century from Catholics, with the main sources of cleavage being state support of Catholic schools and conscription during World War I (Aitkin, 1985, pp. 219–221; Thompson, 1994, pp. 64–65). Only the Canadian province of Quebec presented an instance in which the Roman Catholic Church stood as a bulwark against the expansion of the state until the "Quiet Revolution" and its associated secularization during the 1960s (McRoberts & Posgate, 1980, p. 30).

Just as a similar dream propelled our societies in the middle third of this century, a shared sense of disillusionment began to set in during the 1960s. This became especially manifest in the restlessness of youths and intellectuals. It reached pronounced levels in the mid-1960s and persisted into the early 1970s. Such skepticism focused on the slowed or halted momentum in building up the state's capacity for intervention. It acutely felt the systemic obstacles to more thoroughgoing pursuit of the welfare state.

By the late 1960s, the Anglo-American nations began to experience severe pressures on available resources for government intervention. In the United States, Johnson's simultaneous pursuit of the Vietnam War and the War on Poverty overheated the economy. The damage left the United States sputtering at the most crucial phase of economic globalization. Britain began to face the consequences of the loss of its empire. It, too, had done a poor job of retooling for the postindustrial era and found itself the major European power least equipped to contend with the loss of markets resulting from the explosion of Asian enterprise. Its late entry into the European Community would delay the process whereby it could gain access to continental markets.

Canada's economy always closely follows the fortunes of that of the United States. Thus, it slipped into stagflation in the early 1970s—just as the U.S. economy had. The energy crises of 1973 and 1979 placed an added burden on Canada, especially because the eastern part of the country relied heavily on imported oil. As Britain oriented its future toward the European Community, Australia began to suffer serious losses in markets for agricultural products. In addition, sluggish global economic performances, beginning in the early 1970s, meant that demand for minerals became unstable. Australia began its struggle with diversification from an economy based on the farm and the quarry. New Zealand, much more reliant on the farm than the quarry, proved that much more vulnerable.

The Great Depression had sparked support for an interventionist state in our five countries. However, the chilling excesses of fascism and Nazism, followed by the postwar threat of communism, had deepened the demands on leaders to secure liberal democracies. Most saw more equitable distribution of resources as key to this process. And this reflex had a strong run throughout the 1950s and 1960s. However, in most advanced democracies, less auspicious economic circumstances began to constrict the social democratic vision in the 1970s (Rose & Peters, 1978; Arendt, 1978).

The explosion and then retrenchment of state intervention followed similar lines in our five countries. However, some notable differences revealed themselves. Britain faced the constraints of decline even at the outset of its construction of the welfare state (Hennessey, 1992), owing both to the gargantuan task of recovering from World War II—for instance, the government did not end rationing until 1954—and adjustments associated with the relentless decline of the empire. Even though Britain's social programs achieved comprehensiveness long before those of our other nations, they ran on relatively scant resources. In this respect, Britain was no Sweden. As well, a scarcity syndrome prevailed whereby even the Conservatives embraced economic planning and some state ownership of the means of production.

In the United States and Canada, social programs generally received relatively generous resource support. However, their adoption and implementation became somewhat uneven. In both countries, the federal government negotiated patchworks of funding and administration arrangements with state/provincial governments. Therefore, programs and benefits varied widely among jurisdictions. Even Canada's celebrated universal health care system is actually 10 systems that differ considerably among provinces. Each of the welfare states stalled short of "cradle to grave" coverage. For instance, Medicare—provision for the elderly—and Medicaid—health care for the poor—proved the best that the United States could achieve.

The United States' slow progress resulted from the states' rights movement in the 1950s and 1960s and the separation of powers in the federal government. In Canada, much of the delay stemmed from the country's highly decentralized federal system. The constant claims on the part of Quebec for special arrangements exacerbated this difficulty. As noted above, the Quebec case offers the only exception to the assertion that sectarian struggles had little effect on expansion of the welfare state in our five countries.

In Australia, the right-of-center Liberal Party dominated federal politics during the rise of the welfare state in Anglo-American democracies. This meant that Australia moved cautiously toward social intervention. When the political will congealed, however, the actual mechanics of the process went much more smoothly than in the United States or Canada. Three factors entered this equation. First, Australians share a relatively egalitarian societal view which facilitated the adoption of redistributive policies (Castles & Mitchell, 1992, p. 18). Second, the society lacks the depth of regional and sectarian attachments that might have slowed the advancement of the welfare state. Third, the federal system in Australia clearly favors the commonwealth government, especially regarding taxation. Thus, once the federal government embraced one or the other element of the welfare state, it enjoyed both the resources and the leverage to establish programs and monitor their implementation.

New Zealand shares with Australia a strong egalitarian tradition (Richards, 1994, pp. 50–52), with the added advantage of being a unitary government. Further, liberals embraced key elements of the welfare state—such as social security—at an early point. They paved the way for the Labour Party's pursuit of core legislation in the 1930s by legitimizing the theoretical underpinnings of social democracy. Ironically, when the Labour Party last came to government in 1984, it had jettisoned social democracy in favor of economic rationalism.

THE EMERGENCE OF NEOLIBERALISM

As noted earlier, the emphasis on the individual accorded by liberal democracy connects our five systems more than anything else. Unlike the advanced political systems in continental Europe, none of the systems in our nations places a high value on organic views of society. None of our systems fosters in citizens strong notions that the sum of the parts of society exceeds that of its individual components. Nor do religious movements within our societies exert sufficient sway so that the perceived interconnectedness of the community of believers begins to impinge upon the relationship between the state and the individual.

There is some variation here. The U.S. system gives much greater deference to the individual than do the others—although Canada's 1982 charter of human rights quickly has introduced a similar emphasis in that nation. Still, the political leadership and publics of our five countries generally have enlisted pragmatic argumentation in support of greater state intervention, eschewing grand ideologies. They also normally have avoided divisions based on sentiments about the prerogatives of religious communities.

A climate of economic growth and prosperity prevailed during the 1950s and 1960s. Under the circumstances, the publics of our respective countries viewed benignly the gradual expansion of social programs. It proved relatively easy for political leaders to stir sentiments supportive of individuals' responsibility toward society—especially the less advantaged. The residual effects of the Great Depression generalized the salience of such appeals. Many of those who enjoyed the benefits of prosperity had suffered during the 1930s. They recognized that social safety nets serve a function in society.

In time, the perilous years of the Great Depression began to fade from public memory. Declining economic growth began to constrict support of government spending. During the period of expansion, government programs actually helped fan the economy and produce tangible improvements in individual standards of living. As decline began to work its effects, social expenditure began to function as a drag on the economy. New programs gave very little added value to living circumstances.

By the mid-1960s, significant questions arose about the continued expansion of the welfare state. Initially, these focused on issues associated with the effectiveness and efficiency of programs. Analysts looked at the margins of expenditure to see how resources could be used more wisely. As conditions worsened during the 1970s, questions got increasingly hard. Ultimately, analysts began to grapple with the most fundamental issue: Should government involve itself at all in myriad areas?

In the 1960s, a school of economics called public choice developed (Buchanan & Tullock, 1962). Critics of this approach have argued that it has fostered a minimalist view of what government should do (Self, 1993), often on the basis of scant or dubious empirical grounding (Green & Shapiro, 1994, pp. 11–12; Blais & Dion, 1991; Campbell & Naulls, 1991). For instance, this approach holds that governments breed programs far beyond what the public expects or requires. This stems from the desire of government officials to devise ways to build their own empires (Niskanen, 1971). Empires require resources, and one must exert great entrepreneurial skills in devising and expanding programs that can command ever-expanding resources. Public choice theorists urged electorates to select representatives who would clip the wings of government officials. Such representatives would apply automatic devices for eliminating programs and cutting expenditures, that is, methods that would proscribe special pleading from bureaucrats.

Our five systems ran through the entire decade of economic decline in the 1970s before political leaders advocating views akin to public choice—or its political manifestation, neoliberalism—took power (Self, 1993, pp. 64–68). Margaret Thatcher came first, forming a government in Britain in 1979. Joe Clark soon followed in Canada. However, he lacked a majority and lost power in 1980. Ronald Reagan installed a strong neoliberal administration in that same year. Bob Hawke—though head of a left-of-center party—seized control from the conservative coalition in Australia in 1983. Labor had successfully co-opted the neoliberal appeal. The electorate had associated the right-of-center party with economic decline, and Labor exploited a rare opportunity to occupy the center. In New Zealand, the 1984 election of Labour under David Lange began the most defined period of neoliberal rule yet achieved among Anglo American democracies, although the National Party took the baton in 1990. Finally, Brian Mulroney brought Canada's Progressive Conservatives back to office in 1984.

From that time until Bill Clinton's inauguration in 1993, neoliberalism dominated the Anglo-American political scene. In fact, neoliberalism proved highly resilient in all of our countries except Canada. In Britain, competing views of Thatcherism made John Major's efforts at executive leadership a living hell. In Australia, many believed that Bob Hawke's successor, Paul Keating, would not be able to renew Labor's mandate against a Liberal Party that finally had staked out a strong neoliberal agenda. In the 1993 election, however, the Liberal Party's message struck many voters as too strident. Since 1987, labor had become adept at presenting itself as a government that embraced a form of neoliberalism that retained a social conscience. In January 1994, even the president of the Australian Liberal Party publicly praised Labor for attaining such balance. However, Labor uncharacteristically fell off the high wire in 1996 in an election in which the Liberal Party brilliantly underplayed its true neoliberal self. Furthermore, neoliberalism has developed fault lines in New Zealand. Thus, the National Party had difficulty renewing its mandate in 1993. The next election—which will operate under a newly installed Mixed Member Proportional (MMP) representation system—will probably result in a coalition government, which may deny the coalition parties the clarity of mandate required to continue with unvarnished neoliberalism.

The Clinton administration, though hardly neoliberal at its core, had to acknowledge from the outset the sway that the approach enjoyed both in Congress and in the populace (Jones, 1996; Quirk & Hinchliffe, 1996). The administration eschewed the introduction of significant tax increases as part of its deficit reduction initiatives. Its failed health care reform package went through Rube Goldberg–like contortions to make itself look like a private-sector solution to a public crisis. The administration even enshrined a neoliberal icon— the North American Free Trade Agreement (NAFTA)—much to the chagrin of bedrock Democratic Party supporters such as unions and voters in the industrial northeast and midwest. All of this proved to be too little too late and Congress swung radically to the neoliberal side of the ledger in the November 1994 elections (Burnham, 1996).

In Canada, the federal Progressive Conservative's variant of neoliberalism received a stinging rebuke in the October 1993 federal election. Brian Mulroney deeply antagonized voters by playing footloose and fancy-free with the viability of Canada as a nation. Whatever its appeal as an economic theory, the free trade agreement with the United States seemed to have decimated the Canadian manufacturing sector. In addition, Mulroney's willingness to cede federal functions to the province of Quebec, along with the funds necessary to run related programs, struck voters as cavalier in the extreme. The repudiation— which was directed at the Progressive Conservatives under Mulroney's hapless successor, Kim Campbell—went beyond electoral defeat of a neoliberal regime. The collapse of the party to two seats in the 1993 election amounted to their defrocking as a parliamentary party. Ironically, the Liberals' budgets have made many tough, neoliberal choices that the Progressive Conservatives, notwithstanding all the lightning and thunder, never could bring themselves to make. In this respect, Jean Chretien's government has tried to replicate what the "economic rationalists" of Bob Hawke's Labor government accomplished in Australia during the mid-1980s. Members of his government have presented themselves as neoliberals with heart.

We have seen, especially in the last few years, that neoliberalism is not a panacea. To an extent, voters continue to embrace it because they have yet to return to political leaders who articulate more positive views of the function of the state. It has even become clear that neoliberal politicians must make their appeals more palatable. Thus, George Bush spoke of a kinder and gentler American, John Major pushed the concept of a "Citizens' Charter," and the Australian Labor government stressed the importance of equity as it pursued "economic rationalism." When New Zealand went into budgetary surplus in 1993, the National Party had to deal with appeals for "spreading the gain."

THE CRISIS OF EXECUTIVE LEADERSHIP

To be sure, neoliberalism took hold much more pervasively in all Anglo-American systems than it did anywhere in continental Europe. This speaks volumes about the susceptibility of the Anglo-American mind to argumentation based on individual-centered versus organic views of society. However, neoliberalism—and the minimalist governance that has stemmed from it—has come at a cost. Voters have begun to experience the pain of excessive retrenchment of government. However, they remain very chary of supporting parties that provided administrations during the most traumatic phase of economic malaise—the late 1970s and early 1980s.

Thus, a type of electoral schizophrenia has emerged. If voters renew the mandates of neoliberal administrations, they do so grudgingly. This has been the case in Britain, Australia, and New Zealand, where ambiguous mandates have led to a cacophony of voices in previously tidy neoliberal regimes. If, on the other hand, voters decide to embrace a former governing party that had fallen into disrepute during the economic crisis of the late 1970s, they do so reservedly. Certainly, this pertained in the United States, where many voters lodged a protest vote by selecting Ross Perot, thereby denying Bill Clinton a strong mandate. In November 1994, they compounded the confusion by voting in a Republican Congress. A similar process has occurred in Canada. There, English-speaking Canadians of all stripes swamped the Liberal Party in the eleventh hour. They recognized that a minority government in a parliament whose official opposition was the separatist Bloc Quebecois would becalm the ship of state.

At the end of the heyday of the welfare state, problems with the implementation of social legislation—owing to irreconcilable pulls of government organizations and special interests—proved the bread and butter of analysts (Lowi, 1969; Pressman & Wildavsky, 1973). The cumulative evidence of contradictions in policy outcomes and unintended consequences helped lay the groundwork for neoliberalism. Even those broadly committed to the social agenda began to note a crisis in faith (Heclo, 1981) regarding the governability of the complex welfare state (King, 1975). We, of course, can assume that what is good for the goose is good for the gander. However, neoliberalism—perhaps because it has become the flavor of the month and has only recently taken shape in actual policies—has so far received relatively light treatment. Many observers have taken it on around the fringes. Few have made frontal attacks similar to those aimed at the welfare state in the 1970s. But works both by columnists (e.g., Phillips, 1990; Keegan, 1992) and scholars (Donahue, 1989; Marmor, Mashaw, & Harvey, 1990; Durant, 1992; Self, 1993; Savoie, 1994; Henig,

1994) suggest ways in which neoliberalism has served up its own arrays of contradictions and worked unintended consequences. These include the danger of building down the state below what is required to sustain society and the apparent emergence of an insidious process whereby style has supplanted substance in governance.

WHY STYLE HAS SUPPLANTED SUBSTANCE AND FUELED THE SHIFT TO NEOLIBERALISM

In Anglo-American systems other than the United States, observers have become increasingly absorbed with the issue of "presidentialization" (Weller, 1983; Jones, 1983; Jones, 1991). This concern has emerged whenever prime ministers make appeals directly to the public, attempting to bypass cabinet opponents. In Britain, Canada, Australia, and New Zealand, some observers see this approach as a threat to the integrity of the constitutional system. Strong conventions in all four systems prescribe that prime ministers consult with their cabinets before committing their governments to a course of action.

The term "presidentialization" implies that prime ministers who "go public" and outflank opposition in cabinet follow a strategy that comports more with the U.S. Constitution than with parliamentary government (Kernell, 1986; Rose, 1991). In reality, very serious concerns have arisen in the United States about the tendency of U.S. presidents to go public. In such cases, incumbents have tried to override the counsel of both cabinet colleagues and members of Congress who oppose a proposal. Through speeches, campaign-like tours, endorsements, and well-placed leaks, they have employed the immense power of media attention to turn public opinion against their opponents. President Clinton's 1993 campaign to gain approval of NAFTA, against stiff opposition from the leadership of his own party in the House of Representatives, is a classic instance of going public. In fact, the encounter between Vice President Al Gore and Ross Perot on *The Larry King Show* brought the art form to new heights.

The new era of electronics affords executive leaders of any type immense capacity for bypassing constitutional institutions and making policy directly with the people (Seymour-Ure, 1991). The dysfunctions of this approach apply across systems, regardless of whether we are assessing the performance of a president or a prime minister (Campbell, 1993, pp. 394–398). First, executive leaders who go public run the risk of not sufficiently drawing on the constructive contribution potentially made by other institutions in the constitutional system. Second, such leaders can undermine the legitimacy of institutions, the bureaucracy, cabinet, legislators, and public interest organizations that form the building blocks of liberal democracy. In other words, each instance of going public—especially circus-like events such as the Gore-Perot debate—pushes the system toward populism and institutional approaches to resolving disputes within the body politic. Third, executive leaders can do themselves a great deal of harm by going public beyond what the public can bear. The approach can be easier than dealing with institutions—remember George Bush's lament in 1990 that he would rather deal with Saddam Hussein than with Congress—but it is not always the smart way to proceed (Jones, 1996).

Executive leaders in all five of our countries increasingly have become products and exploiters of electronic appeals. That Ross Perot—utterly unencumbered by institutional buttresses—bought his way into a strong third-place performance in the 1992 election suggests the proportions of the problem in the United States.

Kim Campbell's rise and fall in Canada gives us a view of how a-institutionalism might develop in parliamentary systems (Dobbin, 1993). Campbell caught the eye of Brian Mulroney soon after her election to the House of Commons in 1988. He rapidly promoted her to justice minister and then to defense minister. She became his heir apparent and a media darling. Once leader and prime minister in the summer of 1993, she spent virtually all her time nurturing her relationship with the electorate, attending an endless succession of festivals and fairs to the delight of the fawning media. She did not convene parliament and she rarely met with the cabinet. She completely reorganized the bureaucracy—actually, she simply rubber-stamped a plan worked out by Mulroney and his top mandarins—and then absented herself from the tough work of implementing the reforms.

This approach held together until the real campaign started in the fall. Then the press and public began to question Campbell's ability to engage herself as an executive leader. Time and again, she stumbled in public utterances about her policies. She became detached, even from her organization, speaking only occasionally to her campaign manager. In a colossal gaffe, she asserted that she could not discuss how she would cut the deficit. She implied that such issues went beyond the ken of the electorate—adding that she would decide them privately when she became prime minister.

The Campbell experience points up two things. First, political leaders in parliamentary systems can establish themselves through electronic means with facility close to that of presidential aspirants and incumbents. Second, there still might be a threshold for a-institutional appeals. In this regard, the electorate's chagrin over Ross Perot's performance in the NAFTA debate might help us locate the fault line in the United States. Voters might tolerate a demagogic style in a presidential campaign. However, they might expect a certain respect for office when a private citizen engages an incumbent vice president in a television debate. The explosion of electronic links between politics and the public has radically transformed both campaigning and incumbency. In addition, all of our countries underwent a radical retreat from the interventionist state during the past 15 years.

To gain power, even executive leaders who head left-of-center parties have presented themselves as neoliberals bent on building down the state. This tack can pave the way to gaining office, but it eventually can become an albatross. Problems that require some sort of public attention still emerge. Voters expect leaders to respond. However, they have been fed the line that taxes can be cut. They expect leaders to solve problems with ever-shrinking resources.

Changes in the conditions of governance spawned a convergence of executive leadership in Anglo-American countries that—to a degree—functions independently of structural factors. The various dimensions of this convergence include a shift from selecting "insiders" as chief executives to choosing "outsiders"; a decreased salience of collective means for decision making within the executive branch; and a preference for preserving political viability over solving problems.

Any examination of the U.S. system soon brings home an important point that observers in other Anglo-American systems should bear in mind. Prime ministers who behave "presidentially" have simply imbibed the headier wine of executive leadership in the electronic era. This gives a huge advantage to political leaders—be they presidents or prime ministers—who occupy center stage in the political arena. The hunger of the media for sound bites and events entices chief executives into making direct appeals to the public, over the heads of cabinet colleagues and legislatures. When they connect, modern chief executives begin to believe that they can manipulate the core themes that will rivet the public consciousness.

For most such leaders, a high degree of acuity in directly rallying public support ultimately will lead to monocratic behavior. Only the most disciplined leader recognizes that even an effective device can be used once too often. The majority goes blithely on with little regard to the hostility building among cabinet members and legislators over their preemption from the most critical initiatives of the administration. At the same time, most chief executives do not recognize that the public gives about the same run to an average political spellbinder as it does to most TV series.

TOWARD RECASTING EXECUTIVE LEADERSHIP

Individual chief executives will function in unique ways. However, they should invest a great deal more time and care in discerning their strengths and weaknesses and sculpting their management styles and the institutions through which they will work accordingly. In Anglo American systems during the past 15 years, the tremendous adaptations brought on by the politics of constraint have exacerbated the difficulty of this task. Leaders have tended to take various paths of least resistance: disengagement from institutions, personalization, and even self-mythologization. All of these strategies have come at a cost: the bloated deficits of the United States, United Kingdom, and Canada; the United States, the United Kingdom, Canada, and Australia all banking on service-sector expansion while allowing much of manufacturing to atrophy; the emergence of racial and regional underclasses in the United States and the United Kingdom; the exhaustion of the Canadian spirit through prolonged constitutional brinkmanship; and kudos for New Zealand's unvarnished neoliberalism with scarcely a mention of the resulting social dislocations. The time has passed when placebos and grand gestures can count as leadership.

The dawning of the twenty-first century might tempt us to think grand thoughts about the types of executive leaders that we will require in Anglo-American societies in the next 104 years. But we must discipline ourselves by sticking to the more modest task at hand: How do we get these aging democracies on a footing that will allow them to think creatively about their missions in the twenty-first century?

In the first and second thirds of the current century, the Anglo-American nations galvanized as bulwarks of democracy. Notwithstanding the preoccupation of the Anglo-Saxon political mind with individuals' rights, these nations also became places in which attaining equality of opportunity served as a centerpiece of statecraft. Since the early 1970s, technology—through electronics—has served up leaders poorly qualified for statecraft of any kind. Further, globalization has clipped the wings of our countries' economies. The demise of the Keynesian world of steady growth, low inflation, and high employment has stymied the candy-store possibilities of the interventionist state. To many in our nations, equality of opportunity as a democratic goal became the carry-on baggage that passengers leave behind if their plane crashes.

We find ourselves in a trend toward improvement at the end of a century and the beginning of a new millennium. Experience seems to count more in the selection of chief executives. This might mean that electorates have become more cautious about electronic appeals that blithely skate over political and economic realities. The economies of our five countries appear as well to have stabilized. All have experienced considerable slippage in the definition of full employment; that is, all tolerate higher levels of unemployment before adopting special measures for those without work. In addition, concerns have emerged in each nation about whether the economy has left completely behind substantial numbers of young and middle-aged workers who lack the skills required to find work. Yet our systems seem to have gotten themselves out of wild gyrations in unemployment. Our economies also remain recession prone. The bond markets have become neuralgic about any hint of inflation, and all of our systems have encountered problems with perceptual lags whereby voters believe they still suffer from episodes of recession when the economy has actually recovered and their personal circumstances have improved. Still, confidence seems to increase as each passing year lightens the memory of the late 1970s and stagflation.

Thus, as we begin a new century, we might well be moving into an epoch that invites chief executives to pursue more positive statecraft than we have seen over the past 20 years. As Bill Clinton discovered with his failed health care reform, the new environment probably will not sustain major or intricate attempts to redefine the role of the state. However, they will go beyond the smile-with-a-name-tag on the status quo that characterized John Major's Citizens' Charter.

The emergence of a renewed vision of statecraft will call, initially, for hard-nosed assessment of the unintended consequences of the build-down of government. This renewed vision will then look to pressure points. Where can government make a difference? What essential functions have gone into free fall and need rescuing? What new, unaddressed problems have emerged from the age of minimalist government that urgently require attention? Many chief executives and the cabinet officers and officials upon whom they rely might prove temperamentally ill-disposed to this type of statecraft; that is, they will bring to office either nostalgia for the interventionist era or inertia from the age of contraction. We really are looking here for chief executives who do not choke when they hit turbulence and recognize that they will not be able to soar.

The new breed of chief executives must center their appeals much more than before on palpable economic benefit. We have given a great deal of attention to the degree to which Anglo-American societies eschew organic views of society. On occasion, individuals in these nations will assent to policies not based on narrow self-interest. However, such situations have become relatively rare. The expansive programs of the 1960s and 1970s strained the capacity of our political cultures for governance beyond managing the interface between the state and the market. This reality poses daunting difficulties for those trying to capture segments of the population that still harbor high expectations for governance. No matter how much their hearts bleed in the right place, chief executives heading traditional left-of-center parties have encountered backlashes whenever they have tried to move their appeals rightward.

Bill Clinton's encounter with health care reform has become almost emblematic of the obstacles faced by leaders trying to inch social welfare forward: The cost of health insurance became a central concern of corporations in the early 1990s. At the same time, the sizable constituency for efficiency and effectiveness revealed some embarrassing facts about American, market-style health care. For instance, it consumes a greater proportion of the gross national product than any other health care system and costs much more to manage. Thus, the opportunity presented itself whereby an astute leader could wed concern about costs with concerns about social issues. The system does provide Cadillac coverage to a portion of the population. But it offers nothing to huge categories of individuals. Most troubling here are those whose treatment costs have exhausted existing coverage and those without insurance because of unemployment or a change of job.

Clinton tried to form a grand coalition around health care reform but failed. His concept, managed competition, would have expanded coverage by regulating the insurance market and limiting costs. Much of the insurance and care provision establishment saw this new government role as threatening. Those concerned about the noncovered did not receive sufficient assurance of universality. Middle-income Americans with coverage saw the specter of an immensely complicated system that seemed bent on forcing them into managed care. Clinton himself now recognizes that he bit off too much in trying to bring about comprehensive reform with a shaky coalition. However, even incremental changes have encountered difficulty.

In the final days of the Reagan administration, Congress passed legislation providing protection for the elderly who fell victim to catastrophic illnesses that threatened their life savings. The Bush administration got Congress to rescind the legislation. It could not take the flack from wealthy elderly taxpayers reacting to the additional levy against their income designed to pay for the new coverage. Therefore, any attempt to meld economic and social justification must consist of one part pragmatism and the other courage under fire.

REFERENCES

Aitkin, D. (1985). The new electorate. In D. Woodward, A. Parkin, & J. Summers (Eds.), *Government, politics and power in Australia*. Melbourne, Australia: Longham Cheshire.

Arendt, H. W. (1978). *The rise and fall of economic growth*. London: Longman.

Barber, B. (1996, September). Strengthening democracy by recreating civil society. Paper presented at the meeting of Independent Sector, "Measuring the impact of the independent, not-for-profit sector on society." Washington, DC.

Blais, A., & Dion, S. (Eds.). (1991). *The budget-maximizing bureaucrat: Appraisals and evidence*. Pittsburgh: University of Pittsburgh Press.

Buchanan, J. M., & Tullock, G. (1962). *The calculus of consent: Logical foundations of constitutional democracy*. Ann Arbor: University of Michigan Press.

Burnham, W. D. (1996). Realignment lives: The 1994 earthquake and its implications. In C. Campbell & B. A. Rockman (Eds.), *The Clinton presidency: First appraisals*. Chatham, NJ: Chatham House.

Butler, D., & Kavanagh, D. (1992). *The British general election of 1992.* New York: St. Martin's Press.

Campbell, C. (1993). Political executives and their officials. In A. W. Finifter (Ed.), *The state of the discipline II.* Washington, DC: American Political Science Association.

Campbell, C., & Naulls, D. (1991). The limits of the budget-maximizing theory: Some evidence from officials' views of their roles and careers. In A. Blais & S. Dion, (Eds.), *The budget-maximizing bureaucrat: Appraisals and evidence.* Pittsburgh: University of Pittsburgh Press.

Castles, F. G., & Mitchell, D. (1992). Identifying welfare state regimes: The links between politics, instruments and outcomes. *Governance, 5*(1), 1–26.

Dobbin, M. (1993). *The politics of Kim Campbell: From school trustee to prime minister.* Toronto: Lorimer.

Donahue, J. D. (1989). *The privatization decision: Public ends, private means.* New York: Basic Books.

Durant, R. F. (1992). *The administrative presidency revisited: Public lands, the BLM, and the Reagan revolution.* Albany: State University of New York Press.

Esping-Anderson, G. (1990). *The three worlds of welfare capitalism.* Cambridge, MA: Polity.

Feigenbaum, H. B. (1985). *The politics of public enterprise: Oil and the French state.* Princeton, NJ: Princeton University Press.

Green, D. P., & Shapiro, I. (1994). *Pathologies and rational choice theory: A critique of applications in political science.* New Haven, CT: Yale University Press.

Heclo, H. (1981). Introduction: The presidential illusion. In H. Heclo, & L. M. Salamon (Eds.), *The illusion of presidential government.* Boulder, CO: Westview.

Henig, J. R. (1994). *Rethinking school choice: Limits of the market metaphor.* Princeton, NJ: University of Princeton Press.

Hennessy, P. (1992). *Never again: Britain 1945–1951.* London: Jonathan Cape.

Jones, C. O. (1996). Campaigning to govern: The Clinton style. In C. Campbell & B. A. Rockman (Eds.), *The Clinton presidency: First appraisals.* Chatham, NJ: Chatham House.

Jones, G. W. (1983). Prime ministers' departments really create problems: A rejoinder to Patrick Weller. *Public Administration, 61*(1) 79–84.

Jones, G. W. (1991). Presidentialization in a parliamentary system? In C. Campbell & M. J. Wyszomirski (Eds.), *Executive leadership in Anglo-American systems.* Pittsburgh: University of Pittsburgh Press.

Keegan, W. (1992). *The spectre of capitalism: The future of the world economy after the fall of Communism.* London: Radius.

Kernell, S. (1986). *Going public: New strategies of presidential leadership.* Chapel Hill: University of North Carolina Press.

King, A., (Ed.). (1975). *Why is Britain becoming harder to govern?* London: BBC Books.

King, R. (1986). *The state in modern society: New directions in political sociology.* London: Macmillan.

Lowi, T. J. (1969). *The end of liberalism: Ideology, policy and the crisis of public authority.* New York: Norton.

Marmor, T. R., Mashaw, J. L., & Harvey, P. (1990). *America's misunderstood welfare state: Persistent myths, enduring realities.* New York: Basic Books.

McRoberts, K., & Posgate, D. (1980). *Quebec: Social change and political crisis* (2nd ed.). Toronto: McClelland and Stewart.

Newton, K. (1993). Caring and competence: The long, long campaign. In A. King (Ed.), *Britain at the polls 1992.* Chatham, NJ: Chatham House.

Niskanen, W. (1971). *Bureaucracy and representative government.* New York: Aldine and Atherton.

Phillips, K. (1990). *The politics of rich and poor: Wealth and the American electorate in the Reagan aftermath.* New York: Random House.

Pierson, C. (1991). *Beyond the welfare state?: The new political economy of welfare.* University Park: Pennsylvania State University Press.

Pressman, J. L., & Wildavsky, A. (1973). *Implementation.* Berkeley: University of California Press.

Quirk, P. J., & Hinchliffe, J. (1996). Domestic policy: The trials of a centrist democrat. In C. Campbell & B. A. Rockman (Eds.), *The Clinton presidency: First appraisals.* Chatham, NJ: Chatham House.

Richards, R. (1994). *Closing the door to destitution: The shaping of the Social Security Acts of the United States and New Zealand.* University Park: Pennsylvania State University Press.

Rockman, B. A. (1984). *The leadership question.* New York: Praeger.

Rose, R. (1991). *The postmodern president: George Bush meets the world* (2nd ed.). Chatham, NJ: Chatham House.

Rose, R., & Peters, G. (1978). *Can government go bankrupt?* New York: Basic Books.

Self, P. (1993). *Government by the market?: The politics of public choice.* Boulder, CO: Westview.

Seymour-Ure, C. (1991). The role of press secretaries on chief executive staffs in Anglo-American systems. In C. Campbell & M. Wyszomirski (Eds.), *Executive leadership in Anglo-American systems.* Pittsburgh: University of Pittsburgh Press.

Thompson, E. (1994). *Fair enough: Egalitarianism in Australia.* Sydney: University of New South Wales Press.

Weller, P. (1983). Do prime minister's departments really create problems? *Public Administration, 61*(1), 59–78.

Chapter **6**

The Necessity
for Studying Organizational
Advocacy Comparatively

John D. McCarthy and Jim Castelli

INTRODUCTION

Brian O'Connell, founding president of INDEPENDENT SECTOR, in his incredibly widely cited claim, termed advocacy "the quintessential function of the voluntary sector" (O'Neill, 1989, p. 114). The subtext of that claim undoubtedly accounts for its broad resonance among functionaries in the nonprofit sector: nonprofit organizations (translated into the latest resonant language, "civil society institutions") can be expected to leap into the breach to represent the interests of the poor and physically disadvantaged who are unable to represent themselves in the rough-and-tumble of U.S. interest group politics. That sense of advocacy is the focus of our interest and motivation for the analysis that follows, even though we are convinced that advocacy cannot be understood by studying it in isolation.

Regardless of the key functions of a sector, few analysts have attempted to specify the extent and impact of advocacy by the formally constituted organiza-

John D. McCarthy • Professor, Department of Sociology, Pennsylvania State University, University Park, Pennsylvania 16802.   Jim Castelli • President, Castelli Enterprises, Inc., Buke, Virginia 22015.

Measuring the Impact of the Nonprofit Sector, edited by Patrice Flynn and Virginia A. Hodgkinson, New York, Kluwer Academic/Plenum Publishers, 2002.

tions in the nonprofit sector. As a result, little information is available for deciding whether or not these organizations have more than a token impact on the outcomes of public policies that affect the poor and physically disadvantaged. Additionally, of the few existing studies of nonprofit advocacy, most concentrated on a narrowly circumscribed set of organizations, termed "advocacy organizations," which, a priori, are assumed to have advocacy as their main function irrespective of their substantive focus. These advocacy organizations are typically studied in isolation from other categories of nonprofit organizations, not to mention for-profit and governmental organizations. Consequently, assessments of their relative extent within and their impact on the nonprofit sector is prohibited.

However, we will show that advocacy is widespread across the entire range of nonprofit organizations. Consequently, we argue research on advocacy by nonprofit organizations should be expanded to include this entire range in order to move toward eventual comparisons with advocacy by both for-profit organizations and governmental agencies, which is also widespread. This broadened research perspective would constitute an agenda for the study of policy advocacy by organizations parallel to the exhaustive, ongoing study of civic and political participation by individual citizens that has long occupied political scientists and sociologists. Given the consensus among social scientists that the density and impact of formal organizations in the U.S. is growing (Coleman, 1982; Scott, 1997), it is surprising that the systematic study of policy advocacy by organizations with equivalent probability sample survey methodologies has languished.[1]

The ultimate goal of the research agenda we imagine is represented by measuring the relative impact of policy advocacy by organizations in the nonprofit sector. But first we must clearly specify and measure organizational advocacy, a task that remains to be completed in any systematic way. A number of considerations should guide our efforts toward this goal. First, both direct and indirect advocacy must be studied. Organizations may operate through a wide array of direct advocacy strategies aimed at shaping public opinion and policy, but they may also operate indirectly, through the mobilization of advocacy by individual citizens. This set of tactics is now known as "grass-roots lobbying." The range of techniques was invented by organizations known as advocacy groups, but it has now been widely adopted by corporations and their subsidiary political organizations (e.g., political action committees or PACs) as well as by labor unions.

Second, state and local advocacy should not be neglected at the expense of national advocacy, which has been heavily emphasized in early research on advocacy organizations. A great deal of advocacy, both direct and indirect, occurs at the state and local levels, and it should also be included in our efforts to measure the extent and variety of organizational advocacy. The heavy emphasis of past work was on studying widely known, national advocacy groups (e.g., Children's Defense Fund, Mothers Against Drunk Driving, and Operation Rescue). The findings implied an impact on understanding the role of nonprofit advocacy that may be erroneous, especially in light of accelerating trends toward the decentralization of decision making. The "wedding cake" imagery of criminologists who counsel against trying to understand the operation of the criminal justice system through the lens of rare "celebrity trials" may be appropriate here, leading us to question whether the behavior of the most celebrated advocacy groups is a good indication of the sum of nonprofit advocacy.

Third, research on advocacy in the nonprofit sector should be comprehensive and include all organizations within the sector since policy advocacy is widespread among nonprofit organization not know as advocacy groups, for example, and by factions within religious and educational organizations,.

Finally, nonprofit advocacy must be placed in *the broader context of advocacy* by for-profit, governmental, and formally registered political organizations (such as PACs and political parties) where advocacy is widespread and, it can be argued, has been expanding and growing more sophisticated recently. Only by comparing the extent and variety of nonprofit sector advocacy with that of other sectors can we begin to assess its independent contribution to shaping public opinion and public policy as well as its independent impact upon the mobilization of individual advocacy by citizens.

In what follows, we: (a) propose a definition of organizational advocacy (or organizational political participation) parallel and complementary to that of individual citizen advocacy (or political participation), (b) discuss the difficulties of identifying a special class of advocacy groups, (c) review a number of studies that convincingly demonstrate the widespread nature of advocacy across the nonprofit sector, and, (d) suggest three research strategies to assess policy advocacy. Of these, two are designed to assess the extent and nature of advocacy across the entire range of formally constituted organizations, and the third, to assess the relative impact of various categories of organizations, for instance, nonprofits versus others/foundations versus grass-roots groups.

TOWARD AN OPERATIONAL DEFINITION OF ADVOCACY

Advocacy is a term widely employed in public discourse in the United States today, and one that carries even more weight among nonprofit functionaries and researchers. Yet, the term has typically been used without well-specified empirical referents. Among the most widely cited definitions of advocacy by nonprofit researchers is Jenkins': "any attempt to influence the decisions of an institutional elite on behalf of a collective interest" (Jenkins, 1987, p. 297). However, this does not clearly specify the actual range of behaviors that constitute policy advocacy. One approach toward more substantive content of a definition derives from the body of law governing nonprofit advocacy. Hopkins, prefacing his discussion of charity advocacy and the law, delineates six categories of nonprofit advocacy (1992, pp. 35–43):

- *Programmatic Advocacy*. Advocating positions on policy issues as part of work in carrying out their charitable purposes. (This form is now more widely known as issue advocacy.)
- *Legislative Activity*. Lobbying members of legislative bodies.
- *Political Campaign Activity*. Participating or intervening in political campaigns in support of or opposition to candidates for public office.
- *Demonstrations*. Public support or opposition to an issue or a policy.
- *Boycotts*. A conspiracy to prevent the conduct of business by preventing or inducing potential customers from doing business with the object of conspiracy.
- *Litigation*. Involving legal action to advance a cause, recruit members, assist in fund raising or the preparation of *amicus curiae* briefs.

Hopkins' category scheme is quite valuable for structuring the vast variety of concrete behavior that actually constitutes advocacy by any type of organization, including nonprofit, but it needs to be supplemented with the empirical detail of the advocacy behavior of samples of all types of organizations. Fortunately, a number of inductively derived lists of concrete advocacy tactics exist. They were created to survey advocacy-type nonprofits and can allow the first steps in enumerating concrete advocacy behavior by organizations (McCarthy & Castelli, 1994; reviewed by McCarthy, Smith, & Zald, 1996). For example, the following tactics, described in one or another of those studies, would constitute programmatic advocacy: distributing literature, organizing public meetings, canvassing door-to-door, building organizational coalitions, publishing a newsletter, disseminating information at booths during public events, op-ed campaigns, cultivating press relations, running advertisements, making media appearances, and sponsoring public service announcements. This list is certainly not exhaustive, but it illustrates what we believe to be the most fruitful direction for generating a comprehensive operational definition of several dimensions of policy advocacy.

An organization may participate in any of these advocacy activities as may any individual citizen. However, Hopkins' category scheme does not include what has become one of the most widespread activities, grass-roots lobbying, which encourages individual citizens to participate in any of an organization's

activities as individuals rather than as representatives of the encouraging organization. We refer to the encouragement by organizations of individual citizen
advocacy as *indirect advocacy*[2] following Hrebenar (1997). The essence of this
form includes efforts by organizations to build grass-roots constituencies for
policy positions so that citizens may directly, and apparently independently,
bring pressure to bear in favor of the positions (Faucheux, 1995; Bailey, 1996;
Walters, 1983; Rampton & Stauber, 1995). By one estimate, $790 million was
spent on this form of advocacy in 1993–1994, with more than half representing
in-house organizational expenses (Faucheux, 1995, p. 21). As we shall see below, much indirect advocacy occurs in routine contacts between organizations
and their members. Consequently, the financial extent of indirect advocacy is
clearly underestimated by that assessment which relies heavily on information
related to campaigns by national associations. The lines between indirect advocacy and issue advocacy, especially through the mechanism of media campaigns,
are not clearly drawn in most previous analyses of grass-roots lobbying.

THE DIFFICULTY OF IDENTIFYING ADVOCACY-ORIENTED NONPROFIT ORGANIZATIONS

In order to study a subclass of nonprofit organizations, such as advocacy
organizations, their key features need to be identified, both conceptually and
empirically, before they can be sampled. Many overlapping approaches for doing so are available and we briefly discuss a number of them here. O'Neill's
depiction captures the view of many nonprofit researchers and overlaps, to some
extent, with other attempts to define citizens' groups, social movement organizations, public interest groups, and challenging groups, each of which is embedded in a disciplinary research tradition. He states:

> Advocacy organizations are primarily involved with lobbying and dissemi-
> nating information directed toward broad societal objectives or collective
> goods rather than outcomes of benefit only to their own members. Even
> when advocacy organizations represent a particular group—such as women,
> members of minority groups, physically handicapped people, victims of
> drunk driving, and potential victims of handgun attacks—there is an im-
> plicit assumption that actions benefiting these people will benefit all of
> society. (1989, p. 110)

The key to this definition is that groups primarily engage in advocacy and
they do so on behalf of collective goods. Salamon and Anheier (1992b) define
advocacy organizations as those "that protect the rights and promote the interest of specific groups of people—for example, physically handicapped people,

the elderly, children and women." Schlozman and Tierney offer a definition which more explicitly includes the connotation implied in the foregoing in stating: "Other citizens' groups that we call *advocacy groups* seek selective benefits on behalf of groups of persons who are in some way incapacitated or are otherwise unable to represent their own interests" (1986, pp. 45–63). Describing collective action aimed at influencing public policy as advocacy implies selfless behavior on behalf of the defenseless, the key to the term's resonant use:

> **Advocacy.** 1: The profession or work of an advocate.
>
> **Advocate.** 1: One who pleads the cause of another. 2: One that argues for, defends, maintains or recommends a cause or proposal.
>
> 2: The action of advocacy, pleading for or supporting. (Gove, 1986)

Walker (1991, p. 57) defines citizens' groups in a similar vein stating that they "have open memberships, and their membership appeals are unrelated to a profession and usually focus on broad ideals or issues." Schlozman and Tierney, consistent with extensive research among political scientists , state: "A public interest group can be defined as one seeking a benefit, the achievement of which will not benefit selectively either the membership or the activists of the organization." (1986, p. 29) McCarthy and Zald define a social movement organization as "a complex, or formal organization that identifies its goals with the preferences of a social movement or a countermovement (preferences for changing some element of the social structure or reward distribution of society)" (1987, p. 20). All of these definitions depend upon delimiting a category of nonprofit organizations by features of their stated goals rather than their patterns of action.

Utilizing the criterion that nonprofit groups only qualify as advocacy groups if they engage primarily in advocacy creates serious difficulties for their identification since groups may change their mix of activities (provision of services, membership benefits, advocacy) over time and the predominance of advocacy in that mix cannot easily be established a priori for many organizations. Nevertheless, taxonomers of the nonprofit sector have continued to attempt to use the category to develop a class of advocacy organizations. For instance, Salamon and Anheier (1992a, b) follow the lead of the National Taxonomy of Exempt Entities in locating advocacy groups in a category defined primarily by civil and legal rights.[3] Using the "primarily advocacy" and "collective benefit" criteria, one would expect to find advocacy groups in other functional categories of their taxonomy, especially groups classified under environment, animals, and economic, as well as social and community development categories. We do not intend this as a general criticism of their scheme, which we find quite useful for other purposes. Instead, this illustrates the difficulties encountered in attempting to classify nonprofit organizations with respect to the type and extent of their advocacy since it represents a distinct dimension, separate from that of function, on which the general classification scheme rests. This is the same point O'Neill makes.

For several reasons there are no statistics of advocacy groups comparable to those on other nonprofit organizations. Advocacy groups are variously classified as "social welfare" entities, civic groups, membership organizations, and legal-assistance agencies. Many nonprofits whose primary activity is religion, health, education, or social services are also engaged in advocacy, within the limits of such activity imposed by the Internal Revenue Service. Advocacy organizations are often largely or exclusively volunteer-based and sometimes fall below the limit of $25,000 in annual revenue required for registering with the IRS. Some advocacy organizations with one tax identification number have dozens or hundreds of local subunits. "Finally, it is possible that some advocacy organizations, by nature suspicious of government, exercise an old American tradition by declining to register with the authorities" (O'Neill, 1989, p. 111).

Schlozman and Tierney (1986) make the same point about the use of the phrase "cause groups" by political scientists—the intensity of concern about issues is not confined to certain groups, but varies across issues, time, and groups.

Finally, most organizations frame their goals in terms of broad public benefits. As a consequence, relying on the stated goals of organizations to determine their actual behavior is rarely accomplished easily. For these reasons, then, identifying a class of organizations as advocacy groups is problematical. We maintain, however, that our ability to undertake a research agenda aimed at understanding organizational advocacy does not depend on resolving this problem.

ADVOCACY ACROSS THE NONPROFIT SECTOR

Most observers agree that advocacy by nonprofit organizations is widespread and is not restricted to charitable nonprofits. For instance, O'Neill states, "Virtually all types of nonprofits engage to some extent in lobbying and public information campaigns," (1989, p. 110). Individual survey evidence, based upon reports of organizational members and participants, reveals considerable *indirect advocacy*.

National Surveys of Political Participation. Based on their national survey, Verba and his colleagues report that citizens affiliated with a wide range of organizations, mostly nonprofit groups, indicated that 61 percent of them, on average, take stands on political issues. Table 6.1 shows these range from lows

Table 6.1. Percentage of Members of Nonprofit
Organizations Who Say They Were Asked
to Take Political Stands by Type
Membership Organization

Organizational type	Percentage
Liberal or conservative	95
Candidate, party	94
Political issue	93
Women's rights	79
Unions	67
Senior citizens	61
Nationality, ethnic	61
Business, professional	59
Veterans	59
Civic, nonpartisan	59
Neighborhood, homeowners	50
Educational	43
Service, fraternal	30
Other	30
Religious	27
Cultural	25
Hobby, sports, leisure	18
Youth	18
Literary, art, study	16
Charitable, social service	16

Source: Verba, et al., 1995. Adapted from Table 3.5, p. 63.

of 16 percent for literary, art, and study groups, as well as charitable social service groups, to highs in the mid-90 percent for expressly political groups. Significant percentages of their respondents also report having been asked to take political action (vote or other action), and this is reported across the range of groups, even in those groups that do not take stands on political issues (1995, p. 63). As shown in Table 6.2, almost a third of their respondents report having been asked to take such action on the job, in church, or by nonpolitical organizations with which they are affiliated. These findings constitute strong evidence of how widespread indirect advocacy is among both nonprofit and for-profit organizations, and, in our judgment, underestimate its extent because of the narrow focus of the questions pertaining to political activities.

These figures are consistent with 1985 survey data reported by Baumgartner and Walker (1988, p. 922) where respondents were asked whether the groups with which they were affiliated took stands on public issues. Verba and his colleagues also indicate that 39 percent of union members reported having been asked to vote or act politically (for instance, sign a petition, write a letter, con-

Table 6.2. Percentage of Those Institutionally Involved Citizens Who Reported
Being Asked to Take a Politically Relevant Act, by Organizational Type

Location	Type of Act			
	To contact	To vote	To act politically	Any of the above
On the Job	19	10	18	33
In a nonpolitical organization	12	12	24	28
In a religious organization	5	12	31	34

Source: Adapted from Verba, et al., 1995.

tact a public official) 34 percent of church members report having been asked
in church, and 28 percent report having been asked in their most important
nonpolitical organization (1995, p. 147).

Postal Rate Commission. The U.S. Postal Rate Commission looked at a probability sample of 2,520 mailings from nonprofit permit holders to measure the
extent of advocacy among nonprofit organizations. The commission found that
active political advocacy (encouraging writing to a politician, sending money,
voting for a particular candidate, demonstrating) and political opinion advocacy (messages aimed at influencing a recipient's opinions on issues) were widespread across charitable, nonprofit organizations. A sample of their results is
shown in Table 6.3. They summarize the findings of the study:

> All types of nonprofit organizations send some advocacy mail ranging from
> a high of 60 percent for Agricultural organizations to a low of 4 percent
> for Scientific organizations. Educational, philanthropic, and religious or-

Table 6.3. Use of Third Class Mail for Political Advocacy Purposes

Organization type	Percent of pieces containing advocacy	Percent of organizations sending advocacy	Percent of mailings containing advocacy	Percent of total advocacy mail
Agricultural	60	47	23	4
Veterans	35	34	13	8
Labor	24	29	23	1
Fraternal	16	13	7	2
Scientific	4	15	3	1
Educational	20	19	9	29
Philanthropic	24	11	13	37
Religious	17	8	2	19
TOTAL	21	13	7	100

Source: Adapted from Postal Rate Commission, 1987.

ganizations account for 84 percent of nonprofit mail and 85 percent of mail containing political advocacy. However, the percent of their own mail pieces or mailings containing any advocacy is small relative to Agricultural, Veterans, and Labor organizations which have the largest percentage of mailings which contain advocacy. For example, only 2 percent of Religious organizations' mailings contain advocacy but they account for 19 percent of all advocacy mail sent, while 23 percent of Agricultural organizations' mailings contain political advocacy but they only account for 4 percent of the total advocacy mail. (U.S. Postal Rate Commission, 1987, p. 4)

Religious Organizations. Hertzke has said, "[T]here is evidence to suggest that major changes are afoot, and that religion and politics are more deeply intertwined than at any time in recent history. Indeed, what is striking about current political engagement is its tremendous breadth and ideological diversity" (1988, p. 4).

A recent survey by The Pew Research Center for the People and the Press (Kohut, 1996), summarized in Table 6.4, revealed that large numbers of regular churchgoers reported that their clergy spoke out on public issues, constituting primarily programmatic advocacy. Some 21 percent indicated that their pastors had spoken out on specific candidates and elections.

Internal Revenue Service Filings. At the request of Congressman Ernest Istook, the U.S. Government Accounting Office recently analyzed a sample of IRS 990 long form filings for 1992 to determine the extent of lobbying expenditures by nonprofit organizations also receiving federal grants. Analysis of this

Table 6.4. Percentage of Regular Worshipers Who say
Clergy at Their Place of Worship Speak Out
on Public Issues

Public issues	Percentage
Hunger and poverty	87
Abortion	60
World trouble spots such as Bosnia or Rwanda	59
Prayer in public schools	56
Pornography laws	41
Laws regarding homosexuals	36
Right-to-die laws	29
Death penalty	27
Health care reform	26
Candidates and elections	21

Source: Adapted from Kohut, 1996.

alternative source of evidence showed that less than 2 percent of the 501(c)3 long form filers reported any lobbying expenses (Gandhi, 1995). This certainly underestimates the extent of such expenses for advocacy, as Salamon's research, summarized below, shows.

A number of studies document the extent and variety of direct advocacy by nonprofit organizations of all types.

Studies of Associations. Two studies of diverse nonprofit organizations provide additional evidence about the extent of advocacy among nonprofit organizations not specializing in advocacy. Young, Ian, and Bailey's (1994) evidence developed from a survey of a sample of human services, health care, education, religion, and arts associations, listed in the 1992 *Encyclopedia of Associations*, focused primarily on organizational structure. They found that 33 percent of all of the surveyed associations reported engaging in policy advocacy. More of the trade associations, 36 percent, reported engaging in advocacy than other kinds of groups, but not by substantial margins.

Knoke's (1990) survey evidence was generated from a sample of national associations based upon three national directories of associations (*National Trade and Professional Associations of the United States*; *National Recreational, Sporting and Hobby Organizations of the United States*; and the *Encyclopedia of Associations*). Table 6.5 displays the extent of advocacy for the four types of nonprofit groups surveyed. Labor unions engage in the most advocacy of each type, but with the exception of working in campaigns and demonstrating, the other kinds of nonprofit groups are quite engaged in both direct and indirect, membership mobilization advocacy.

Salamon (1995) reports results from a survey of almost 3,400 nonprofit, public benefit organizations (excluding hospitals and institutions of higher

Table 6.5. Organizational Advocacy and Membership Mobilization for Advocacy of a Sample of 459 Nonprofit Associations

| | Organizational Type | | | | |
	All	Labor	Trade	Professional	Recreational
Activity					
Change societal values	50	59	38	57	36
Influence public policy	49	86	58	53	22
Encourage members to					
Contact government officials	37	87	42	45	21
Write to newspapers	32	63	22	35	34
Work on election campaigns	6	71	3	3	1
Demonstrate or picket	6	71	3	1	4

Source: Adapted from Knoke, 1990.

education) that was conducted in sixteen communities in the early 1980s. Agencies were asked if " . . . they engaged in either or both of two varieties of advocacy activity—'advocacy for particular client groups' and 'advocacy for political, legislative issues'; second, respondent agencies were asked to indicate what share of their expenditures they devoted to 'legal services or advocacy' as one of nine functional areas of activity" (pp. 2–3). The findings are summarized in Table 6.6. Mirroring the preceding studies, these data show that advocacy is widespread among nonprofit public benefit organizations, and that it varies significantly across type of organization. Salamon believes that the evidence on expenditures probably overstates the extent of that kind of advocacy somewhat because "legal services" were included in his measure of advocacy.

We have reviewed a number of studies that demonstrate that both direct and indirect advocacy is widespread across the nonprofit sector, but unique among those studies is Salamon's effort to begin to account for variation in advocacy across nonprofit organizations.[4] His results suggest that the more dependent nonprofit groups are upon both governmental and/or private sources of funding, the more likely they are to engage in advocacy, although the strength of these relationships is quite modest. As well, the more professionalized the organization's staff and services, the less likely they are to engage in advocacy, but the strength of these relationships, too, is quite modest.

Based on these various sources of evidence, it is very clear that advocacy is practiced not only among typical "advocacy organizations," but also among organizations across the entire sector.

Table 6.6. Advocacy by Nonprofit Human Service and Arts Agencies

Organization type	Percent reporting advocacy
All	18.0
Legal Services	78.5
Multi-Service	31.0
Housing	22.2
Employment and Training	18.3
Mental health	17.2
Social services	16.7
Institutional, residential care	13.7
Education and research	12.5
Health	10.0
Arts and Culture	4.9

Source: Adapted from Salamon, 1995. Based on survey responses from 3,332 human service and arts agencies.

A Grid for Mapping the Extent and
Variety of Organizational Advocacy

Figure 6.1 represents a crude map of the full range of organizational types against our tentative list of advocacy forms. By gathering systematic samples of organizations across the entire range and surveying them concerning their advocacy activities, we could estimate the full extent and variety of organizational advocacy.

As an example, consider the policy contests over whether or not to: (1) classify tobacco as a drug, thereby allowing the Food and Drug Administration to regulate its sale and use and (2) link the amount of federal transportation funds to each state's having met the .08 Blood Alcohol Content (BAC) standard for determining the legal intoxication of drivers. Each includes a wide variety of organizational actors including organizations from each of the four types: (1) industry groups from the private sector (including tobacco companies, restaurant owners, and beer manufacturers); (2) nonprofit organizations (including public health groups and Mothers Against Drunk Driving); (3) political groups (including a number of PACs); and (4) governmental regulatory agencies with interests in the issues (including the FDA and the National Highway Transportation Safety Administration). Conceivably, we could map all of the direct and indirect advocacy on these policy issues and display its extent in our grid shown in Figure 6.1. Of course, we would expect certain patterns to emerge because

Organizational Type				
Advocacy Dimension	Private Sector	Nonprofit Sector	Political/ Party	State/ Governmental
Programmatic/Issue				
Legislative				
Political/Campaigns				
Demonstrations				
Boycotts				
Litigation				
Indirect/Grassroots				

Figure 6.1. A grid for mapping organizational advocacy type.

the law discourages some classes of organizations from engaging in certain forms of advocacy. We will refer back to the grid as we describe the main outlines of three alternative research strategies for studying organizational advocacy.

RESEARCH STRATEGIES FOR STUDYING ADVOCACY

Each of the three research strategies we outline below is designed to answer a different set of questions. The first aims to describe the extent and variety of direct organizational advocacy; the second addresses the extent and variety of indirect advocacy; and, the third focuses on assessing the impact of various organizational types on policy outcomes. (See Baumgartner & Leech, 1998, for a parallel discussion.)

Samples of Organizations. In order to establish the extent and variety of direct organizational policy advocacy, it is necessary to sample the entire range of organizations. To develop adequate samples, all formally constituted organizations need to be enumerated. For the three organizational types, other than nonprofit organizations, this is a manageable task because strict registration requirements provide sources for accomplishing such enumeration. Nevertheless, creating probability samples requires clear specification of the population unit of analysis and a method for sampling the population of units: this is most problematic for nonprofit organizations.

Unit of Analysis. On behalf of their organizations, nonprofit organizational leaders and functionaries may engage in both direct (for instance, lobbying) and indirect advocacy (aimed at encouraging advocacy among organizational members or constituents or the general public). Importantly, since much indirect and some small amount of direct advocacy depends on the most local units of national networks of organizations (e.g. denominations composed of many congregations, labor unions composed of many locals, or subunits of chaptered national organizations with a single IRS tax registration including Mothers Against Drunk Driving), we follow Salamon and Anheier in believing that the "establishment" rather than the organization should be the research unit of analysis. They state, "An establishment is essentially a place of operation of an organization. In other words, it is a smaller unit than an organization. An organization may consequently run a number of different establishments" (1992b, p. 281). Further, since a large number of small, local, volunteer-led nonprofit groups are involved in advocacy, but are not registered with authorities, the size of the "underground" nonprofit economy[5] is of great importance in sampling nonprofit organizations for studying advocacy.

Sampling Strategies. Making establishments the unit of organizational advocacy analysis—coupled with the fact that a large number of membership establishments, many of which engage in advocacy, are small local groups, many of which are not formally nonprofits, that is, registered with the IRS (Smith, 1994; McCarthy, Smith, and Zald, 1996)—raises major difficulties for sampling the appropriate population of nonprofit organizations in order to study advocacy within the nonprofit sector. Three well-known ways of attempting to generate a representative (or stratified) sample of such organizations exist, each of which aims to counter these difficulties. They have been widely used in studying nonprofit groups of all types and advocacy nonprofits in particular:

1. Probability sampling of lists of organizations formally registered with the state (such as IRS registration). This method of enumerating populations severely underenumerates volunteer-led nonprofit groups that advocate.
2. Probability sampling of lists of organizations created for other purposes (such as the *Encyclopedia of Associations*). This method is also likely to underenumerate the small, volunteer-led groups.
3. Creating lists of organizations (usually circumscribed geographically) using triangulated strategies that include cross-checking preexisting lists, consulting many sources, sometimes with the addition of snowball nominating procedures, and then developing probability samples of them. This method nets more of the small volunteer-led groups than the previous two methods (Gamson, 1990; Grønbjerg, 1992, 1993).

Hypernetwork samples of indirect advocating organizations. In the previous research approach, organizational representatives may be surveyed about their organization's indirect advocacy efforts. Another means to assess the extent and variety of indirect advocacy is to begin with samples of individual citizens, asking them about their experiences with organizations that have encouraged them to become active advocates and then developing lists of encouraging organizations from their responses. This consists of creating lists of organizations from the reports of membership by respondents in probability samples of individuals, in order to develop weighted probability samples of that population of organizations (McPherson, 1982; Kalleberg, 1994; Spaeth & O'Rourke, 1994). Known as hypernetwork sampling, this method appears to provide a solution for creating a probability sample of organizations, including nonprofits, in a community which have members or have engaged in indirect lobbying efforts. It will, however, miss organizations which directly advocate but do not have members.

Issue Advocacy Campaigns. The two previous sections have described research designs that depend upon creating samples of organizations of all types. A very different approach to studying advocacy by nonprofit organizations focuses upon the participants in specific issue advocacy campaigns or the regular participants in policy arenas.

Here, the population of organizations is defined as those organizations that take part in advocacy around a specific issue. This approach allows a more direct focus upon the interacting process of advocacy within issue domains and the mapping of organizations within domains. Keck and Sikkink (1998) use a similar concept in their attempt to describe the international environmental issue arena.

A major advantage of this strategy is that groups which take part in advocacy campaigns many times leave traces (as organizations or through the individuals they have mobilized),and populations of advocating organizations can be identified from such traces and sampled. In most extensive issue advocacy campaigns the population of organizations identified is likely to be far broader than advocacy organizations, and even broader than nonprofit organizations engaging in a bit of advocacy since it is likely to include firms and governmental agencies as well

Employing a prototype of the strategy we are suggesting here, Laumann and Knoke (1987) elucidate the role of advocacy by organizations across the entire range of formal organizations in their study of two policy domains—health and energy. Their empirical mapping of organizational mobilization and interaction in the policy domains and around key policy decisions within these domains provides another illustration of the usefulness of focusing upon issue campaigns for studying the role of organizational advocacy. The several campaigns they analyzed reveal the extensive advocacy role of many nonprofit organizations, sometimes in concert and sometimes in conflict with similar advocacy by for-profit organizations and government agencies.

Two other studies use traces of involvement in issue advocacy efforts to provide a glimpse of the possibilities of this research strategy. DeGregorio and Rossotti (1995) sampled organizations identified in public sources that became advocates in the Bork and Thomas Supreme Court nomination confirmation process. The sample of groups they assembled, which took part on both sides of these two widely controversial decisions, represent a wide range of nonprofit groups. Some of the sample might be easily identified as advocacy groups by common criteria, but many of these are nonprofit groups of different kinds.

Bykerk and Maney (1995) used U.S. House of Representatives and Senate Committee hearings on consumer protection issues to identify nonprofit groups and governmental agencies involved in advocacy around consumer issues. They found wide involvement among affected and interested governmental agencies, as well as among nonprofit groups, including business associations, labor unions, professional associations, and advocacy groups.

CONCLUSION

We framed the study of advocacy to this point in ways that avoid the heated controversies over many of the questions that could be addressed with the sorts of evidence we have suggested be collected. Are religious groups violating the terms of their tax exempt status by the ways in which they encourage their congregants to take part in elections? Have conservative foundations had inordinate influence in shaping the public discourse on social issues during the last decade? Have corporate, grassroots lobbying campaigns overwhelmed the voices of majorities of unorganized citizens in policy contests in recent years?

Many of the most interesting debates about the forces that shape the creation of public policy can be addressed with one or another of the research strategies we have outlined. We began our thinking about these issues with questions about the relative impact of the nonprofit sector on public policy outcomes. But, of course, nonprofit organizations line up on opposing sides of many policy issues. Consequently, some of the most interesting questions that can be addressed in studying organizational advocacy comparatively relate to the changing role of different kinds of nonprofit organizations. What is the changing role of foundations in advocacy over the last three decades? What is the consequence of the fact that large proportions of nonprofit organizations are effectively excluded from partisan political activity? Is "civil society" in decline (Putnam, 1993, 1995; Foley & Edwards, 1996)?

NOTES

1. There exists an extensive interest-group literature that focuses primarily upon direct lobbying by both for-profit and nonprofit organizations but it does not articulate very closely with the nonprofit advocacy research. See Petracca (1992) for an introduction to the more recent trends in interest group research.
2. We know much more systematically about the demography of individual citizen participation than we do about the demography of organizational advocacy. Typologies of individual citizen participation were developed inductively from extensive surveys of self-reported behavior. Research on individual citizen participation has generally assumed that it is the result of self-motivation rather than the result of encouragement from outside instigators.
3. Developing taxonomies of social elements is unsung labor among social science researchers. Steven Jay Gould says of the work of taxonomy that "it occupies a low status among the sciences because most people view the activity as a kind of glorified bookkeeping dedicated to pasting objects into preassigned spaces in nature's stamp album. [But] classifications are. . . theories of order, not simple records of nature. . . . Actively imposed, not passively

imbibed, they shape our thoughts and deeds in ways we scarcely perceive because we view
our categories as 'obvious' and 'natural'." (1990, p.73)
4. We summarize, and oversimplify, his multiple-regression analysis results aimed at determining
   which organizational factors best predict the level of advocacy.
5. This is what Smith (1994) calls the "dark matter" of the nonprofit sector.

REFERENCES

Bailey, C. W. (1996). Snakes in the grass. *Washington Monthly, 28* (September), 24–27.
Baumgartner, F. R., & Walker, J. L. (1988). Survey research and membership in voluntary asso-
    ciations. *American Journal of Political Science, 32,* 908–928.
Baumgartner, F. R., & Leech, B. L. (1998). *The importance of groups in politics and political sci-
    ence.* Princeton, NJ: Princeton University Press.
Bykerk, L. & Maney, A. (1995). Consumer groups and coalition politics on capitol hill. In A. J.
    Cigler & B. A. Loomis (Eds.), *Interest group politics* (4th ed., pp. 259–279). Washington,
    DC: Congressional Quarterly Press.
Coleman, J. S. (1982). *The asymmetric society.* Syracuse, NY: Syracuse University Press.
DeGregorio, C., & Rossotti, J. E. (1995). Campaigning for the court interest group participation.
    In A. J. Cigler & B. A. Loomis (Eds.), *Interest group politics* (4th ed., pp. 215–238). Washing-
    ton, DC: Congressional Quarterly Press.
Faucheux, R. (1995). The grassroots explosion. *Campaigns and elections,* (December/ January),
    20–25, 53–56, 66–67.
Foley, M., & Edwards, R. (1996). The paradox of civil society. *Journal of Democracy, 7,* 38–52.
Gamson, W. (1990). *The strategy of social protest.* Belmont, CA: Wadsworth.
Gandhi, N. M. (1995). Personal correspondence to Honorable Ernest Istook. Washington, DC:
    U.S. Government Accounting Office.
Gould, S. J. (1990). Taxonomy as politics. *Dissent, 28* (Winter), 73–78.
Gove, Philip Babcock (Ed.). (1986). *Webster's Third new International Dictionary.* Springfield,
    MA: Merriam-Webster.
Grønbjerg, K. A. (1992). Developing a universe of nonprofit organizations: Methodological con-
    siderations. *Nonprofit and Voluntary Sector Quarterly, 18,* 63–80.
Grønbjerg, K. A. (1993). *Understanding nonprofit funding: Managing revenues in social services
    and community development organizations.* San Francisco: Jossey-Bass.
Hertzke, A. (1988). *Representing God in Washington: The role of religious lobbies in the American
    polity.* Knoxville, TN: University of Tennessee Press.
Hopkins, B. R. (1992). *Charity, advocacy, and the law.* New York: Wiley.
Hrebenar, R. J. (1997). *Interest group politics in America.* Armonk, NY: M.E. Sharpe.
Jenkins, J. C. (1987). Nonprofit organizations and policy advocacy. In Walter Powell (Ed.), *The
    nonprofit sector* (pp. 296–318). New Haven: Yale University Press.
Kallenberg, A. L., Knoke, D., Marsden, P. V., & Spaeth, J. L. (1994). The national organizations
    study. *American Behavioral Scientist, 37,* 860–871.
Keck, M. E., & Sikkink, K. (1998). *Activists beyond borders: Advocacy networks in international
    politics.* Ithaca, NY: Cornell University Press.
Knoke, D. (1990). *Organizing for collective action.* New York: Aldine de Gruyter.
Kohut, A. (1996). *The diminishing divide: American churches, American politics.* Washington, DC:
    Pew Research Center for the People and the Press.

Laumann, E. O., & Knoke, D. (1987). *The organizational state: Social choice in national policy domains*. Madison, WI: University of Wisconsin Press.

McCarthy, J. D., & Castelli, J. (1994). *Working for justice: The campaign for human development and poor empowerment groups*. Washington, DC: Life Cycle Institute, The Catholic University of America.

McCarthy, J. D., Smith, J. & Zald, M. N. (1996). Accessing public, media, electoral and governmental agendas. In D. McAdam, J. D. McCarthy and M. N. Zald, (Eds.), *Comparative perspectives on social movements: Political opportunity, mobilizing structures and cultural framings* (pp. 291–311). New York: Cambridge University Press.

McCarthy, J. D., & Zald, M. N. (1977). Resource mobilization and social movements. *American Journal of Sociology, 82*, 1212–1241.

McPherson, J. M. (1982). Hypernetwork sampling: Duality and differentiation among voluntary associations. *Social Networks, 3*, 25–250.

O'Neill, M. (1989). *The third America: The emergence of the nonprofit sector in the United States*. San Francisco: Jossey-Bass.

Petracca, M. P. (1992). *The politics of interest: Interest groups transformed*. Boulder, CO: Westview Press.

Putnam R. D. (1993). *Making democracy work: Civic traditions in modern Italy*. Princeton, NJ: Princeton University Press.

Putnam R. D. (1995). Bowling alone: America's declining social capital. *Journal of Democracy, 6*, 65–78.

Rampton, S., & Stauber, J. C. (1995). Yes, in your backyard: Flacking at the grass-roots level. *PR Watch, 2*, 5–11.

Salamon, L. M. (1995). *Partners in public service: Government-nonprofit relations in the modern welfare state*. Baltimore, MD: Johns Hopkins University Press.

Salamon, L. M., & Anheier, H. K. (1992a). In search of the non-profit sector I: The question of definitions. *Voluntas, 3*, 125–151.

Salamon, L. M., & Anheier, H. K. (1992b). In search of the non-profit sector II: The problem of classification. *Voluntas, 3*, 267–309.

Scott, W. R. (1997). *Organizations: Rational, natural and open systems* (4th ed.). Englewood Cliffs, NJ: Prentice-Hall.

Schlozman, K. L., & Tierney, J. T. (1986). *Organized interests and American democracy*. New York: Harper and Row.

Smith, D. H. (1994). The rest of the nonprofit sector I: The nature of grassroots associations in America. Prepared for Annual ARNOVA Meeting, Berkeley, CA.

Spaeth, J. L., & O'Rourke, D. P. (1994). Designing and implementing the national organizations study. *American Behavioral Scientist, 37*, 872–890.

U.S. Postal Rate Commission (1987). *Study of political advocacy in third-class nonprofit mail*. Washington, DC: Postal Rate Commission.

Verba, S., Schlozman, K. L., & Brady, H. E. (1995). *Voice and equality: Civic voluntarism in American politics*. Boston, MA: Harvard University Press.

Walker, J. L., Jr. (1991). *Mobilizing interest groups in America: Patrons, professions and social movements*. Ann Arbor, MI: University of Michigan Press.

Walters, J. (1983). Multiply your clout with a grassroots lobbying network. *Association Management, 35*(April), 56–61.

Young, D. R., Ian, N. B., & Bailey, D. (1994). The structure of national nonprofit associations: survey results. Working Paper. Aspen Institute: Washington, DC.

Chapter 7

The Distributional Impacts of Nonprofits and Philanthropy

JULIAN WOLPERT

Who benefits from nonprofits and philanthropy, that is, the third sector? The answer in general terms is that we all benefit directly or indirectly, tangibly and intangibly, from nonprofit hospitals, museums, universities, religious institutions, and social services. We also benefit from the public interest advocacy by nonprofits, from their contributions to our civic society, and from our own voluntary participation in their efforts.

Yet, the inputs into the nonprofit sector are far easier to assess than its outputs and benefits. Surveys and analyses of donors and nonprofit agencies have taught us a good deal about the inputs of revenue, labor, and volunteer time. We know that annual donations approximate $130 billion, that nonprofits spend $600 billion each year, and that 9 percent of the labor force works for nonprofits. These are undoubtedly substantial resource inputs, but specifics about outcomes, impacts, performance, and beneficiaries cannot yet be measured with precision. We cannot catalog the total direct and external impacts or even categorize all the forms of benefit.

Furthermore, our knowledge of the *incidence of benefit* or who benefits and how, the subject of this chapter, is almost entirely lacking. The beneficia-

JULIAN WOLPERT • Henry G. Bryant Professor of Geography, Public Affairs, and Urban Planning, Woodrow Wilson School of Public and International Affairs, Princeton University, Princeton, New Jersey 08544.

Measuring the Impact of the Nonprofit Sector, edited by Patrice Flynn and Virginia A. Hodgkinson, New York, Kluwer Academic/Plenum Publishers, 2002.

ries are clients of social services, patrons of museums, students in private universities, patients in nonprofit hospitals, members of churches, as well as taxpayers who pay less tax because of donor and volunteer efforts.

Do some benefit more than others from nonprofit activities? Does some invisible hand guide benefits to those groups, causes, and institutions that need it most and use it best? The narrow connotation of *distributional effects* typically refers to income distribution, but can relate to other types of distribution as well. Philanthropy and nonprofits have not had primary responsibility for ameliorating conditions for the powerless and those in need in American society since the Depression and the New Deal. Their distributory role is now supplementary and as a partner with (or occasionally a critic of) government's efforts (Salamon, 1995). Their primary activities are targeted more to civic purposes, amenities, and the delivery of services.

My objectives here are: (1) to clarify the distributional issues that pertain to nonprofits and philanthropy; (2) to evaluate potential indicators of the sector's distributional impacts and their advantages and limitations; (3) to suggest data series that are needed to improve our measures; and (4) to outline major research priorities for the work that needs to be done.

WHY BE CONCERNED ABOUT DISTRIBUTIONAL CONSEQUENCES NOW?

Perceptions that nonprofits benefit the powerless and people in need exist in the public mind and among a significant share of donors as well as among members of Congress and state legislators who have accorded a privileged status to the sector. These perceptions need periodic reinforcement with hard evidence to support the claims of fairness and equity in providing services. However, the evidence will likely show that nonprofits have little impact on income distribution but have other distributional consequences that are deemed beneficial. The current discussions in Congress and state legislatures about allowing tax credits only for donations to those nonprofits that target their activities to poverty relief and direct services to the poor are indicative of the special attention accorded to questions of income distribution. Furthermore, much of the current media and regulatory focus on the accountability of nonprofits relates to their record of delivering services in an ethical and economical way to intended beneficiaries, that is, the focus is on ensuring that consumers of services benefit more than donors, boards of trustees, and staff.

Distributional information can also inform us about groups that are bypassed or underserved by government or nonprofits, or that may need additional assistance or more active advocacy and lobbying on their behalf. Tracking beneficiaries of nonprofits may not provide a comprehensive assessment of distributional impacts, but it should at least be possible to address broad issues such as the effectiveness of nonprofits in targeting various groups, service gaps in various communities or sections of the nation, and so on. It should also be possible to extend and improve our case study information and back-of-the-envelope estimates even if the outcomes are not totally comprehensive.

It is important as well to be able to address critics who maintain that philanthropy serves only elite institutions or that nonprofit services target benefits to the poor only to the extent of their subsidized government grants and contracts. The issue of who benefits is not a neutral question to critics but a challenge for philanthropy and nonprofits to do more for those who are most underserved by America's institutions. However, it is vital to keep in mind during discussions of distributional impacts that philanthropy and the nonprofit sector have neither the resources to bring about any major realignment of income, wealth, or service access in the United States nor much control to retarget current patterns of gaps in support.

INFORMATION GAPS

Why is better information about the distribution of nonprofit benefits not more readily available? First, the prior task of defining and identifying net benefits of the nonprofit sector as a whole and of its hundreds of thousands of diverse organizations and agencies is itself a resource-taxing and challenging task. How can the distributional effects be assessed before we can even measure the (direct and external) benefits themselves? The tally of direct beneficiaries or service clients must be supplemented by a tally of those who benefit indirectly in diverse ways, including clients' families and communities, taxpayers, private-sector suppliers, donors and volunteers, nonprofit employees, and so on.

Determining who benefits and how is a daunting task: Who would do it? How would the diverse information be aggregated? Who would use it, and for what purpose? Would the benefit of the effort match its costs? Would improved information be beneficial or harmful for the sector's image and reputation? Many individual agencies, especially those with grants and contracts from government or umbrella groups, are currently expected to enumerate their clients by income, ethnicity, and age categories, but even these minimal data are very spotty. Smaller agencies generally lack the resources, staff, and background for detailed tabulations of services to their consumers. Furthermore, agencies are generally not optimistic that their outputs, performance, and targeting of types of clients can be measured adequately; for instance, the benefits and beneficiaries of a natural history museum, private education, or nursing home care. In

addition, neither nonprofit leaders nor researchers (with some notable exceptions) have given the issue of benefits and their distributional consequences
much emphasis. The issues have become more timely only now that the nonprofit sector has been challenged by Congress to assume a larger share of service provision and by their critics to defend the benefits and targeting of their
services.

HOW ARE DISTRIBUTIONAL ISSUES EXAMINED IN THE PUBLIC SECTOR?

The distributional role of nonprofits cannot be examined in isolation from
public-sector activities to improve public welfare, redistribute income, guarantee safety nets, or ensure entitlements (Salamon, 1995). Some would maintain
that progressive welfare states "crowd out" the distributional agenda of philanthropy and nonprofits. In comprehensive and benevolent welfare societies,
nonprofits are freer to focus on civic, religious, and quality-of-life issues. Where
and when government condones severe disparities in income and access to services, nonprofits have more significant distributional and advocacy functions.
If infant mortality rates, for example, are higher among the poor than among
the rich despite government efforts, then nonprofits would be inclined to become involved in direct service or advocacy for more public-sector attention.
Thus, the distributional impacts of nonprofits loom as a more or less significant
topic depending on what government has agreed to do: assessing this supplementary or residual role initially requires knowing what the public sector is or
is not accomplishing in dealing with gaps and disparities.

Distributional impacts of the *public sector* are generally framed in terms of
equity and fairness and are an important component in the literature of welfare
economics and political theory (see, for example, Okun, 1975, and Rawls, 1971).
These discussions are instructive for defining the comparable task of assessing
who benefits from third-sector activities. Distributional effects of public-sector
policies and programs refer conventionally to the incidence of benefits and
costs among subgroups of the population, typically, who pays or is harmed, and
who benefits.

Presumably, if one could start all over again in a rational and just society,
the first step would be to reserve roles for public, private, and nonprofit sectors
that most effectively and equitably address goals for society's quality of life,
efficiency-in-service provision, and minimum thresholds for well being. However, our society relies on government as the primary agent for establishing
entitlements and safety nets and for fine-tuning incremental shifts to retarget
responsibility and resources within and among the three sectors.

The most meaningful criteria for making these shifts relates to their comparable benefits—the total net benefits and the incidence of benefit. Benefits can, of course, never be equalized among all groups of the population, and not everyone can be raised to the same level of well-being. But conventions are adopted on the margin, such as targeting the most severe disparities for remedial action or ensuring minimum thresholds of service provision or safety nets for all members of society. These conventions vary with the social and political agenda, as does the degree of reliance on public as opposed to charitable interventions.

Most germane for our comparative discussion here are government programs or regulations, such as minimum wage, public school financing, or progressivity of income taxes, that aim to improve general welfare by reducing inequality in opportunity, income, health services, or some other criterion of well-being. Analysts concerned with public sector impacts measure distributional effects of interventions using indicators of direct and indirect impacts on the rich, the middle class, and the poor; children and senior citizens; African Americans and Hispanics; urbanites and rural people; Easterners and Westerners. Examples include the effects of various flat-tax proposals on income distribution, the effects of Medicaid expenditures on the longevity of the elderly poor in rural areas, and the impact of banning lead in gasoline on test scores of center-city children. The goals for policy or program outcomes are justified by welfare and quality-of-life considerations and also by political judgments and the clout of constituencies that effect agendas and priorities for targeted remedial actions. Nonprofit boards act in a similar fashion.

The analytic approach used implicitly to evaluate government programs targeted to specific goals arrays potential services in a tableau format. The total costs and benefits of alternative program remedies are assessed along with the incidence of these direct and external benefits and costs among income or other subgroups of the population (Figure 7.1).

Presumably, government decisions are made on the basis of cost/benefit differences but subject to incidence criteria that assess the distributional consequences of each program. Of course, costs and benefits and their distributional consequences cannot be measured fully, but the tableau at least provides a format for identifying and estimating the major expected impacts and for enumerating the uncertainties and intangibles.

Government programs to promote equity overwhelmingly involve income maintenance and cash transfers (e.g., Social Security, Medicare and Medicaid, Supplemental Security Income (SSI), Temporary Aid to Needy Families (TANF) [which replaced Aid to Families with Dependent Children (AFDC)], farm subsidies, disaster assistance, and unemployment compensation). Direct and induced benefits from these programs and their distributional consequences can

	Goal/Mission 1 Program/Service Alternative		Goal/Mission 2 Program/Service Alternative		Goal/Mission 3 Program/Service Alternative	
	1	2	1	2	1	2
Benefit 1						
Direct						
Incidence a						
Incidence b						
Incidence c						
Indirect						
Incidence a						
Incidence b						
Incidence c						
Benefit 2						
Direct						
Incidence a						
Incidence b						
Incidence c						
Indirect						
Incidence a						
Incidence b						
Incidence c						
etc.						
Cost 1						
Direct						
Incidence a						
Incidence b						
Incidence c						
Indirect						
Incidence a						
Incidence b						
Incidence c						
Cost 2						
Direct						
Incidence a						
Incidence b						
Incidence c						
Indirect						
Incidence a						
Incidence b						
Incidence c						
etc.						
Summation						

Figure 7.1. Benefit and cost tableau for assessing nonprofit distributional effects.

be assessed with some rigor. It is possible to gauge, therefore, such impacts as the share of elderly or children who are lifted out of poverty by these income transfer programs.

THIRD SECTOR'S CRITERIA FOR ASSESSING DISTRIBUTIONAL CONSEQUENCES

No sector—public, private, or nonprofit—would maintain that distributional equity is its primary goal. However, government and, to a somewhat lesser degree, the nonprofit sector are held accountable for the distributional impacts of their policies and programs, and these impacts are considered a vital part of their legitimate functions in our three-sector economy. Many nonprofits have also assumed a watchdog role as advocates for a caring society and as a voice for the needy and powerless in promoting distributional equity in government programs and nonprofit activities. Yet nonprofits are mainly locally based, have no formal entitlement responsibilities to address equity or service gaps, and lack the national tier structure that government has evolved. Their fragmented structure is analogous to a public sector composed of only self-governing local constituencies. However, it is interesting that nonprofits are somewhat more integrated nationally only in the human services subsector through umbrella groups, such as United Way, Catholic Charities, Jewish Federations, Salvation Army, and Red Cross, in order to carry on activities that require a national perspective.

If government activities balance the pursuit of allocative efficiency against the promotion of distributional equity, then which goal leads nonprofits to disregard equity in their targeting of services? It would be difficult to build the case that the fragmented and atomized nonprofit sector shares the pursuit of efficiency as its primary alternative to distributional equity. However, a case can be made that the presence of nonprofit services in our three-sector economy does foster an efficient service market that helps to keep service quality high and costs low. More significant perhaps, the pursuit of equity by nonprofits is balanced principally by the competing goal of enhancing the variety and quality of life through improved health, education, civic, religious, and cultural life, especially if government is deemed to be addressing overall equity concerns more or less satisfactorily.

Nonprofits also have a distinctive distributional agenda that may differ from the goals of the public sector. They foster pluralism and diversity in viewpoints and in provision of many services that government may not foster or support (e.g., the Children's Defense League). Some nonprofits are advocates for minority perspectives and fledgling groups that median voters would not otherwise represent. Nonprofits often have access to information about clients' needs and improved intervention strategies that may not be available to or accepted by government agencies or private service providers, for instance, the "tough love" approach in social service programs. Nonprofits are also able to garner additional revenues from donors for services that would not otherwise be made available through tax payments to government. The contributions are motivated by donor preferences for a distinctive nongovernmental approach to service delivery that the recipient nonprofit organization is able to provide. The "exit and voice" options of donors help set the distributional agenda of nonprofits.

Assessments of who pays and who benefits can be much the same for the private sector as for the public sector, even if their missions are different. In fact, the evaluation of third-sector benefits can be assessed against the counterfactual of service provision by the private sector or by the government, directly, especially if the service is equivalent (which is rare). Yet, the precise evaluation of the benefits from service provision, whether provided by the public, private, or nonprofit sector, is a much more challenging empirical task than assessing the impacts of income transfers. Imagine trying to assess the benefits of organized religion or attendance at a ballet performance. Third-sector activities typically involve the direct provision and delivery of services, but can also include advocacy, political mobilization, or more intangible contributions to a civic society. Incidence of access to and use of services can potentially be tallied, but the obstacles in going beyond these elemental measures are severe. However, a version of the same tableau implicit in public sector assessments can potentially be useful for organizing the data collection and evaluation (Figure 7.1).

TYPOLOGIES OF THIRD-SECTOR ACTIVITIES

Classification by Nonprofit Mission

The assessment of distributional impacts is important not only for the sector as a whole but also for its various components and subsectors. To analyze the incidence of benefits, third-sector activities can be arrayed within a triangle whose three corners represent the alternative goals of *philanthropy* (i.e., enhancement of civic institutions), *charity* (i.e., redistribution), and *service* (i.e., provision and delivery of services) (Figure 7.2).

Some nonprofit activities are solely charitable or philanthropic or service oriented, but most reflect, as suggested by their position within the triangle, some combination of the three objectives. Location within the triangle also

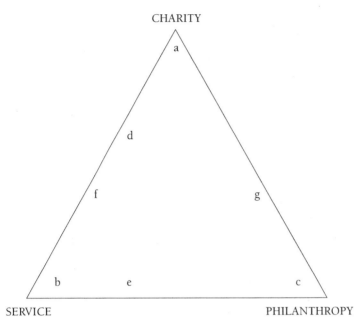

Figure 7.2. Nonprofit typology by type of mission.

identifies the targeted beneficiaries and hints at measurement schemes for assessing impacts. Agencies mapped at positions *f* and *d*, for example, reflect a balance between charity and service orientation.

Philanthropic activities (i.e., by foundations and large donors) target the establishment and enhancement of institutions such as hospitals, universities, museums, and community social capital. These activities can be assessed at least in the abstract by measuring their broad contribution to the quality and variety of life in the communities they serve (e.g., the art museum or the public interest environmental group). However, the measurement of their specific benefits and distributional consequences will be challenging, especially since most of the benefits are likely to be indirect.

Charitable organizations (e.g., Salvation Army, Catholic Charities) transfer resources from the more fortunate to the needy and can be assessed by metrics such as the income difference between donors and recipients or the percentage of the lowest income groups that has been assisted.

Nonprofit service organizations aim to foster mutual benefit and pluralism; serve "thin" markets not served by private or public sectors; and enhance quality, variety, compassion, and efficiency in service delivery. The impacts of their activities can be assessed through surveys of target population subgroups; these surveys might evaluate efficiency, income differences between donors and re-cipients, or effectiveness or client satisfaction relative to comparable govern-ment or private market services. Impacts would need to be evaluated relative to assessments of service needs and demands. Other distributional indicators would include efforts to democratize boards, the use of sliding fee schedules, the na-ture of outreach efforts, and so on.

Benefits of activities that reflect combinations of philanthropy, charity, and service clearly must be gauged through these multiple criteria. Churches, for example, provide most of their benefits through services to their own congre-gations but may engage in charity by cross-subsidizing fees for their lower in-come members or by providing a temporary shelter for homeless people.

The analysis of distributional effects based on this classification would proceed from an examination of the organizations' mission statements, valida-tion that the services and targeting of beneficiaries were consistent with the mission, and a tally, with various breakdowns, of the consumers of the services. Aggregation of these data for the nation as a whole and by various communities would provide some sense of overall targeting of benefits.

Classification by Nonprofit Subsector

The most obvious typology that can be useful for examining nonprofit benefits is the functional classification based on type of service. The nonprofit subsectors of health, education, religion, culture and the arts, human services, foundations, and so on are distinctive enough in mission and intended benefi-ciaries that assessing distributional consequences by subsector becomes very relevant, even if nonprofit organizations in each of the subsectors are not en-tirely homogeneous. In fact, the major study of the distributional consequences of having a third sector (Clotfelter, 1992) used this functional categorization. The general issues of how to assess benefits and who benefits are laid out in an initial chapter, followed by separate statements on religion, human services, health, education, the arts, and foundations.

Salamon's essay in that collection (Clotfelter, 1992) as well as his volume, Partners in Public Service (Salamon, 1995), provide a good deal of insight about the challenges in identifying and measuring benefits and their distributional consequences in the human services subsector, which is widely regarded as the most redistributive of nonprofit components. Salamon shows how it is pos-sible, at least theoretically, to assess agency revenues and their sources against receipt of services by beneficiaries of various groups. This would make it pos-sible, for example, to compare the income distribution of "input" sources with that of "outputs" and thereby assess the income redistributive effects of the agency's operations. The same framework is used by Netzer for culture and the arts; Margo for foundations; Biddle for religious congregations; Salkever and Frank for health services; and Schwartz and Baum for nonprofit education (Clotfelter, 1992). All the contributors to the Clotfelter volume acknowledge that the evidence from use of such measures shows very little net redistribution from nonprofit services (with some variation between subsectors), while readily admitting that the databases for assessment are partial and incomplete.

Salamon and others point to the lack of information about users of social services, service performance or satisfaction, and potential clients who need services but are not served (Salamon, 1995). Very little is known about the intended beneficiaries of service programs and almost nothing about the targeting efficiency (i.e., the success in providing benefits to targeted groups) through these efforts. We know little about the distributional effects of secondary benefits to clients' families and communities, to employees of nonprofits, to their private-sector suppliers, or to the value of property that neighbors nonprofit institutions. One would expect, however, that these secondary and induced impacts are less redistributive than are the intended benefits for targeted beneficiaries.

POTENTIAL INDICATORS OF THE DISTRIBUTIONAL IMPACTS OF NONPROFITS

Is better assessment of the distributional consequences feasible and practicable? Improvements in the Internal Revenue Service's Master Business File accompanied by the National Taxonomy of Exempt Entities (NTEE) classification and the Census of Services can be useful for assessing the share of nonprofit resources channeled into the various subsectors in regions and communities around the nation. These data also reveal some details about agency revenue sources, expenditure patterns, and targeted beneficiaries that can provide better clues to distributive impacts. Analyses can show, for example, the share of nonprofit resources that flow to the relatively more or less redistributive subsectors; the relative density of nonprofit services in rich and poor, white and minority communities; and the characteristics of areas, including their quality of life, that have low or high nonprofit activity.

The following indicators provide some starting points for assessing the distribution effects of nonprofits:

- The assets, revenue sources, and expenditures of nonprofits by subsectors.
- Tallies of beneficiaries by type, for example, service clients, students, audiences, patients, physically and mentally handicapped, homeless, substance abusers, or volunteers.

- Tallies of beneficiaries by income, age, ethnicity, race, immigrant status, etc.
- Locations of nonprofit facilities relative to community composition.
- Nonprofit board and staff composition relative to clients.
- Nonprofit outreach and community-building activities.
- Income (plus ethnicity and race) differences between donors (or tax-payers) relative to service users.
- Community well being, quality of life, and amenities relative to non-profit representation and activity.
- Advocacy and lobbying activities by nonprofits.
- Community-service inventories and needs-assessment activity by nonprofits.
- Nonprofit efforts to raise levels of donations and reduce donor targeting of contributions.

DATA SERIES THAT CAN IMPROVE OUR MEASURES

A sample survey supplement to the IRS 990 file of tax returns from non-profit organizations can glean additional information from agencies, such as the agency's mission or intended beneficiaries; the share of revenue derived from donors and from federal, state, and local government; service fee schedules; detailed breakdowns of administrative and operating expenditures; information about the services that are rendered; and specific demographic, social, ethnic, and economic information about service users and their households.

An additional sample survey instrument could help collect more information on service outcomes, agency effectiveness, client satisfaction, and community attitudes about the agency's performance. Multivariate analysis would be used to analyze survey responses to examine the consistency of the various distributional indicators and their determinants.

MAJOR RESEARCH PRIORITIES

The tasks that have been identified are difficult, long-term, and costly and they require cooperation from many nonprofit agencies that would need to be convinced that the effort is feasible and worthwhile. A planning committee could be established to scope the tasks and to recommend interim and long-term activities in cooperation with a similar committee that focuses on identifying and measuring benefits. It would be useful, for example, to start with some detailed case studies based on field analysis in order to define various components of the nonprofit sector that are involved in assessing distributional effects. Such case studies would ease the task of (a) identifying existing secondary data that could serve as useful indicators and (b) designing the survey instruments. The planning committee could also define interim back-of-the-envelope calculations from existing indicators that address some of the currently high priority distributional areas, such as:

- Nonprofit service coverage to those most in need.
- Nonprofit advocacy efforts where government is most deficient in addressing disparities and needs.
- Nonprofit leveraging of government grants through fund raising and voluntary efforts.
- Beneficial impacts of nonprofits on the communities they serve.
- Nonprofit efforts to streamline costs so as to make more of their services affordable to low-income populations.

CONCLUSION

Some major points need to be reviewed and stressed in this summary. The issue of who benefits from nonprofits is of much greater concern now than in the past. We all benefit from the activities of nonprofits in myriad ways. Yet it is difficult to assess the distribution of benefits because prior efforts to measure the direct and indirect benefits of nonprofits were relatively primitive. But it is not accidental that so little attention has been devoted to identifying the outcomes and benefits and tracking even the direct beneficiaries of nonprofit services. The measurement task is challenging, costly, and perhaps even threatening.

Nonprofits are not primarily responsible for the pursuit of equity in American society. That is not government's primary role either, but nonprofits and government are held accountable for reforms and interventions that address opportunities and disparities in the nation and in our communities. Thus, nonprofits are partners with government in helping to bring about distributional equity in addressing needs and delivering essential services. But nonprofits have a distinctive and independent agenda in their distributory role that is based on enriching civic life, ensuring quality and variety in community services, and responding ethically to community needs. Existing studies of distributional effects have uncovered little direct—and even less indirect—redistributive impacts of nonprofits, but the data sources for these studies have been very incomplete.

The task of measuring the benefits and distributional consequences of nonprofit activities can be undertaken more systematically for the diverse set of organizations that constitute the third sector if they are initially classified by type of mission and service subsectors. There are no simple and ideal indicators of distributional effects, but some conventional measures and indicators can be useful as starting points, such as support streams targeted to the more or less distributive nonprofit services; economic, social, and ethnic differences among donors, taxpayers, and service consumers; nonprofit activity levels in pockets of affluence and need; democratization of nonprofit boards and staff; nonprofit advocacy, outreach, and support for divergent and minority perspectives and financially struggling fledgling groups; and efforts to improve assessment of service outcomes and client and community satisfaction with nonprofit services. The research agenda for the difficult task of enhancing our information base on distributional effects should be incremental, with initial efforts devoted to some well-chosen and diverse case studies that allow intensive examination of the measurement task; a sample survey of nonprofits that builds on Internal Revenue Service 990 data and the National Taxonomy of Exempt Entities classification; and a reputational survey in representative communities that probes service outcomes and satisfaction.

REFERENCES

Clotfelter, C. T. (Ed.). (1992). *Who benefits? The distributional consequences of the nonprofit sector*. Chicago: University of Chicago Press.
Okun, A. M. (1975). *Equality and efficiency: The big tradeoff*. Washington, DC: Brooking Institution.
Rawls, J. (1971). *A theory of justice*. Cambridge, MA: Harvard University Press.
Salamon, L. M. (1995). *Partners in public service: Government–nonprofit relations in the modern welfare state*. Baltimore: Johns Hopkins University Press.

Chapter **8**

Can Public Life Be Regenerated?

DAVID MATHEWS

These days, we seem willing to consider the possibility that democracies need something more than written constitutions, multiple parties, free elections, and representative governments. They also depend on a strong public life, a rich depository of social capital, a sense of community, and a healthy civil society (Sandel, 1996).

Now comes the obvious follow-up: Is it possible to "reweave the social fabric" (Cortes, 1994), to generate social capital where it is lacking, to build a sense of community in a fragmented, polarized city, to invigorate public life at a time when many Americans are seeking security in private sanctuaries? No one knows. Maybe a democratic civil society takes centuries to develop, building layer upon layer like a coral reef. Maybe the places we admire most result more from happenstance than we would like to admit.

These reservations notwithstanding, we do have cases in which a civil order changed its character in a relatively short period of time. Modern Spanish democracy emerged from Franco's fascism in only forty years, according to Pérez-Díaz (1993). And Grisham (1997) reports that Tupelo, Mississippi, changed its civic character in roughly the same amount of time, the result being that the poorest city in the poorest county in the poorest state of the union became a progressive community with a per capita income close to that of Atlanta.

So maybe—just maybe—it is possible for towns and cities, perhaps even

DAVID MATHEWS • President and Chief Executive Officer, Charles F. Kettering Foundation, Dayton, Ohio 45459.

Measuring the Impact of the Nonprofit Sector, edited by Patrice Flynn and Virginia A. Hodgkinson, New York, Kluwer Academic/Plenum Publishers, 2002.

counties and states, to change their politics. Maybe public life can be regenerated. I say "regenerated" because I am assuming that some vestige or memory of public life exists almost everywhere. I think modern public life is rooted in the earliest institutions and norms created for collective survival. So my instincts tell me that strengthening public life is best accomplished by following the advice of J. Herman Blake, a very effective community organizer, whose practice is to "build on what grows." With that as a predicate, let us consider the question of how people might change the character of their civil order.

There is some urgency surrounding this question; I sense a danger in trying to strengthen public life with only a thin concept of the public, civil, or communal to guide the way. That would create a problem akin to trying to paint a barn red without clearly distinguishing red from pink or orange. There is a tendency to take descriptions of cities with a rich reservoir of social capital and try to replicate their features. If they have a lot of festivals, why not generate public life with a pig roast? (Actually, a foundation in Europe was asked to do just that.) But are community barbecues and festivals the product of something that happens prior to the events, of some precondition that we haven't been able to identify? Are we in danger of mistaking the symptom for the cause? If we make such an error, our strategies for building civil society will be the equivalent of dress-for-success strategies that tell us we can get ahead in the world by wearing the right tie or dress.

DEVELOPING A CONCEPT OF PUBLIC LIFE

Here is what I will try to do in this chapter: Drawing on what the Kettering Foundation is learning from its research and observations and from studies others have done, I will propose a way of thinking, a paradigm, about public life. Kettering has been developing a hypothesis about what public life is in order to have a better idea about how to strengthen it. The way we understand the structure and function of a public suggests ways to regenerate public life. As no one knows the answer to the question of whether such life can be renewed, surely the thing to do is to spell out our assumptions, which can be tested by experience.

We aren't making empirical claims when we develop a hypothesis. Yet our experiences influence our imagination of what might be. For fifteen years, Kettering has been observing public life in communities from Grand Rapids, Michigan, to El Paso, Texas, and from Newark, New Jersey, to Orange County, California. We have also commissioned independent research on public life. And we have been influenced by studies such as Pérez-Díaz's (1993) on Spain, Grisham's (1997) on Tupelo, Putnam's (1993) on north central Italy, and that of the Heartland Center for Leadership Development (1992) on the difference between dying and prospering rural communities, among others.

Putnam and Grisham reinforced our own impressions that the "soft side" of the social order or an intangible such as social capital is critical to public life. Social capital is said to consist of networks of civic associations, along with norms of reciprocity and social trust, that result in high levels of voluntary cooperation. This capital is generated where public life is strong, that is, where people are involved in public matters and in relationships that run horizontally (among equals) instead of vertically (between haves and have-nots). While Putnam found these characteristics in some areas in Italy, they were noticeably absent in others. People in the "uncivil" areas did not participate in either local politics or social organizations, and their relationships tended to be hierarchical, with the have-nots dependent on the haves.

Similar studies have found towns and cities in the United States with many of the characteristics of those in north central Italy. Tupelo is often cited as an example. Small (its population is about 30,000) and located in a rural area, Tupelo has no special advantages: no large body of water, no nearby metropolitan center, and no government installation with a large federal budget. Until 1980, there wasn't even a four-lane highway within seventy-five miles. Today, its prosperity extends into the surrounding area. In each of the past twelve years, Lee County has added more than a thousand new industrial jobs and even more service jobs.

According to Grisham, who has spent the better part of his career studying Tupelo, a large proportion of the people there have a strong sense of community (of what they share together) as well as a willingness to take responsibility. The citizenry "owns" the town's major civic projects; participation levels are high. Tupelo has a rich array of organizations and networks that provide opportunities for people to define and redefine their problems and make decisions about how to act. Of course, this is not a perfect town. The local development foundation has been compared with the political "bosses" who ran local governments at the turn of the century. Some prominent citizens don't believe in public participation and think decisions should be in the hands of a small elite. Most, however, are convinced that the upper tier of leadership has to create even stronger ties to rank-and-file citizens because as the town grows, new people and new problems create new challenges. On the whole, Tupelo appears to be a town with a flourishing public life, which has been able to reproduce itself decade after decade.

You might ask whether the strong economy isn't the reason for this town's strong public life. Obviously, each reinforces the other. But when Putnam investigated a similar question in his study, he found that it was public life rather than the economy that made the difference, that north central Italy was not civil because it was rich but rich because it was civil. The people of Tupelo agree. They say that their prosperous economy has been the result of community development; their economic strategies have been what I would call public-building strategies.

While citizens of Tupelo would say that they have a rich community life, I would call it public life because the word "public" helps capture the natural dissonance within a democratic community. A public, for me, is a society of diverse people who are joined through ever-changing alliances in the practical business of addressing common problems. I have always found Palmer's characterization of a public as a "company of strangers" (1981) useful. Citizens share some things with one another and don't share others. Interests differ and still people are able to work together in always temporary alliances. I suspect that norms of cooperation and trust may be by-products of this public work. Without denying the importance of such factors, I want to give due weight to the pragmatic and practical. Our experience at Kettering, especially our international experience, leads us to believe that people don't have to be close to or even like one another in order to work together effectively.

We have found it useful to distinguish between different forms of social capital, not to deny that all political capital is a kind of social capital, but to call attention to the particular type of capital directly related to politics, or the capacity of a community to solve its problems.

To be sure, public life rests on an informal social system. Social gatherings help people form closer ties to their communities. People chat before and after church services; they talk at weddings and festivals; they sound off at bars and bingo parlors. Many of their conversations are about issues of the day, common social and economic problems, and deep political concerns. Oldenburg (1989) has called the sites for these conversations the "great good places" of a community. They are remarkably similar to good homes in the comfort and support they offer.

In order for these social gatherings to strengthen public life, however, some have to have particular characteristics; we would say that they have to build *public* capital rather than purely social capital. Our research suggests that, in order for public capital to be generated, there must be occasions where people can get to know one another as citizens; it's not enough for community members to know each other on the basis of social status or family background. Also, people must have opportunities to engage in a larger conversation about the well-being of the community as a whole. And there must be inclusive gatherings, inclusive with respect to who organizes them as well as to who takes part in them. Citizens must be able to find others who have similar or related interests (The Harwood Group, 1995b).

GUESSES ABOUT STRUCTURE AND FUNCTION

Focusing on the more public forms of social capital, we have begun to create something like an anatomical framework for giving order to what we are learning about public life. We felt we needed to develop a reasonably comprehensive and coherent account of what constituted public life and how it functioned in order to be able to make reasonable assumptions about how to strengthen or regenerate it. We have come up with a half-dozen or so categories for capturing the essential elements of public life. Here they are in brief:

We think that public life consists of particular kinds of *relationships* or, better said, *ways of relating*. These public relationships are a source of political power, so we put them together in one category. We think that public relationships are governed by certain *precepts* or *mind-sets* about how things get done. At Kettering, Hal Saunders calls these "pictures in the mind" or mentalities. We suspect that, where public life is strong and democratic, the concept of politics is strikingly different from politics as usual.

In addition to relationships and precepts, we believe it is useful to look at the distinctive structures that are characteristic of public life. We have in mind an array of ad hoc associations and more formal organizations that provide space for public relationships to form, that create connective tissue, and that serve as channels of communication among disparate elements within a geographic community. So *civil infrastructure* is another of our categories.

Public life, we have long thought, is expressed in particular *practices*. By "practices" we mean what the Greeks meant—ways of acting that have intrinsic worth or value to people, as contrasted with techniques, or purely instrumental ways of getting things done. For example, hammering a nail is a technique; no one hammers for hammering's sake. Painting, singing, and dancing are practices; they have intrinsic worth to the practitioners, as well as social benefit. People genuinely like to paint, sing, and dance. An example from politics: The dialogue used to solve problems seems to have intrinsic value to citizens. They like the dialogue; it changes people, adding a public dimension to their lives.

We have identified several practices we think are critical in public life: (a) naming problems, (b) making collective decisions about how to act on these problems, (c) acting together, and (d) judging the results of action.

Finally, in observing and reading about places where public life is strong or growing, we have been impressed by how much those communities are like good students. They are voracious learners, picking up everything they can from both their own experience and the experience of others. That seems to be how they maintain the vitality of their public life. We have been calling this *civic learning*.

Having now summarized what is to follow, let us look in more detail at what we see as the major elements of public life.

Relationships

Mind-sets about a different way of doing politics take concrete form in the way citizens relate to one another and to those in office. Public relationships are those that people form with one another in the course of attending to public matters. They are different from relationships based on kinship, affection, or friendship. To paraphrase Palmer (1981), they are ties that bind relative strangers in the practical work of attending to common problems. Public relationships, we think, abound in public life.

Gerald Taylor (1993), of the Industrial Areas Foundation (IAF), tries hard to build these relationships in the communities where he works. Though he sees public life and private life overlapping, he thinks they are separate spheres governed by different rules of behavior. Public relationships begin in different interests and in acknowledging those differences rather than trying to homogenize them. Public relationships are personal, human, and face-to-face, but they are also relationships among different interests; they are connections in which one set of interests influences another.

Here is an account of how IAF operated in Baltimore to build public relationships by connecting interests: "When leaders of Baltimore BUILD, the nation's largest mainly black local organization, first met with Senator Paul Sarbanes, he smiled, took out his notebook and asked 'What can I do for you?' 'Nothing,' replied the leaders. 'We're here to get to know you. We want to know why you're in the U.S. Senate, what are your interests and concerns. We think that will help us develop a working relationship over time'" (Boyte, 1990, p. 516).

Taylor believes there is political power in the ability to form public relationships, the kind of power that comes from different people combining their capacities. These combinations are held together by promises people make to one another in public. You might call them commitments or covenants (Elazar, 1985). Promises, made in public and subject to public review (Did you do what you said you would?), are Taylor's equivalent of trust.

Organizers trying to build public relationships aren't just trying to solve specific problems; they are trying to change the way people deal with one another. While they say that public relationships are subject to change and that alliances may shift (because there are no permanent enemies or friends, only interests), they hope that public ways of relating can become ongoing habits. Their ambition is to create public life even when interests differ and conventional power is unequally distributed. Public relationships don't require equality among the parties or promise equal distribution of outcomes. Though filled with tensions, they are a nonviolent alternative to dealing with the potential clash of differences.

Precepts and Norms

We distinguish the social norms that influence public behavior from what we refer to as precepts, mind-sets, or mentalities. Norms mean to us social pressures that result in noncognitive, adaptive behavior. Precepts are more like guiding principles for political behavior, which grow out of a shared image of how things get done. Precepts are more cognitive than norms, which though powerful, appear to be by-products or derivatives of precepts. So, without dismissing them, we have been looking more at the role of mentalities or what some call "conventions" (Brown, 1995).

As I said earlier, we suspect that where democratic public life flourishes, the mind-set about how things get done is strikingly different from the perspective that informs politics as usual (Mathews, 1994, Chapters 8, 9). One difference is that where public life is strongest, people seem to have a broad, interconnected concept of their community, rather than a compartmentalized perspective, which separates everything into discrete categories.

Grisham (1997, Chapter 2) calls precepts "guiding principles." In Tupelo, they include such injunctions as "Never turn the work over to agencies that don't involve citizens." Widespread, inclusive participation is an absolute maxim. Some of the guidelines are commonsensical: "Build teams and use a team approach." Others are counterintuitive: "See everyone as a resource."

John McKnight, a student of community organization, helps explain why this last principle—seeing people as a storehouse of capacities rather than only as needs—is so critical. Thinking of communities as the sum of the capacities of citizens has the potential to change the understanding of public participation from a right to an asset. Everyone can be seen as a glass half empty or half full, McKnight says. By labeling people with their deficiencies (that is, their needs), we miss what is most important to them—opportunities to "express and share their gifts, skills, capacities, and abilities" (McKnight, 1989, p. 7). The only way communities can become stronger, he argues, is by harnessing the sum of everyone's abilities. That precept has evidently guided the citizens of Delray Beach, Florida, whose recent civic projects have been based on the principle "err on the side of inclusion" (White, 1995, p. 43). Don't leave a lot of people on the sidelines.

Where public life is strongest, we also expect to find a different mind-set about power. Conventionally, power means control over scarce resources and a legal license to act. This kind of power is in limited supply. Particular people and institutions are thought to have the power or authority to act, while others are seen as powerless. So those without power must be empowered by the powerful. Yet, as Follett (1918) pointed out, the power given by others isn't real power; no one can really empower someone else because it grows out of each person's unique experiences and talents. Consequently, this traditional concept of power is bound to leave a great many people feeling powerless or in need of being empowered.

For public life to be robust, there would surely have to be a broader concept of power, a notion of how even those who have no formal authority or control over existing resources could accomplish something. And, in fact, some citizen groups are quite aware of types of power that people generate themselves, such as the power of personal commitments. These groups think that power grows out of people's innate capacities and is amplified through their ability to band together (Susskind & Cruikshank, 1987).

Seeing power as innate leads to the conviction that "local people must solve local problems," which is another of Tupelo's guiding principles. In other communities, citizens have said, "We are the solution," echoing an old song from the civil rights movement: "We Are the Ones We Have Been Waiting for." These expressions are affirmations of responsibility, evidence of people "owning" their problems.

That people have to claim their own responsibility may be the most important precept of all for democratic public life. In an area of western Connecticut hard hit by plant closings, one citizen explained the need to claim responsibility this way: "All workers have to realize that we're responsible for our own condition. If we don't devote some time to our unions, our political party, our church organization, and the laws being enacted, we'll wake up and find ourselves with empty pension funds, bankrupt companies, disproportionate sacrifices, and a run-down community" (Brecher & Costello, 1990, p. 93). A newspaper editor in Wichita expressed the same conviction: "The only way... for the community to be a better place to live is for the people of the community to understand and accept their personal responsibility for what happens" (Merritt, 1992, p. 9).

Civil Infrastructure

Public relationships depend on organizations and institutions that provide space or occasions for them to form. The same thing is true of all human relationships. Families are social organizations that allow relationships of love and caring to develop. Trade associations create commercial relationships, and so on. For public life to flourish there must be space, that is, events and meetings, where people can join to talk about and organize action on common problems. There must be institutions and associations willing to organize those gatherings. We call the sum total of this public space, along with the way it is ordered and connected, a community's civil infrastructure.

One of the distinctive features of a community with a healthy public life is the amount of effort that goes into building this civil infrastructure, which also provides channels of communication. On the "ground floor," numerous ad hoc associations (small groups such as local development councils and neighborhood alliances) open doors for people to get "involved." Associations like those Alexis de Tocqueville found in the nineteenth century still provide opportunities for public deliberation on key issues. In the case of the public forums of Grand Rapids, Michigan, for example, a loose alliance of thrity to forty civic and education organizations has convened the community to deliberate on three major issues each year for more than a decade. The forums depend on the voluntary efforts of citizens, and their only structure is a steering committee that organizes a kickoff to introduce the issues and a wrap-up meeting to report on results.

The next tier in the infrastructure consists of formal civic clubs, leagues, and nongovernment organizations, which usually have offices with signs on the doors, staffs, and budgets. We think that, if public life is to be healthy, some of these organizations have to serve as umbrellas or boundary spanners, encouraging a community-wide exchange, developing a sense of interrelatedness, building networks, and promoting resource sharing. The Wilowe Institute, established in Arkansas in 1982, has been a classic boundary spanner. Dorothy Stuck, one of the founders, described the mission of the organization simply as "connecting people." The Institute convened statewide assemblies of citizens as citizens (rather than citizens as representatives or delegates) to work on issues from education to economic development.

Practices

Associations and organizations that develop public relationships also provide public space for citizens to work on their common problems, using the four civic practices mentioned earlier.

Community problem solving, or any problem solving for that matter, follows a familiar pattern. Something untoward happens; someone gives the problem a name and proceeds to make decisions about how to act; someone acts; and then someone assesses the results. Too often, the public is pushed aside at each of these crucial points. Problems are named in technical, legal, or ideological terms. Leaders make the decisions; citizens never struggle with the choices. Results are evaluated in a way that undermines the public's sense of ownership and accountability. Public life grows weaker at every step. So at Kettering we asked ourselves what it would take to put the public back into the picture, what genuinely public problem-solving practices would look like. Here are the results of our thinking:

Naming Problems and Framing Issues in Public Terms

Who names the problems in a community and the names that are chosen—even the terms that are used—are critically important. They determine the way a community will approach a problem and who will be involved. They even shape the outcomes of the actions taken to solve problems. While the tendency is to use names foreign to them, citizens have their own "take" on problems. They respond to those described in ways that reflect everyday experience and the things people consider most valuable. For example, many Americans are inclined to see stopping drug abuse as a family or community issue rather than simply a matter of enforcing the law or preventing drugs from entering the country. That perspective captures deeply held concerns about the collapse of the family and the loss of personal responsibility. Naming the problem in legal and governmental terms shuts out those who see drug abuse every day in their neighborhoods and connects the problem to what is happening in the social order and economy.

Studies have shown that people will not take the first step into public life unless they see a connection between civic matters and their personal concerns (The Harwood Group, 1993). People aren't just looking for down-home stories or words with fewer than three syllables. The obstacles that keep them from becoming involved can't be overcome by just using everyday language. Problems have to be named in ways that show their connection to the things people consider most valuable. I don't mean "values"; I mean basic motives, such as being secure from danger or being treated equally (see Rokeach & Ball-Rokeach, 1989). Naming problems to capture the deeper concerns of the whole community builds a sense of shared fate; it helps move people off the sidelines.

Although naming problems is a critical first step in community problem solving, it's only one step. Framing issues for presentation to the public is equally important. (Ask any lawyer!) A name identifies a problem but doesn't say what our options are for solving it. The name doesn't tell us what has to be decided or what is really at issue. And what is really at issue are tensions among the many things we consider valuable. Framing issues in public terms sets the stage for confronting our competing motives. Our various concerns often lead to different approaches to dealing with issues, which may be in conflict.

When it comes to health care, for example, we want what is best, and we also want what is most affordable. Yet the better the care, technically, the more costly and less affordable it is. Any strategy for dealing with the costs of technically advanced health care runs squarely into this dilemma, which is typical of the dilemmas posed by major public issues. Furthermore, every option for action will have in it both positive and negative implications for what we hold dear.

Unless citizens see and confront these conflicts and the costs of every option, they won't make sound decisions. (A sound decision is one in which people understand and are willing to accept the consequences of the option they like best.) Citizens will not move beyond individual first impressions to shared, mature public judgment. Therefore, we believe that public judgment, as opposed to popular opinion, is essential to healthy public life (Yankelovich, 1991).

The Role of Public Dialogue

Naming problems and framing issues in public terms set the stage for making choices together so that people can act together. At one of the recent Grand Rapids forums, a mother who had lost two sons to random violence said simply but with conviction, "We have to band together to stop the killing." Communities can't band together, however, unless they can make decisions about the purposes and direction of action. As I have just noted, these decisions are always difficult. Conflicts inevitably arise because a great many things are valuable to us, and we have no way of being certain which of our concerns should guide us.

How have people been able to arrive at decisions when the stakes are so high and the uncertainty about what to do so great? They have called on the human faculty for making judgments and have employed that form of thinking that is tied to a particular way of talking to one another, which we call "deliberation." The Greeks of ancient Athens knew about deliberation, colonists used it in America's town meetings, and it flourishes today in Grand Rapids. To deliberate, people have to talk face-to-face in order to examine a wide variety of perspectives and weigh the pros and cons of every option. That is what deliberation is—carefully weighing various approaches to an issue against what is truly valuable. Deliberative dialogue is different from popular expression (sounding off), information gathering, and debate. Deliberation explores several basic questions: What is valuable to us when we think about a particular issue? What are the costs and consequences of the various options for acting on that issue? What are the tough choices or dilemmas that make the decision so difficult? The final question can take a variety of forms: What are we willing to do to solve the problem? What trade-offs are we willing (or unwilling) to make? Where do we want a policy on this issue to take us? In responding to these questions, people are also "working through" conflicts over which of the many things that are valuable to them should inform their actions (see Yankelovich, 1991, pp. 63–65).

Deliberation is a process of decision making that is tied to action. While it doesn't necessarily result in agreement, deliberation can produce a general sense of direction and point to shared or interrelated purposes. We do not think of deliberation as the same thing as building a consensus or mediating differences. Forums identify a range of actions that people can live with. They locate the area between agreement and disagreement, the area of the politically permissible. Better said, deliberative forums *create* this area, as people sort out what they are and aren't willing to do to deal with an issue.

By watching thousands of National Issues Forums (NIFs) across the country—locally controlled, financed, and convened by civic and education organizations—the Kettering Foundation has been able to learn more about the outcomes of deliberative dialogue. NIFs are part of the programs of thousands of civic, service, and religious organizations, as well as of libraries, high schools, and colleges. Neighborhood associations, prison literacy programs, community leadership programs, and a diverse array of other organizations are also part of the NIF network. The forums take their name from the NIF books they use, which are prepared by the Kettering Foundation and Public Agenda, both nonpartisan research organizations.

We thought initially that deliberation would prompt changes in attitudes. While that happens in some cases, the forums are more likely to change a person's perception of another person's opposing views than to get the two to agree. In other words, participants don't change their own opinions as much as they change their opinions of others' opinions. They say they understand opposing views better. Deliberation allows us to "take in" other people's experiences. As we internalize their views, we are changed, our perceptions of others are changed, and we see possibilities for acting together that we hadn't seen before (see Doble Research Associates, 1996, and Farkas & Friedman, 1995). That sense of possibility generates civic energy for implementing decisions.

Difficult decisions about how to act are made in stages, never all at once. So deliberation has to become a habit; one or two forums won't have much effect. People usually begin by blaming the difficulties on others before working through the emotions provoked by having to face unpleasant costs and consequences (see Yankelovich, 1991). Working through an issue takes a long time, goes on in many different settings, and moves in fits and starts. Conversations may begin as friendly backyard exchanges long before they become seriously deliberative. Typically, we start talking about personal concerns and then try to find out whether anyone else shares our worries. For example, neighbors may begin talking about the drug paraphernalia they found alongside the streets (The Harwood Group, 1993, pp. 11–12). Informal conversations may turn into a larger dialogue at a neighborhood gathering. Later, a forum may be held on the issue. Months of deliberation may pass before people determine what they can do together.

Public life in America has benefited from the deliberation of citizens since the first town meetings in the 1630s. So, in analyzing public life today, we look at community decision making to see how public and deliberative it is, and we look to see if there is enough patience for deliberation to become a habit. Pérez-Díaz's account of the emergence of civil society in Spain (1993, pp. 57, 101) reinforces this view. He suggests that among other factors, a public discussion of different versions of common interests helped the country take initiatives to solve its collective problems.

Acting Publicly

Another phenomenon some of us think is characteristic of public life is a particular kind of action, which we have called public action. A good argument can and has been made that the most important feature of public life is the nature of action or "public work" (Boyte & Kari, 1996). One of the limitations of the term "public life" is that it tends to underplay the dynamic quality of what a public does. A public is a body of political actors, and public life is a life of action. We assume that public life is characterized by a way of acting that is quintessentially public.

Public action may be seen as a pattern of acting, an ongoing process integral to the political culture of some communities. Just after World War II, observers recalled that the trains in both England and Germany had run on time. In Germany, they had been on time because someone had ordered them to be punctual. In England, they had been on time because that had been "the custom." Public action is a custom of acting, an ethos for acting.

How else might we understand public action? While studies of towns and cities with a vibrant civil society give some indication of what public action is, we thought we might be able to describe it more fully by asking what action would be like if it had the qualities associated with publicness.

For example, the word "public" is closely linked with what is common, shared, or for the benefit of all. Public action, then, would be that action focused on the overall or common well-being of people—although the common good might be found at the intersection of different self-interests. "Public" also refers to that which is open to all, unrestricted, and therefore diverse. So public action would be the action of a diverse array of citizens. A "public" is an organized body of people, so public action would be the action of cooperating citizens. The term could be used for a type of civic action we suspect is found in public life—action that is complementary and mutually reinforcing rather than fragmented and compartmentalized, an "alloy" of initiatives drawing on different capacities and fused the way different metals are to make a superior material. The many initiatives that make up public action shouldn't be merely amassed; they should reinforce each other so that the whole of the effort becomes greater than the sum of the parts.

Case studies of areas where civil society is strong do, in fact, report action with these public qualities. For instance, the Delray Beach project could be called public because it included an array of citizens; no one was left on the sidelines (White, 1995).

In describing civil society relationships as horizontal, Putnam's study of

Florence gives us another clue to the nature of public action. While not anti-thetical to governmental or institutional action, which is vertical as well as uni-form, linear, and coordinated by an administrative agency, public action surely has a different character. Institutional action is necessarily vertical. The fire department lays out rules for exiting a building safely. It sends an inspector around from time to time to supervise a fire drill. The interactions are from officials down to citizens or, in some cases, from citizens up to officials. Public action, on the other hand, is a repeating collection of lateral efforts; it isn't linear, beginning at one point and ending at another. Neighbors working to-gether to take care of their parks—pitching in to remove trash, plant trees, or build benches—might be an example. The interactions are horizontal, shoulder-to-shoulder, citizen-to-citizen.

We don't think of public action as a substitute for carefully planned ac-tions by organizations, although it has certain qualities that other forms of ac-tion lack. Economists would say that it is efficient because its transaction costs are lower. Even though it requires a degree of coordination (everyone can't show up at the park to mow grass and pick up trash), it isn't administratively regulated (North, 1990).

Our guess is that cities where there is little public action—where every-thing that is done has to be highly organized and planned in detail—miss the initiative and inventiveness that allow them to be optimally effective. What's more, institutional action may be less productive when it isn't reinforced by public action. Consider the way a good neighborhood watch program helps a police department do its job. Because official interactions are vertical, while public interactions run the other way, they can support each other. If the two are woven together, as with threads, the result should be the strong "whole cloth" of community action. (If it were not for the threads crossing one another in the fabric of our clothes, our elbows would come through our shirtsleeves.)

Though public action isn't the product of an administrative plan, we don't see it as spontaneous or magical. We believe it can grow out of deliberation, which, if it goes well, results in a sense of direction. Yet while public delibera-tion seems a necessary condition for stimulating public action, we don't think it is a sufficient one. Communities also have to deal with the obstacles posed by conflicting interests. Ideally, common interests should override the particular interests that often clash, but that is not always the case. We have all seen inter-ests in direct conflict such as in instances in which developers and environ-mentalists clash. Other kinds of self-interest, which are not mutually exclusive, may also hamper public action. People simply may not see the interdepen-dence of their interests clearly enough to be mutually supportive. The interest of the police officer on the beat may be to preserve order, while the social worker in the area may be more concerned with the harmony of family life. These interests are different and, while not mutually exclusive, they aren't necessarily related either. Each professional can, and often does, go about his or her business without the assistance of the other. So, after deliberative forums, citizens and organizations have more work to do in order to identify the interdependence of different interests. Deliberation lays the foundation for that discovery. Seeing where particular interests are interdependent should prompt more complementary public action.

Judging Results

Another practice that we think has a great deal to do with public life is the means used to evaluate the outcomes of action. Americans insist on knowing results because they want to be successful—and well they should. If they didn't, efforts to strengthen public life would degenerate into the worst kind of therapy: warm but illusory feelings of momentary comfort. Results must be known and evident to more than those directly involved. Unfortunately, the conventional way of assessing outcomes can undermine the very thing that makes for success—a strong sense of public responsibility.

For instance, a community might decide to improve its schools by having experts, educators, and key leaders set measurable standards of "success." Although local districts might have wide latitude in implementing the standards, the outcomes would be calculated against a predetermined criterion, the way a carpenter calculates whether a board is a certain length. That would limit the public to measuring success by standards it hadn't set, which would undercut its sense of accountability—of citizens holding *themselves*, not just officials and institutions, responsible. When people don't feel responsible, when they don't hold themselves accountable, their communities seem far less likely to change.

Success, getting the results we want in the affairs of our communities, may not be reducible to simply promulgating standards and measuring results; it may require an ongoing process of judging results publicly. To prevent the loss of "ownership," we may need the kind of accountability in which citizens participate in determining success rather than just receiving reports of what others have done. This public accountability would require a mechanism for direct examination of outcomes by citizens in much the way that a jury sees evidence and hears witnesses.

If the essence of public accountability is judging results publicly, as we think it is, then not only does the judging have to be done by the public, it also has to employ the appropriate mode of reasoning. Judging is the act of determining the worth of something when there is no authority to tell us what its value is and when people are likely to reach different conclusions.

As you may recognize, we are drawing on the classical definition of judging the worth of an action. Isocrates first described the difference between this kind of practical reasoning and both scientific and philosophic inquiry using

the device of a fictional jury trial for Timotheus, a general who was accused of
being a bad officer because he pacified rather than annihilated his enemies.
Isocrates laid out the criteria for determining the worth of action as he showed
how the general's tactics were consistent with what Athenians considered most
valuable to the city and pointed out that friendly allies are better than bitter
subjects (Isocrates). We have used the classical criteria in constructing our standards for judging publicly.

To determine the worth of political actions, citizens have to look both at
what happened as a result of those actions and, simultaneously, at the effects of
what happened on what they consider most valuable. Those two determina-
tions are the essential steps in judging success. In simplest terms, people have
to ask themselves, "Did we get what we really want?"

This process is unlike that used in the hypothetical case of school evaluation, in which one of the elements in the determination of success—what people
wanted or considered most valuable—was not subject to reconsideration by
the public. We anticipate that in the process of judging, people will change
their definitions of success. We expect them to do in public life what they do in
private life where it is common to change our minds—such as when we change
our minds about what we really need after buying something that does what
the manufacturer said it would do but doesn't do what we wanted done. (In the
South we say, "I felt like the dog that caught the car," to let people know that
we've changed our definition of success.)

We certainly don't mean to imply that judging results involves nothing
more than applying a simple two-part formula. We recognize that there will be
difficulties because (a) many things are important to people, so defining success is not simple; (b) actions to get what we want always have both negative
and positive consequences; and (c) our actions usually produce unanticipated
and unintended effects. Furthermore, judging publicly won't result in clear-cut
declarations of success or failure because success is a moving target. However,
this way of evaluating outcomes should produce a more realistic understanding of actions and consequences. Most important, it should prompt the civic
learning so essential to public life. Judging publicly should help communities
decide what to do next, opening people's eyes to possibilities for moving ahead.

Civic Learning

In introducing this report on our efforts to paint a picture of public life, I
said that we have been impressed by the importance of the community learning
described in Grisham's account of Tupelo. We have seen the same kind of learning in other places where public life seems to be growing, such as the "wiregrass"
area of southeastern Alabama. At first, we meant no more by "civic learning"

than studying what others are doing. Tupelo, for instance, has made a habit of sending investigative groups and bringing in scores of outsiders for advice and counsel.

We have suspected, however, that learning from others involves more than looking for good models to replicate. Modeling would seem to drive out learning. When Scott Foster was with the Council for Economic Development, he reported at one of our board discussions that communities successful in reviving their economies had gotten beyond the impulse to copy others, which was fatal to the strategy that worked best, namely, building a new economic base rather than resurrecting dying industries. We continue to believe that civic learning is adaptive, not imitative. Rather than importing models from elsewhere, learning communities seem to create their own.

More recently, we have begun to look at how communities with a strong public life learn from their own experiences. Rather than trying projects, finding them imperfect, and giving up, the Tupelos of the world seem to learn from their failures. Or, as Charles Kettering once said of inventors, they know how to fail successfully.

In contrast, we have noticed that politics as usual seems to preclude civic learning. Leaders often take months to study issues and make decisions among themselves, yet allow the public little opportunity to learn. The custom is to promote the proposals of leadership groups with a collection of supporting facts intended to convince the public of their merits. Leaders put their energies into doing "a real selling job." They don't seem to recognize that, if it takes the best informed people a long time to decide how to respond to a problem, it is likely to take those less familiar with the issues at least as long. Perhaps leaders assume that citizens are very accepting of the conclusions reached by prominent folk in positions of authority. If so, it is an assumption that they might want to reconsider in today's cynical, antiauthoritarianism climate.

Civic learning surely involves more than people hearing proposals and amassing facts. Citizens have to understand the perceptions that others bring to problems because no one has exactly the same experience with any given issue, and differing experiences lead to differing ways of approaching problems. The new road that gets one person across town more quickly may block someone else's access to neighbors. In order to know how a community sees a problem such as improving transportation, people have to synthesize a number of quite different perceptions. They can't really know what *they* think about an issue until *they* have talked about it. They have to construct a shared sense of what is happening; that takes time and patience, which are often in short supply.

Civic learning seems to allow us to know those things about our communities that we can know only by learning together—and never by learning alone. That means understanding what is valuable to us as a community, what our shared or interrelated interests are, whether we have compatible purposes, and what we think we ought to do in responding to common problems. People don't discover those things as much as they create them; they don't preexist their talking together in the kind of talk that people use to teach themselves before they act.

FROM WHAT TO HOW

We believe civic learning is indispensable to the reinvigoration of public life because it is compatible with the kind of politics that citizens "own" and does not undercut the sense of responsibility that is so crucial. Consequently, rather than trying to find ways for a third party to intervene, the better strategy for strengthening public life might be to think of ways that citizens can accelerate civic learning in their communities. This learning might occur most around those activities in which the public has been least involved, naming problems and framing issues, making decisions about policies or courses of action, figuring out how to act together effectively, and determining whether actions have been successful. All of these, taken together, would seem to be rich in opportunities for learning and for developing an idea about a more public form of politics.

Our towns and cities are more alike than is popular to say, yet strengthening public life requires that each of them find its own way. While no one should expect the way to be neat, linear, and systematic, neither does it have to remain mysterious. Although we think that it may be possible to strengthen public life by putting the public back into the act at critical points, we certainly don't assume that there is a science or set of rules that can be followed to a predictable outcome.

We don't expect public-forming strategies to work overnight. One round of naming problems in public terms or one deliberative forum won't change anything. These strategies have to become habits and be embraced as practices. Still, we may not have to wait for centuries for our neighborhoods, cities, and states to change their ways of doing business, to strengthen their public lives. We can start experimenting now.

There isn't space to spell out the implications of our concept of public life for leadership. Many would argue that the only way to strengthen public life is through leaders. We aren't sure that is an adequate answer. Some research suggests that established civic leaders can be one of the principal obstacles to involving more of the public because they think they *are* the public. Even those leaders who are convinced that their communities need a more active public aren't sure of what to do to bring that about. One problem is that a public is an abstraction difficult for them to distinguish from voters, an aggregate of interest groups, or a body of clients (The Harwood Group, 1995a, pp. 16–19).

Communities where public life is strong may not have what would normally be considered the "best" leaders. Yet they have so many leaders in so many places that they are "leaderful." In robust communities, some forms of leadership initiative appear to be expected of everyone (Grisham, 1997). When citizens talk about their leaders, they seem to recognize that they are talking about themselves.

We have also noticed that, where public life is strong, those exercising leadership appear to know a great deal about how to enrich public life. For example, they seem more likely to be door openers—those who get others involved and connected—than the more conventional gatekeepers—those who grant or withhold approval for civic initiatives. I have always liked Ronald Heifetz's definition of leaders (1994, Chapter 4) as good coaches for civic learning (my language, not his).

For those who share these or similar assumptions about public life and how it might be strengthened, the next task is to find out more about how civic learning can be accelerated through the public experiences of naming problems, making choices, and the like. That is what Kettering is attempting to do now. We also want to find out which existing institutions will provide the public space needed for civic learning or, if these institutions don't provide enough of this space, how to build new democratic organizations that will.

Finally, we believe that people learn how to live a more public life not practice-by-practice but by first getting a sense of the whole, which is more than the sum of the parts. As I said early on, mentalities seem to shape relationships, practices, even structures. So ultimately, people have to decide whether they want to live a different kind of political life—one that would put them at the center of a stronger, more public form of democracy.

REFERENCES

Boyte, H. C. (1990). The growth of citizen politics: Stages in local community organizing. *Dissent, 37,* 513–518.

Boyte, H. C., & Kari, N. N. (1996). *Building America: The democratic promise of public work.* Philadelphia, PA: Temple University Press.

Brecher, J., & Costello, T. (Eds.). (1990). *Building bridges: The emerging grassroots coalition of labor and community.* New York: Monthly Review Press.

Brown, D. W. (1995). *When strangers cooperate: Using social conventions to govern ourselves.* New York: Free Press.

Cortes, E., Jr. (1994). Reweaving the social fabric. *Boston Review, 19,* 12–14.

Doble Research Associates. (1996). *Responding to the critics of deliberation.* Dayton, OH: Kettering Foundation.

Elazar, D. J. (1985). America and the federalist revolution. *This World, 10,* 52–71.

Farkas, S., & Friedman, W. (1995) *The public's capacity for deliberation.* New York: Public Agenda for Kettering Foundation.

Follett, M. P. (1918). *The new state: Group organization, the solution of popular government.* New York: Longman, Green and Co.

Grisham, V. L. (1999). *Tupelo: The evolution of a community.* Dayton, OH: Kettering Foundation Press.

The Harwood Group. (1993). *Meaningful chaos: How people form relationships with public concerns.* Dayton, OH: Kettering Foundation.

The Harwood Group. (1995a). *America's struggle within: Citizens talk about the state of the Union.* Washington, DC: Pew Center for Civic Journalism.

The Harwood Group. (1995b). *Forming public capital: Observations from two communities.* Dayton, OH: Kettering Foundation.

Heartland Center for Leadership Development. (1992). *Clues to rural community survival* (8th ed.). Lincoln, NE: Author.

Heifetz, R. (1994). *Leadership without easy answers.* Cambridge, MA: Harvard University Press, Belknap Press.

Isocrates. *Antidosis.* (G. Norton , Trans.). Loeb Classical Library: 1929.

Mathews, D. (1996). *Is there a public for public schools?* Dayton, OH: Kettering Foundation Press.

Mathews, D. (1994). *Politics for people: Finding a responsible public voice.* Urbana: University of Illinois Press.

McKnight, J. L. (1989). Do no harm: Policy options that meet human needs. *Social Policy, 20,* 5–15.

Merritt, D., Jr. (1992, December). Transcript of the Public Journalism Seminar sponsored by the Kettering Foundation and New Directions for News, Dayton, OH.

North, D. C. (1990). *Institutions, institutional change, and economic performance.* Cambridge, MA: Cambridge University Press.

Oldenburg, R. (1989). *The great good place: Cafés, coffee shops, community centers, beauty parlors, general stores, bars, hangouts and how they get you through the day.* New York: Paragon House.

Palmer, P. J. (1981). *The company of strangers: Christians and the renewal of America's public life.* New York: Crossroads Publishing.

Pérez-Díaz, V. M. (1993). *The return of civil society: The emergence of democratic Spain.* Cambridge, MA: Harvard University Press.

Putnam, R. D. (1993). *Making democracy work: Civic traditions in modern Italy.* Princeton, NJ: Princeton University Press.

Rokeach, M., & Ball-Rokeach, S. J. (1989, May). Stability and change in American value priorities: 1968–1981. *American Psychologist, 44,* 775–784.

Sandel, M. J. (1996, March). America's search for a new public philosophy. *Atlantic Monthly, 277,* 57–74.

Susskind, L., & Cruikshank, J. (1987). *Breaking the impasse: Consensual approaches to resolving public disputes.* New York: Basic Books.

Taylor, G. (1993, June). The contours of public relationships [Photocopy]. Dayton, OH: Kettering Foundation.

White, O. (1995, February). The best-run town in Florida. *Florida Trend, 17,* 36–43.

Yankelovich, D. (1991). *Coming to public judgment: Making democracy work in a complex world.* Syracuse, NY: Syracuse University Press.

Part **IV**

Measuring the Impact
of Various Subsectors
and Special Populations

Part IV consists of six chapters evaluating the issues of research and measurement among selected subsectors and special populations of the nonprofit sector. Representing a variety of disciplinary perspectives, each author attempts to review the state of research and/or provide a research approach that might improve upon the state of measuring a sector's impact on society.

McCarthy (Chapter 9) argues that not only a disciplinary but also a multidisciplinary lens is needed to study women and philanthropy. While citing the importance of history, sociology, political science, and economics to women's studies, a multidisciplinary approach is also needed to measure the impact of women's philanthropy on society. Research on women has shown the importance of literacy, religion, and independent sources of income upon the development of women and the societies in which they lived or live. While she finds intrinsic value in qualitative research, McCarthy argues that an important first step for quantitative measures is to collect statistical data by gendered categories in studies of nonprofit organizations and in women's giving. In other words, it is difficult to measure the impact of various special populations unless statistical systems identify women's organizations or women separately.

In Chapter 10, Connell and Klem argue that traditional approaches to evaluation in education reform efforts have done little to provide the body of evidence necessary to evaluate the effectiveness or lack thereof of education reform either to public or private donors. They present a plan built on a theory of change, a method for collecting data to evaluate whether the implementation of steps to accomplish that change are working, and a plan to document the longer term impact of an educational program on the lives of children. They conclude that measuring outcomes and impact must be a comprehensive exercise uniquely tailored to each specific change situation.

Gray (Chapter 11) discusses the large sector of health care that is going through rapid change both in ownership characteristics (public, nonprofit, and for profit) and in types of institutions (health maintenance organizations). He argues that although many traditional measures such as number of patients served or number of beds are useful, they do not measure community benefit, which might provide the best way to distinguish between nonprofit, for-profit, and public hospitals and their contributions to community. Gray provides a broad definition of the items that might be included in a definition of community benefit to better delineate the level of contributions by ownership in health care and its impact on communities. Unfortunately, data covering community benefit items are not widely collected, but Gray argues that should such data be collected, it could help communities and local governments make more informed decisions when organizations consider converting to for-profit status.

Wyszomirski (Chapter 12) takes on the task of evaluating what might need to be done to measure the impact of the arts on society. She acknowledges that currently impact is measured by such variables as audience surveys, the number of agencies, and level of expenditures. To measure the impact of the arts would demand a new approach and collection of information that might be put into a series of indexes such as economic impact, organizational health, educational impact, and community effect. Wyszomirski argues that the challenges of such measures are formidable, but other indices have been developed, and this approach might help to overcome the "virtual invisibility" of the impact of the arts on society.

Greenway (Chapter 13) provides a survey of the types of outcomes assessment conducted by major human services agencies. She reviews the pitfalls of such assessments, arguing that there are no agreed-upon definitions of what "success" means. She focuses on program outcomes, or the benefits participants receive as a result of their involvement in a program. Community outcomes are defined as the cumulative results from a multiplicity of policies, programs, citizen action, and environmental factors that lead to social change such as reducing the impact of infant mortality in a community.

Greenway reviews current approaches to measuring outcomes, for example, national studies that measure participant outcomes in programs; national surveys of local program participants to assess current or past perceptions of the impact of programs; national assistance programs to local affiliates; national certification programs that require outcomes measurement; and locally developed evaluations using national models. She finds that human service organizations generally measure outputs (e.g., number of people served) but not outcomes, defined as changes in values, attitudes, knowledge, skills, behavior, and conditions. Moreover, a key problem for organizations is not having a clear target or benchmark for success. For example, if a program serving homeless individuals moves 20 percent of clients to self-sufficiency, is this a good or a bad outcome?

She also finds that most efforts focus on program review and not on community level outcomes. Community outcomes are far more dependent on external conditions such as public policies, the state of the economy, and a whole range of other support systems including families, schools, and churches. Greenway argues that much more research must be done on the development of systems and measures that can draw connections between outcomes of programs and community factors.

In the final chapter of this part, Wuthnow (Chapter 14) explores how to document the role of religious institutions upon society. While recognizing that the congregational series inaugurated by Independent Sector is new and not adequately analyzed, he suggests that religious institutions are engaging in a wide range of activities not regularly charted in available data series. These include interfaith coalitions, community development partnerships that bring nonprofit and government organizations together, and various volunteer networks. Wuthnow recommends in-depth research at the community level in order to understand the complexity of the mix of organizations and affiliations and partnerships that occur in communities. Only by understanding these complex mixes can aggregate data be created. He also considers how good quantitative studies have built upon in-depth qualitative studies.

Chapter **9**

Women and Philanthropy
Charting a Research Agenda

INTRODUCTION

The upsurge of research on the voluntary sector during the past decade has
been extraordinary. We now have databases and detailed studies of nonprofit
activities of a quantity and quality that few would have predicted when the
Independent Sector hosted its first Spring Research Forum in 1983. To date,
the majority of this work has focused on the nonprofits themselves: their numbers, their activities, their managerial concerns, and the effect of government
cutbacks. However, far less attention has been devoted to what might be termed
the human equation: the social, political, and economic impact of giving and
voluntarism.

In order to address this need, in 1993, the Center for the Study of Philanthropy began commissioning papers from scholars around the world to examine the role of women's philanthropy in their various countries. To date, essays
from more than twenty nations representing every continent have been commissioned, providing opportunities for comparison on a wide range of issues
from the impact of tradition, religion, government, and law in shaping the

KATHLEEN D. MCCARTHY • Professor of History and Director, Center for the Study of Philanthropy,
Graduate School and University Center, City University of New York, New York, New York 10016.

Measuring the Impact of the Nonprofit Sector, edited by Patrice Flynn and Virginia A. Hodgkinson,
New York, Kluwer Academic/Plenum Publishers, 2002.

initiatives women have created through their gifts of money and time, to contemporary funding and organizational concerns. In the process, we sought not only to examine the current challenges facing women's organizations, but also to begin to measure the role of philanthropy in opening a "space" for disadvantaged groups even in public policy making and institutional development.

The reasons for focusing on women's issues, aside from their inherent import and interest, were twofold. First, although religious, governmental, and economic systems can and do differ tremendously, women comprise at least half of the citizenry in every country and thus often constitute a majority. Second, women—even wealthy women—have historically tended to be among the most politically and educationally disadvantaged groups in their societies. As a result, the factors that clear the way for their participation in building civil society tend to stand out in bold relief.

These commissioned papers provide a wealth of data on women's roles as donors, volunteers, and organizational entrepreneurs; they also offer a number of insights into the issues currently surrounding giving, voluntarism, nonprofit development, and social advocacy in a variety of countries. They have enabled us to begin to formulate a series of hypotheses about the societal factors that promote philanthropic activities.[1]

Of the eight hypotheses being tested in the project, four are particularly worth noting in the context of this overview:

1. Religion is the most important factor in shaping women's philanthropy and civil society.
2. Women's organizations have made their greatest impact on public policy-making agendas through "maternalist" programs for mothers and children.
3. Nonprofit organizations are heavily dependent on public funding.
4. Dependency on public funding limits women's ability to pursue advocacy and feminist agendas.

How can we develop useful criteria for studying the sector as a whole, on the basis of this type of qualitative research on philanthropy? And how can we develop these measures in ways that will strengthen the emerging field of nonprofit studies? There are currently three major challenges facing the continued growth and institutionalization of the field. The first is the need to ground our research more firmly within the mainstream of scholarly disciplines. This means not only proselytizing and convincing our colleagues of the importance of the topics we study, but also finding ways to adapt our work to the idioms and discourses of more established fields. The second challenge is to devise testable, qualitative theoretical frameworks that address issues of such broad concern that they cut across disciplines. Finally, we need to bridge the chasm between scholarship and practice, to design research that addresses the day-to-day concerns of contemporary nonprofit work. Three challenges; three idioms; three very different agendas. All are vitally important if we want the field to achieve the legitimacy it deserves. Each has relevance for the ways in which we might begin to measure the impact of philanthropy.

ENTERING THE MAINSTREAM: WOMEN'S STUDIES, HISTORY, AND PHILANTHROPY

The traditional disciplines of economics, political science, sociology, and history have provided powerful analytical tools for research into women's lives and activities, often with the doubtful side effect of isolating the results of feminist inquiry into academic (and disciplinary) "ghettos."

The history of research on women and their activities evolved through a series of reasonably discernible stages. Initially, the goal was visibility: writing women into the historical record from which they had been excluded. By the 1970s, the emphasis shifted to tracing the lineage of feminism and the role of "sisterhood" in transcending the constraints of what Friedan called "the feminine mystique." Berg's *The Remembered Gate* (1978) and Cott's *The Bonds of Sisterhood* (1977) exemplified this line of analysis, while Smith-Rosenberg's lively polemic, "Beauty, the Beast and the Militant Woman" (1985), limned the origins of the revolt against the double standard.

By the 1980s, Marxist analyses had come into vogue. As the prevailing catchwords shifted from "sisterhood" to "social control," historians such as Stansell (1986) and Hewitt (1984) gave context to the record of women's voluntary activity within the framework of emerging class relations.

The 1990s witnessed the rise of what might be termed a "functionalist" approach: efforts to assess the political and economic aspects of women's voluntarism, and their role in "nation building." Thus, Ginzberg (1990) documented the success of female volunteers in securing legislative concessions for their charities, and their economic functions as nonprofit employers. Some of my own work (McCarthy, 1990, 1991) examined the impact of women's organizations in developing parallel power structures and a national "subterranean economy" for marketing goods produced by and for women. Sklar (1995) underscored the emerging theme of "political culture": the ways in which even politically disadvantaged groups shaped public policy making agendas from the perimeters of the electoral politics. Perhaps the most ambitious analysis was that of Skocpol (1995; see also Koven & Michel, 1993), who traced the development of the modern American welfare state back to women's organizational crusades for expanded entitlements for mothers and children at the turn of the century.

The past few years have witnessed a subtle shift in feminist discourse. Feminist scholars initially stressed the themes of victimization, patriarchy, and class. These discussions had an important consciousness-raising effect, spurring both political action and a wave of revisionism that reexamined the record of the past through the prism of feminist concerns. More recently, writers have begun to draw a distinction between "victim feminism" and "power feminism" (p. xvii). As Wolf (1993) explains, victim feminism "casts women...as mythically nurturing, and stresses the evil done to these 'good' women as a way to petition for their rights." Power feminism, on the other hand, "sees women as human beings . . . and lays claim to equality simply because women are entitled to it."

As feminist discourse moves from victimization to empowerment, a new array of questions emerges. How did women of different countries, colors, classes, and religions gain political and economic power in their respective societies, beyond the prerogatives bestowed by marriage and birth? Did they play a political role before they won the vote, for example—and if so, how?

Women's activities were politically invisible in the United States before the right to vote was extended in 1920, so historians and women's studies scholars who sought to examine their early public roles quickly gravitated toward voluntary associations. The record they found was compelling. American women began developing secular charities in the 1790s. The next two decades witnessed their role in the increasing elaboration of religiously-oriented networks—everything from tract and Bible societies to fund-raising groups for ministerial training. By the 1820s, they began to promote social reform as well, later entering the political arena through participation in the abolitionist and suffrage movements, both of which culminated in constitutional amendments. During the Civil War, northern women bolstered the government's military efforts through the fund-raising and administrative activities of the Sanitary Commission, one of the most massive public–private partnerships in the nation's history. Afterwards, the veterans of these wartime activities began to promote new programs for dealing with urban poverty and opened medical, nursing, and educational careers to female practitioners. Individual donors made their mark as well, particularly after the turn of the century. Some, such as Boston's Isabella Stewart Gardner, developed magnificently idiosyncratic institutions of their own, while others, such as Olivia Sage, bolstered higher education and even created foundations. At the same time, a pioneering generation of female professionals, philanthropists, and social advocates played a crucial role in shaping Progressive Era legislative agendas through their lobbying and research. Two generations later, the feminist movement left its imprint on American society as well.

What we do know is that philanthropy provided the primary—if not the only—route to political power for the majority of American women before they won the vote. It was the driving force behind middle class women's entrance into the professions. It played a major role in fostering legislation—both local and national—ultimately setting the tenor of the American welfare state. It even provided a mechanism through which women were able to change the constitution before they secured the right to vote.

Often denied access to direct political participation and barred from remunerative occupations until well into the twentieth century, middle-class women donors, volunteers, and organizational entrepreneurs nonetheless left their imprint on national legislation and institutions in a variety of countries. Through their philanthropic contributions of time, money, and material possessions, they carved out a public niche for themselves in a diverse array of religious, political, and economic regimes.

What we don't know is the extent to which women subsidized the growth of the state through their donations of money and time, issues that are directly related to contemporary scholarly debates about women's roles in "nation building." How can we begin to place a dollar value on the time contributed by female volunteers in the past so that we can compare it with municipal expenditures and private donations in assessing women's relative impact on the creation of the country's public charitable and educational resources? Public–private partnerships are another unstudied but highly promising area of research, particularly for the 1930s through the 1970s, an era for which we have almost no data on women's philanthropic roles. Skocpol argues that women's reform movements and their organizational infrastructures provided the scaffolding for America's first welfare state. What role did women's organizations play in implementing federal programs during the New Deal, World War II, and Lyndon Johnson's Great Society?

Economic functions are also important. Although there is a great deal of concern today that nonprofits are abandoning their "special" mission in the rush to embrace income-generating activities, the historical record indicates that many women's organizations have derived the bulk of their support from these activities since the 1790s. More, certainly, needs to be known about the role of these organizations as employers, merchants, and consumers of local services. In effect, we need to know more about their economic as well as their political roles, issues that speak directly to current scholarly concerns about nation building.

INTERDISCIPLINARY ISSUES:
PHILANTHROPY AND CIVIL SOCIETY

It seems clear that women's studies demands a cross-disciplinary agenda, even as the tools for research are drawn from traditional academic departments. The questions that need to be asked are too often larger than the standard disciplines can accommodate. How might the more theoretical issues be addressed? Is there a way in which we can use women's activities as a lens for studying more encompassing questions, such as the role of philanthropy in developing, expanding, or preserving civil society? How can we begin to identify the factors that have contributed most strongly and most compellingly to the sector's growth over time?

One of the issues that has been vigorously debated during the past decade is whether religion should be included in the nonprofit equation. Are sectarian (and presumably sacramental or ritual) functions "of public benefit," and, if so, should they be included in our definitions and our statistical analyses of the nonprofit sector? This is an extremely important issue in terms of the knowledge base that we are developing, one that has profound implications for our comprehension both of the scope and nature of nonprofit activities and of the significance of philanthropy.

As Americans have consistently tended to donate approximately half of their philanthropic dollars to religious institutions, the exclusion of religious activities threatens to skew our understanding of the role of philanthropy in building and sustaining American nonprofits. But there are other reasons for including religion in our research agenda: the preliminary results from the center's international project reveal that whether one looks at Korea, Australia, India, Russia, or Brazil, religion has been a driving force in facilitating, or in limiting, the growth of philanthropy (McCarthy, 2001).

To take one example that presents a pattern relevant to other countries' experience, Liborakina notes that the earliest women's charity in Russia, inspired by the Church, was for all practical purposes invisible. Because Russian Orthodoxy emphasized and encouraged individual giving (especially almsgiving), numerous women worked quietly, under the auspices of the Church, generously giving alms and food to the needy and shelter to pilgrims and the handicapped. Here the religious (or charitable) impulse was "organized" through the Church and individual women, whose work was, in fact, anonymous.

Russian charity did include female religious communities from at least the 18th century. According to Liborakina (1996):

> Their members were not nuns, but widows or middle-aged women
> with grown children, who joined [religious communities] and spent their

lives in prayer, and in caring for the poor and the sick. [These were founded by generous, pious laywomen, particularly widows who donated their land, money, and time to create unofficial religious communities.] [Their] activities started mostly with the care and shelter of homeless women, as quasi-almshouses. By the middle of the 19th century, following growing concerns about women's education, [the communities] shifted to educational missions. . . . In the process, women contributed to raising the social awareness of Orthodoxy, introducing a more 'civil spirit' into the precincts of the Church. (p. 401)

A number of inviting theoretical questions arise once religion is admitted into the research agenda. Weber wrote his venerable treatise on the *Protestant Ethic and the Spirit of Capitalism* over ninety years ago, arguing that religion and economic development were intimately linked. Although Weber's work has been roundly criticized since then, it continues to foster lively debates and to hold a fascination for people who are trying to understand why different types of institutions and practices emerge more strongly in some cultures than in others.

Our research suggests that it is impossible to understand the nonprofit sector without considering the role of religion. Following Weber's lead, can we begin to develop a series of testable hypotheses as the basis for developing a theory about the relationship between religion, philanthropy, nonprofits, and civil society?

One hypothesis is that Protestantism, particularly evangelical Protestantism, has afforded the greatest leeway for citizen participation (or at least women's participation) in building civil society. This has played out in different ways in different countries. Perhaps the most striking example is Korea. Beginning in the nineteenth century, Western missionaries flooded into the country in search of converts. Korea at that time was an extremely traditional Confucian society in which women were rarely educated and invariably excluded from public roles. Yet by the end of the century, female converts in Korea's Baptist, Methodist, Congregational, and Presbyterian congregations began to establish educational institutions and to lobby for wider educational opportunities. Later, these women used their church groups as institutional bases for launching nationalist campaigns as well.

The key to their participation was literacy. One of the missionaries' first innovations was the revision of the Korean alphabet, reducing the Chinese-based characters to the simplified script used today. This, in turn, made the written language more accessible to women as well as to men. Moreover, the missionaries made a particular point of educating their converts because the ability to read the Bible, oneself, was the very basis of religious belief for them. Once women learned to read, they began to organize. Literacy opened the door to new ideas and contacts beyond their immediate households and communities. In the process, it also paved the way for expanded public and philanthropic roles.

A far different situation existed in the United States. One of the world's oldest democracies, the United States also has the world's most extensive nonprofit sector. American women have constituted a formidable presence on the nonprofit scene since the late 18th century. And Protestantism has played a singularly important role in encouraging and legitimizing their participation. After the American Revolution, American congregations became increasingly feminized. As the number of female adherents increased, so did their importance because churches had to compete for both money and members, and women were the mainstays of religious fund-raising. Moreover, most of these denominations lacked highly centralized organizational structures. Local ministers were chosen by local congregations and they served at the pleasure of their congregations. Since women generally comprised the majority of these congregations, ministers were especially careful to cultivate their good will and enthusiastically encouraged their charitable and fund-raising ventures.

Moreover, the Second Great Awakening that emerged at the beginning of the nineteenth century increasingly emphasized a highly individualistic doctrine of conversion and human perfectibility. The upshot was that female converts were encouraged not only to save themselves and serve the poor, but also to reform the larger society. Taken together, these factors had a significant effect in generating women's philanthropy and in catalyzing the growth and diversification of the American nonprofit sector. They also dictated the nature of women's participation, encouraging giving as well as voluntarism, service delivery as well as social reform. And they did so in ways that accorded women a significant amount of autonomy and control over the money they raised, as well as substantial political roles even without the vote.

Judaism also encouraged both giving and voluntarism, providing a hospitable environment for women's philanthropic activities. However, in the United States, at least in the 19th century, these activities tended to focus primarily on communal concerns, prompting Jewish women to devote themselves to the creation of charities rather than to social reform, patterns that ultimately diminished their political presence.

Religions such as Catholicism, Hinduism, and Islam have tended to place a stronger emphasis on giving than on voluntarism or advocacy, especially among laywomen. Female adherents to these faiths also have had less control over the ways in which their funds were spent because of the presence of strong religious hierarchies or the dominance of male clerics. As a result, women who embraced these religions tended to play very limited political roles, at least through their philanthropic activities. Instead, service provision was emphasized, often rendering women socially and politically invisible as Liborakina (1996) indicated.

The differences between Catholic and Protestant philanthropy were particularly evident in countries such as Ireland and Australia, which had substantial numbers of both groups. In both instances, Catholic women, especially nuns, played a prominent role in the development of charitable and educational institutions. However, it was the Protestants who took the lead in lobbying for suffrage and social reform.

Other factors, such as secularization or political crises, can and did provide an opening wedge for women's increased participation in social reform movements and public policy making in Catholic, Hindu, and Islamic states. Hence, Brazilian women assumed an increasing political presence when the Church adopted an adversarial stance against the military dictatorship that held sway until the 1980s; and Palestinian women moved into prominent leadership positions in area nonprofits when male arrests or military activities created a vacuum in nonprofit leadership.

Finally, some religions and ethical systems, such as Korean Confucianism, are not hospitable to women's philanthropy and possibly impede the growth of the nonprofit sector more generally.

Clearly, we need to know more about the doctrinal and organizational factors that make some religions catalysts for the expansion of civil society while others serve as dampers. In light of the available evidence, religion not only merits inclusion in any consideration of the nonprofit sector; its role is absolutely central.

SCHOLARSHIP AND PRACTICE

One of the greatest challenges currently facing the field of nonprofit studies is the task of bridging the gulf between academic concerns and the interests and needs of nonprofit practitioners. How can the study of women's philanthropy help illuminate contemporary issues and practices?

Many of the papers that we commissioned dealt with contemporary questions. Here, too, women's activities tended to cast these issues in stark relief. Fund-raising and donative patterns, endowments, and related mechanisms for institution building are all areas of central concern to contemporary policy makers and contemporary women's groups.

Moreover, women's philanthropy is changing, and it is important to understand how. Although the incidence of poverty among women is 22 percent higher than among men, women increasingly control their own resources and a growing portion of wealth in the United States. Women constitute 35 percent of the 3.7 million Americans with gross assets of $600,000 or more. What motivates women donors (traditional women philanthropists as well as successful professional women)?

In the United States, the first generation of women to enter the paid workforce en masse is currently reaching the age at which, statistically, they should begin to exhibit accelerating levels of generosity. At the same time, American women continue to hold a considerable proportion of the country's inherited wealth. What does their growing economic importance mean for feminist causes and for the country's nonprofits more generally? Are there gendered patterns of giving and cultivation that will require radically different fundraising strategies in the future? Are there generational differences between the women who earned their own fortunes and those who were precluded from doing so? If so, what implications will these patterns and differences have for the future of American fund-raising? (See McCarthy, 1993 for a fuller discussion of these issues.)

The experience of the Ms. Foundation underscores questions related to increasing women's giving and, most particularly, raising the funds needed to institutionalize women's organizations. How can organizations that are rooted in a strong sense of activism and personal commitment bridge the transition to institutionalization?

Most of the Ms. Foundation's backing currently comes from individual women. This fact raises a host of generational issues. Older women are the most likely to give, but they are more likely to give anonymously or to divert funds to the causes that their husbands embraced. If they do control inherited funds, they may not feel that the money is rightly theirs to give. Career women pose a different set of challenges. Female professionals of the baby boom generation have greater control over their earned wealth. They are just reaching the period in their lives when they will begin to give. The problem here is finding an effective quid pro quo. What sorts of volunteer activities can be devised to capture their attention and bind them to the Foundation over the long term?

Other questions have to do with donor and program visibility, a sense of accomplishment, the issue of sustainability, the value of income-generation projects, and organizational management and growth.

How have women's groups, which are not necessarily a high priority for corporate donors, managed to maintain their activities in other countries where individual giving may still be minimal? Does the acceptance of government funding necessarily spell the end of advocacy in favor of service delivery? What sorts of alternative funding mechanisms are emerging in other countries to support women's activities, and how have they been sustained over time?

Our research strongly suggests that women's organizations have tended to be woefully undercapitalized, particularly in terms of endowment funds. Clearly, endowments are critical to sustaining organizations over the long term. How, where, when, and why have organizations run by and for women managed to attract comfortable endowments, and how have their efforts differed from those of unendowed institutions? What techniques have attracted endowment funding for women's groups, and how replicable are they?

How have women's organizations managed to attract other types of support? In Ghana, for example, several women's professional groups launched a variety of nonprofits by coupling their dues and voluntary activities with in-kind donations from their firms and industry leaders. Are there other models for amplifying the impact of volunteer activities in developing nations that can be culled from women's experiences? And how can these contemporary concerns be translated into a research agenda for measuring the efficacy of women's nonprofits? Clearly, the issues of funding and sustainability are key.

FUTURE RESEARCH NEEDS

The impact of women's philanthropy can be measured in a variety of ways: as an index of participatory democracy; as a means of tracking the empowerment of politically and economically disadvantaged groups; as a window for assessing contemporary trends or for divining the factors that contribute to the growth or stagnation of civil society; or in simple quantitative terms, such as the birth and death rates of women's initiatives, their legislative gains, and the underlying financial and social conditions that influence these trends. International comparisons are particularly useful for tracing the factors that encourage or impede the growth of the voluntary sector. Both quantitative and qualitative analyses are needed; an important preliminary step in gathering statistical data on contemporary trends would be the inclusion of gendered categories in databases on nonprofits and funding trends. In the process, scholars will be better positioned to assess the sector's human dimensions as well as its past achievements and future needs.

NOTE

1. Portions from selected papers for the project appeared in a special issue of *Voluntas*, 7:4 (December 1996). For many of the complete papers, see McCarthy (2001).

REFERENCES

Berg, B. (1978). *The remembered gate: Origins of American feminism.* New York: Oxford University Press.

Cott, N. F. (1977). *The bonds of womanhood: Woman's sphere in New England, 1780–1835.* New Haven, CT: Yale University Press.

Ginzberg, L. (1990). *Women and the work of benevolence: Morality and class in the 19th century United States.* New Haven, CT: Yale University Press.

Hewitt, N.A. (1984). *Women's activism and social change: Rochester, New York: 1822–1872.* Ithaca, NY: Cornell University Press.

Koven, S., & Michel, S. (Eds.)(1993). *Mothers of a new world: Maternalist politics and the origins of welfare states.* New York: Routledge.

Liborakina, M. (1996). Women's voluntarism and philanthropy in pre-revolutionary Russia: Building a civil society. *Voluntas, 7*(4), 397–411.

McCarthy, K. D. (Ed.). (December, 1996) *Women & Philanthropy* (Special Issue). *Voluntas 7*(4).

McCarthy, K. D. (Ed.). (2001). *Women, philanthropy and civil society.* Bloomington: Indiana University Press.

McCarthy, K. D. (1990). Parallel power structures: Women and the voluntary sphere. In Kathleen D. McCarthy (Ed.), *Lady bountiful revisited: Women, philanthropy and power.* New Brunswick, NJ: Rutgers University Press.

McCarthy, K. D. (1993). *The Ms. Foundation: A case study in feminist fundraising* (Working Paper). New York: Center for the Study of Philanthropy.

McCarthy, K. D. (1991). *Women's culture: American philanthropy and art, 1830–1930.* Chicago: University of Chicago Press.

Sklar, K. K. (1995). *Florence Kelley and the nature's work: The rise of women's political culture, 1830–1900.* New Haven, CT: Yale University Press.

Skocpol, T. (1992). *Protecting soldiers and mothers: The political origins of social policy in the United States.* Cambridge, MA: Harvard University Press.

Smith-Rosenberg, C. (1985). Beauty, the beast, and the militant woman: A case study in sex roles and social stress in Jacksonian America. In *Disorderly conduct: Visions of gender in Victorian America.* New York: Oxford University Press.

Stansell, C. (1986). *City of women: Sex and class in New York, 1789–1860.* New York: Knopf.

Wolf, N. (1993). *Fire with fire: The new female power and how it will change the 21st century.* New York: Random House.

Chapter 10

A Theory-of-Change Approach to Evaluating Investments in Public Education

JAMES P. CONNELL AND ADENA M. KLEM

Over the past ten years, corporate and private foundation resources have been energizing urban educational reform initiatives at an increasing rate. But what has resulted? The Institute for Research and Reform in Education (IRRE) concluded that "after nearly 10 years of intensive local, state, and national educational reform efforts, very little meaningful change has occurred in the everyday lives of most urban public school students" (IRRE, 1996). At a time when many students' life chances are threatened by "business as usual" in their schools, the substantial investments made in educational reform should, at a minimum, have provided credible and usable information to guide future reform efforts. Yet, they have not.

Existing evaluations have done very little to buttress, dispel, or explain our rather bleak summary of returns on private and public investments in public education reform. There appear to be two reasons for this. First, all too often, immediate and unrealistic outcomes are expected from reform initiatives, and savvy reformers have, understandably, resisted requests for evalua-

JAMES P. CONNELL • President, Institute for Research and Reform in Education, Toms River, New Jersey 08753.   ADENA M. KLEM • Research Associate, Institute for Research and Reform in Education, Toms River, New Jersey 08753.

Measuring the Impact of the Nonprofit Sector, edited by Patrice Flynn and Virginia A. Hodgkinson, New York, Kluwer Academic/Plenum Publishers, 2002.

tion. Second, even when initiatives are open to evaluation, the specific strategy of a reform effort (in a school or school district) and its projected outcomes are often absent, thus rendering evaluation of such initiatives post hoc exercises.[1]

In response to these conclusions, IRRE recommends a theory-of-change approach to evaluating school- and district-level reform efforts. The following discussion provides a brief overview of this approach, including its advantages over some current approaches and an example of how it is being used to assess one district and school-site reform strategy.

WHAT SHOULD A "GOOD" EVALUATION DO?

Most investors and participants in public education reform have three crucial questions:

1. Is there compelling early, intermediate, and long-term evidence of pay-off in these investments?
2. Can reliable information be obtained about strategies that are and are not producing desired results in order to make mid-course corrections?
3. Are practitioners, policy-makers, and the public learning about effective strategies through the evaluation process?

Unfortunately, as pressure to address these questions is increasing, our confidence in the tools available to do so is waning. The result is that complex interventions, such as district and school-site reform initiatives, have been forced to pursue less than optimal evaluation options including:

- Retreating to process documentation and lowering expectations about obtaining credible evidence of their impacts.
- Trying to force-fit the initiatives, themselves, into existing and acceptable evaluation methods in order to enable estimates of their impacts.
- Waiting until the initiatives are "ready" for evaluation approaches.

Predictably, these options have not—and will not—answer the key questions of investors and participants.

Some theorists have argued that theory-driven evaluations yield more useful information than those that are strictly method-driven (Chen, 1990) or those that do not attempt to specify and test how results are achieved (Weiss, 1995). IRRE, together with our colleagues working on these issues as they apply to the evaluation of community-based initiatives (Connell, Kubisch, Schorr, & Weiss, 1995; Fulbright-Anderson, Kubisch, & Connell, 1998), have defined a theory of change approach to evaluation. This approach can be thought of as a systematic and cumulative study of the links between the activities, outcomes, and contexts of an initiative.

THE THEORY OF CHANGE EVALUATION PROCESS

Connell and Klem (2000) describe a process that can yield a theory of change to guide the implementation and evaluation of education reform initiatives.

Articulating a theory of change is the first stage of the evaluation process. One such theory, presented in Figure 10.1a, b, illustrates how the next steps in

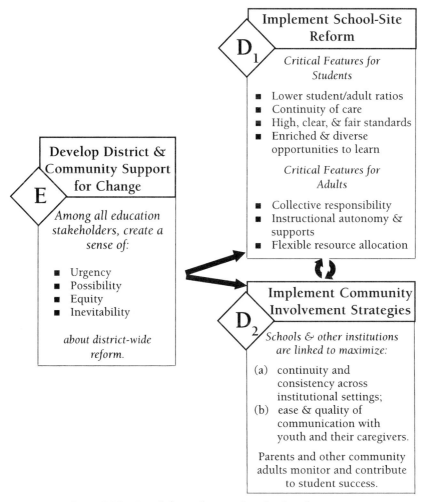

Figure 10.1a. Initial change framework with selected outcomes.

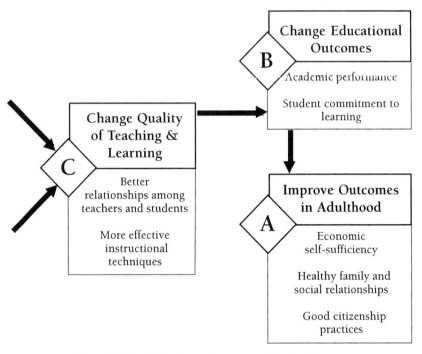

Figure 10.1b. Initial change framework with selected outcomes.

the evaluation process can be implemented. It includes the initiation of an education reform effort; implementation of school reform strategies; sets of changes in teaching and learning; and the effects these changes have on student educational outcomes and, ultimately, on their longer-term outcomes in adulthood.[2]

The second stage is to *specify indicators, target populations, thresholds, and timelines* for each of the outcomes in the theory of change. Stakeholders will need to reach consensus on four key questions pertaining to *each* element of the change framework (Figure 10.1a, b), beginning with element A and finishing with element E:

1. What indicators will tell us that this element's outcomes are changing?
2. Which target populations of people, organizations, or settings are these indicators intended to monitor?
3. How much change on these indicators is "good enough"?
4. What is the estimated time frame to achieve these thresholds?

"Sample answers" to these questions are presented in Figures 10.2 and 10.3. They address elements B and D1 of the change framework shown in Fig-

B	CHANGE EDUCATIONAL OUTCOMES	
	OUTCOME	ACADEMIC PERFORMANCE
	INDICATOR 1	**Reading and Math Achievement Test Scores**
	TARGET POPULATION	All students in the district
	THRESHOLDS	1. 60% of students in the district for more than one year score above the national average on math and reading
		2. Less than 5% score in the bottom quartile on either math or reading for more than one year following enrollment in the district.
	TIMEFRAME 1	Within five years from implementation of the school-site reform (D_1) and the community involvement strategies (D_2).
	OUTCOME	STUDENT COMMITMENT TO LEARNING
	INDICATOR 1	**Attendance**
	TARGET POPULATION	All students in the district
	THRESHOLDS	1. 80% of students in the district for more than one year miss no more than one day per month of school.
		2. No more than 5% of students in the district for more than one year miss more than one day per week of school.
	INDICATOR 2	**Graduation Rate**
	TARGET POPULATION	All students in the district
	THRESHOLDS	90% of district students graduate within five years of entering high school.
	TIMEFRAME 1&2	Within five years from implementation of the school-site reform (D_1) and the community involvement strategies (D_2).

Figure 10.2. Change educational outcomes.

ure 10.1. The answers draw from our own and others' written work as well as from our ongoing consulting work in support of district-wide and school-site reform in urban school districts. For each key outcome in an element, specific indicators and the target population(s) are listed. There are also examples of thresholds—how good is "good enough" on an indicator—and a timeframe

⟨D₁⟩	CRITICAL FEATURES FOR STUDENTS	
OUTCOME	LOWER STUDENT/ADULT RATIOS DURING CORE INSTRUCTION	
INDICATOR 1	Student/adult ratios experienced by students during literacy and mathematics instruction.	
TARGET POPULATION	All students in the district during literacy and mathematics instruction.	
THRESHOLDS	Average ratios experienced during core instruction is less than or equal to 15:1 for 90% of students for at least 10 hours per week.	
TIMEFRAME 1	Within two years from implementation of the District and Community Supports for Change (E)	
OUTCOME	PROVIDE CONTINUITY OF CARE ACROSS THE SCHOOL DAY AND SCHOOL YEARS	
INDICATOR 1	Number of "interruptions" to ongoing learning activities over the course of the school day.	
TARGET POPULATION	All schools.	
THRESHOLDS	Students experience at least two instructional periods per day of 90 minutes or more.	
INDICATOR 2	Number of adults with ongoing relationships with students over multiple years in schools.	
TARGET POPULATION	All schools.	
THRESHOLDS	1. Same group of at least two adults remain with same students for core instruction over at least two years in elementary school, all three years of middle school, and at least two years of high school. 2. All schools broken into small learning communities of 200 students or less.	
TIMEFRAME 1 & 2	Within two years from implementation of the District and Community Supports for Change (E)	

Figure 10.3a. Implement school-site reform.

representing the stakeholders' goal for when thresholds will be achieved. These sample answers can be used as rubrics to help planners and evaluators decide when they have enough information to allow them to move on to the next stage of the process.

The third stage in the evaluation process is to create the research design

OUTCOME	EMBRACE AND EFFECTIVELY COMMUNICATE HIGH, CLEAR, AND FAIR ACADEMIC AND BEHAVIORAL STANDARDS
INDICATOR 1	**Student and teacher understanding of academic and behavioral standards and their connections to their work together.**
TARGET POPULATION	All students and teachers in the district.
THRESHOLDS	1. 80% of students and teachers in the district for more than one year report and demonstrate clear understanding of high academic and behavioral standards and the connection between the standards and their work. 2. No more than 10% of students or teachers indicate low levels of understanding of standards, and none do so for more than one year.
TIMEFRAME 1	Within two years from implementation of the District and Community Supports for Change (E)
OUTCOME	IMPLEMENT ENRICHED AND DIVERSE OPPORTUNITIES TO LEARN, PERFORM, AND BE RECOGNIZED
INDICATOR 1	**Instructional strategies used in classrooms reflect demonstrated best practices.**
TARGET POPULATION	All schools.
THRESHOLDS	70% of students report experiencing enriched and diverse opportunities to learn, perform, and be recognized in their core instructional classes.
TIMEFRAME 1	Within two years from implementation of the District and Community Supports for Change (E)
OUTCOME	ENSURE FLEXIBLE ALLOCATION OF RESOURCES
INDICATOR 1	**School improvement plan reflects site-based allocation of personnel, time, money, and space.**
TARGET POPULATION	All schools.
THRESHOLDS	School resource allocation plan is approved by school staff and school community stakeholders (parents, community partners).
TIMEFRAME 1	Within two years from implementation of the District and Community Supports for Change (E)

Figure 10.3b. Implement School-site reform.

and to *collect data on measures of the indicators.* In creating these strategies, traditional considerations of instrumentation, sampling, and timing of assessments come into play—all of which are shaped by the evaluation priorities of the stakeholders and available resources. Examples of the strategies being used to test the theory of change shown in Figure 10.1 are available through IRRE upon request.

The fourth stage is to *analyze and interpret results from the assessments.* These analyses should yield useful information about whether expected changes are occurring. Are people and institutions fulfilling their commitments? Do changes in practice yield changes in the experience and performance of adults and students?

This issue, establishing causal links between elements in the theory of change, is receiving considerable attention in recent work on comprehensive community initiatives (e.g., Connell & Kubisch, 1998; Granger, 1998; Hollister & Hill, 1995). Specifically, how will stakeholders know whether the reform strategies are causing their intended results? Connell and Kubisch (1998) offer some guidelines. They argue that investors in school-site or district-level reform should be convinced that their investments have had their intended effects if:

1. From the outset, a specific theory of change delineates the expected steps toward specific change thresholds on early, intermediate, and longer-term outcomes (measured against historical baselines).
2. These steps were implemented as planned.
3. The predicted magnitude of change (change thresholds) occurred.
4. No obvious and pervasive external change occurred that could account for these results.

The final step in the theory-of-change evaluation is to use results to *adjust the theory and realign investments,* if needed. In articulating a specific theory of change before implementation, stakeholders should be better able to identify their own and others' responsibilities for results, to take appropriate credit for successes, and to make appropriate adjustments when results are less than optimal.

CONCLUSION

What can a theory-of-change approach to evaluation offer to independent sector investors and participants in public education? It can provide the answers to some important questions.

CRITICAL FEATURES FOR ADULTS

D₁

OUTCOME	INSURE COLLECTIVE RESPONSIBILITY FOR STUDENT OUTCOMES
INDICATOR 1	School practices assuring each student's and the schools' success in achieving targeted student outcomes.
TARGET POPULATION	All schools.
THRESHOLDS	Explicit statement of the school's process and timeline for closing the gap between current and desired levels of student outcomes is approved by school staff and school community stakeholders (parents, community partners).
TIMEFRAME 1	Within two years from implementation of the District and Community Supports for Change (E)
OUTCOME	EFFECTIVE AND ONGOING INSTRUCTIONAL IMPROVEMENT PROCESS
INDICATOR 1	Instructional improvement process adopted by school including: a. Presence of formative and regular assessment of student learning. b. Opportunities for peer and expert observation of instruction. c. Expectations and opportunities for instructional staff to research, discuss, and test new instructional strategies.
TARGET POPULATION	All schools.
THRESHOLDS	80% of "planning time" is observed and reported as leading to effective instructional improvement activities.
TIMEFRAME 1	Within two years from implementation of the District and Community Supports for Change (E)
OUTCOME	ENSURE FLEXIBLE ALLOCATION OF RESOURCES
INDICATOR 1	School improvement plan reflects site-based allocation of personnel, time, money, and space.
TARGET POPULATION	All schools.
THRESHOLDS	School resource allocation plan is approved by school staff and school community stakeholders (parents, community partners).
TIMEFRAME 1	Within two years from implementation of the District and Community Supports for Change (E)

Figure 10.4. Implement school-site reform.

Going into the initiative:
- What early, intermediate, and longer-term outcomes are these investments expected to effect at all levels: community, system, school, classroom, and individual (students and adults)?
- What will these changes look like, how much change is good enough, and when are the changes expected to occur?

During the initiative:
- Are the change strategies being implemented? If so, are they having their intended effects?

Funders, advocates, and volunteers must support and strongly urge public education systems and public schools first to articulate and then to evaluate their theory of change. Why? We need to learn more than we currently are from evaluations of reform initiatives. Also, if investors and participants in urban educational reform are to have any confidence in their reform effort *before* political fortunes are put on the line and *before* individuals and institutions invest their resources, the theory of change guiding the effort must be articulated and its "testability" assured. Our hope is that this approach to planning and evaluating reform initiatives will help to fill these gaps.

NOTES

1. See Anson, Cook, Habib, Grady, Haynes, & Comer (1991) and E.M. Kauffman Foundation (1998) for notable exceptions.
2. Research evidence for the inclusion of the outcomes and linkages in this framework is summarized in IRRE (1996).

REFERENCES

Anson, A. R., Cook, T. D., Habib, F., Grady, M. K., Haynes, N., & Comer, J. P. (1991). The comer school development program: A theoretical analysis. *Urban Education, 26*, 56–82.

Chen, H. (1990). *Theory driven evaluations.* Thousand Oaks, California: Sage Publications.

Connell, J. P., & Klem, A. (2000). You can get there from here: Using a theory of change approach to plan urban education reform. *Journal of Educational and Psychological Consultation, 11*(1), 93–120.

Connell, J. P., & Kubisch, A. C. (1998). *Applying a theory of change approach to the design and evaluation of comprehensive community initiatives: Progress, prospects, and problems.* Washington, DC: The Aspen Institute.

Connell, J. P., Kubisch, A. C., Schorr, L. B., & Weiss, C. H., (Eds.). (1995). *New approaches to evaluating community initiatives: Concepts, methods, and contexts.* Washington, DC: The Aspen Institute.

E. M. Kauffman Foundation. (1998). *Overview of planned research: First things first initiative.* Kansas City, KS: E.M. Kauffman Foundation.

Fulbright-Anderson, K., Kubisch, A. C., & Connell, J. P. (Eds.) (1998). *New approaches to evaluating community initiatives: Vol. 2. Theory, measurement, and analysis.* Washington, DC: The Aspen Institute.

Granger, R. C. (1998). Establishing causality in evaluations of comprehensive community initiatives. In K. Fulbright-Anderson, A. C. Kubisch, & J. P. Connell (Eds.), *New approaches to evaluating community initiatives: Vol. 2. Theory, measurement, and analysis.* Washington, DC: The Aspen Institute.

Hollister, R. G., & Hill, J. (1995). Problems in the evaluation of community-wide initiatives. In J. P. Connell, A. C. Kubisch, L. B. Schorr, & C. H. Weiss (Eds.), *New approaches to evaluating community initiatives: Concepts, methods, and contexts.* Washington DC: The Aspen Institute.

IRRE. (1996). *First things first: A framework for successful school-site reform.* White paper prepared for the E.M. Kauffman Foundation. Kansas City, MO: E. M. Kauffman Foundation.

Weiss, C. H. (1995). Nothing as practical as good theory: Exploring theory-based evaluation for comprehensive community initiatives for children and families. In J. P. Connell, A. C. Kubisch, L. B. Schorr, & C. H. Weiss (Eds.), *New approaches to evaluating community initiatives: Concepts, methods, and contexts.* Washington, DC: The Aspen Institute.

Chapter **11**

Measuring the Impact of Nonprofit Health Care Organizations

BRADFORD H. GRAY

Health care provides an interesting arena in which to consider measurement of the impact of the nonprofit sector. This is a field in which extensive data are available because of the combination of third-party payment and large public programs (Medicare and Medicaid). (For an overview of data sources in health care, see Gray, 1991, pp. 89–96). Yet utilization data are subject to many interpretations, as are many other measures of performance. This is a field that offers many lessons because of its rich array of ownership forms—for-profit, nonprofit, and public. Not surprisingly, form of ownership has become controversial and ideological, with both nonprofit and for-profit ownership viewed with suspicion in some quarters. Health care is also a field that is characterized by rapid change and organizational complexity.

THE NONPROFIT HEALTH CARE SECTOR

Health care accounts for about half of the revenues of the nonprofit sector (Hodgkinson & Weitzman, 1996). Included in the health care category are many

BRADFORD H. GRAY • Director, Division of Health and Science Policy, New York Academy of Medicine, New York, New York 10029.

Measuring the Impact of the Nonprofit Sector, edited by Patrice Flynn and Virginia A. Hodgkinson, New York, Kluwer Academic/Plenum Publishers, 2002.

different types of organizations—hospitals, managed care organizations and health insurers, nursing homes and other long-term care facilities, ambulatory care centers and clinics, home health care agencies, rehabilitation facilities, educational institutions (for medicine, nursing, and many other health occupations), research institutes, and foundations. The nonprofit share differs markedly across these fields, with nonprofit ownership uncommon in a few areas (psychiatric hospitals, blood banks, and nursing homes) and dominant among community hospitals (Marmor, Schlesinger, & Smithey, 1987).

Complicating efforts to measure the impact of nonprofit organizations in health care is the amount of change that characterizes the field. The ownership composition of some health care fields has been volatile. Health maintenance organizations (HMOs) were almost all nonprofit in 1980 but are predominantly for-profit today, with as many as one-third of nonprofit plans having converted to for-profit in the past fifteen years. During the same period, home health agencies have also shifted markedly from their nonprofit dominance, as new for-profit organizations rapidly entered the field.

Even fields that seem stable are undergoing much change. Some 60 percent of the 5,256 acute care hospitals (and 70 percent of the beds) counted by the American Hospital Association in 1994 were nonprofit; 26 percent were public; and 14 percent were for-profit. These percentages have remained largely unchanged for the past thirty years. However, this apparent stability conceals several significant changes and underestimates the extent to which the for-profit sector has grown. First, if measured in terms of beds rather than hospitals, the for-profit sector has almost doubled in size during the period, from 6 percent to 11 percent of short-term general hospital beds between 1965 and 1994; this growth has been at the expense of the public sector (American Hospital Association, 1995). Second, if one includes the approximately 400 psychiatric, alcohol/chemical dependency, and rehabilitation hospitals owned by for-profit companies and the 350 nonprofit and public hospitals that these companies manage, the for-profit sector accounts for almost 32 percent of U.S. federal hospitals and about 23 percent of the beds (Federation of American Health Systems, 1995; American Hospital Association, 1995). The management of nonprofit hospitals by for-profit companies complicates the assessment of nonprofits' impact.

Other rapid changes in health care have resulted both from developments in clinical practice and from the impact of large third-party purchasers. Hospitals have experienced a decline in inpatient services (admissions declined from about 34.8 million in 1980 to about 30.3 million in 1992) along with rapid increases in the numbers of outpatient visits (from about 201 million in 1980 to 361 million in 1994) (American Hospital Association, 1995). Describing hospitals' work only in terms of patients in beds is seriously inadequate.

Organizational change has also been dramatic. Health care organizations have become more complex as a result of several strategies. Some have pursued vertical integration, with hospitals acquiring or building either (a) physicians' practices and health centers that are referral sources for the hospital or (b) home health or long-term care facilities that serve patients after discharge from the hospitals, or both. Horizontal integration into multihospital systems has also been common; at least a third of nonprofit hospitals either own or are owned by another hospital.

Corporate restructuring has also occurred widely among nonprofit hospitals, whereby a nonprofit parent organization is created that has both for-profit and nonprofit subsidiaries, of which the hospital is one. This arrangement enhances revenues and segregates unrelated business income, but it can affect data that might be used to describe important dimensions of performance. For example, charitable contributions that a hospital receives and expends may not be on the books of the hospital itself but in another subsidiary of the parent organization. Organizational complexity can also create misleading situations, as with the use of data from Internal Revenue Service Form 990 to measure numbers or finances of nonprofit hospitals; some large hospitals are subsidiaries of universities and therefore are not coded as health care organizations in the National Taxonomy of Exempt Entities (Gray, 1993).

Perhaps the biggest challenges to assessing the impact of nonprofit health care organizations are conceptual issues regarding what should be counted as impacts. This chapter focuses heavily on these issues and on ways that measures can be misleading. I do not believe it possible to measure the impact of nonprofit health care organizations on society without first dealing with these issues.

SOME GENERAL OBSERVATIONS
ABOUT MEASURES IN HEALTH CARE

Although some measures will be appropriate across types of organizations (for example, number of people served, number of people employed), some measures of output or outcome are specific to the kind of organization involved (for example, the number of heart transplants performed or number of grants made). The simplest types of measures are *volume measures,* or simple counts of the frequency with which services are provided or individuals receive service. Such measures can be disaggregated in almost infinite numbers of ways— by types of people served or types of services provided.

Some measures combine a volume measure with some other piece of information; for example, dividing a hospital's average daily census (a volume measure) by its total bed capacity creates a measure of occupancy. Such aggregations or averages can be compiled at the organizational or sectoral levels. Measures can be expressed in absolute terms, using data only from nonprofits (for example, nonprofit hospitals were the site of 2.8 million births in 1993), or as a percentage of the industry (for example, 72 percent of births in 1993 were in nonprofit hospitals). The latter becomes interpretable only if one knows the nonprofit's share of the industry, which itself can be measured in several ways (for example, nonprofits comprised 60 percent of short-term community hospitals, but 71 percent of beds). How the information should be expressed depends upon the measure involved and one's purpose in looking at it.

Some measures are interpretable only with reference to something else. The point of comparison can be a standard developed by a professional group, government agency, or researcher, or it can simply be a comparison with other organizations. It is not terribly informative to know, for example, that patients stay an average of seven days in nonprofit hospitals or that 85 percent of enrollees in an HMO expressed satisfaction, or that a given percentage of three-year-olds in an HMO had had a recommended set of immunizations unless one knows (a) how long patients *should* stay, (b) what a realistic goal is for patient satisfaction or immunization rates, or (c) what the performance of other organizations is.

For many measures of organizational performance in health care, we know only about ranges or averages in the industry. In some instances, we know that more or less is better: for instance, we can presume that lower levels of patient complaints and higher immunization rates are better. However, in many basic matters we do not know what the "right" rate is. For example, in 1993, when the average length of stay in nonprofit hospitals was 6.9 days, according to the American Hospital Association, the length of stay in for-profit hospitals averaged 6.2 days. Interpreting such numbers presents a dilemma for those who would use them as a measure of performance. Is keeping patients in the hospital longer a virtue that should be chalked up on the ledger of the nonprofit's impact? Not necessarily. Keeping patients in the hospital who do not need to be there should be counted *against* an organization, not *for* it. But the for-profit's shorter length of stay may not mean that they are performing better or more efficiently; it may simply mean that they are admitting fewer patients with very serious or complex problems. This explanation would not be surprising because for-profits include few major teaching hospitals among their ranks.

Thus, simple counts and averages provide some basic measures of performance, but some performance measures gain meaning only in a comparative context. Moreover, being able to collect information about something that sounds important does not mean that one knows how to interpret the information.

A final general observation about measures: Most measures can be collected at the organizational level and aggregated into sector measures. However, depending on one's interests, sector-level measures may be completely unimportant. For example, challenges to tax exemptions of institutions often rest primarily or completely on the performance of particular institutions, not on the characteristics of the sector. The fact that some organizations engage in high levels of meritorious activities can create a misleading impression in sector-level calculations by suggesting that the activity may be commonplace among nonprofits when it is in fact rare. For example, a high percentage of residency programs are in nonprofit hospitals, but most nonprofit hospitals do not have residency programs. Although there is more than one correct way to present the information, we need to be sensitive to the fact that distributions on many matters tend to be quite skewed.

TYPES OF MEASURE

The measures that might be applied to health care organizations can be grouped into three categories that I term (a) basic services, (b) instrumental dimensions, and (c) community benefits.

Basic Services

Basic services are those from which the organization derives most of its income. Health care is a highly commercialized field, with payment for services rendered the predominant form of funding for most types of organizations. Not surprisingly, our most extensive and detailed measures of organizational performance are concerned with the commercial aspects of nonprofits' performance—that is, the services they provide and that someone pays for—because billing and payment create excellent trails of records. Thus, we know much more about what nonprofits do for pay than about their purely charitable activities.

The basic services and activities for which health care organizations are paid include patient care, health professional education, and research. These services are mostly private goods, in that the primary beneficiary is the person who receives the services. Although there are elements of public goods in some services for which health institutions receive payment—particularly research, treatment of infectious diseases, and, some would argue, education—it is nevertheless useful to observe that many of the core activities for most services provided by health care organizations pay their own way.

One starting point for measuring the impact of nonprofit health care organizations is to enumerate the number of patients they serve, the number of students they educate, and the number (or dollar amount) of the research projects they conduct or publications they generate. The most commonly used measures of outputs are utilization measures, such as number of admissions or discharges, number of patients served or surgical procedures performed, days of care, and number of enrollees (e.g., in HMOs), and so on. Thus, for example, the nation's 3,163 short-term general hospitals admitted 2.9 million people in 1993, according to the American Hospital Association (1994), and provided 2.7 billion outpatient visits.

In some ways, measures of the use of services provided by nonprofits are indispensable to thinking about the task at hand; but there are complexities. Such numbers are generally reported the same way, regardless of the form of ownership of the organization; so for-profit and nonprofit hospitals that have the same number of admissions or patient days appear the same on this basic dimension. In that sense, these utilization measures gauge the performance of the organization qua organization, not of a nonprofit qua nonprofit. At least for services for which a commercial market exists, measures of the impact of non-profit organizations are artifacts of the division of a particular market among organizations of different ownership forms. Knowing that about 70 percent of hospital admissions in 1993 were to nonprofit hospitals that owned about 70 percent of the beds in the country may be basic to the task of measuring the impact of the nonprofit sector, but it is not terribly interesting.

In broad terms, we can distinguish among several types of measures of the basic services provided by nonprofits. First, as already mentioned, there are activity measures—how many patients were treated or how many dollars flowed. Second, there are performance measures—what percentage of the women above age 50 in an HMO had a mammogram in the previous two years. Third, there are outcome measures—what percentage of a hospital's coronary bypass surgery patients died before discharge or within one year of discharge, or what percentage of an HMO's diabetics were admitted to a hospital the previous year (admissions is a negative outcome measure for patients whose care should be successfully managed on an outpatient basis). Most available measures concern activities, not outcomes.

Most performance measures regarding nonprofits' basic or core activities were developed to meet the demands of purchasers and have little or nothing to do with ownership form. As already mentioned, few are interpretable in their own terms. But comparing the performance of organizations of different own-ership forms changes the question from "How do we measure the outputs and outcomes of nonprofit organizations in health care?" to "How do nonprofits compare with for-profit or government health care organizations?"

Another complexity regarding measurement can be called the "more is not necessarily better" problem. In a system dominated by fee-for-service payments, economic incentives have encouraged the provision of an ever-greater amount and variety of services, many of which are only marginally useful or are even completely unnecessary. From the standpoint of individual patients and from a societal point of view, providing more services, whether these be procedures, hospital admissions, or longer stays, may not be better.

This situation creates two problems for a project on measuring the impact of a sector. First, we cannot assume that utilization numbers are an unambiguous reflection of the social contributions made by organizations. In fact, under some circumstances, high utilization numbers reflect just the opposite (for example, many hospital admissions for patients with diabetes). Second, the fact that more is not necessarily better does not mean that less is always better than more. Activity measures can be quite misleading without information about matters such as quality, inefficiency, and fraud and abuse. We have nothing approaching sector-level measures on those dimensions.

Instrumental Dimensions

An important aspect of the social impact of nonprofit health care organizations concerns the fact that many people are employed and many goods and services are purchased as part of the process by which the organizations' services are produced. For example, 2.7 million people are employed by nonprofit hospitals, and hospitals are commonly among the major employers in their locales. All of the supplies bought by and capital expenditures made by nonprofit health care organizations could also be counted as part of the impact of the sector.

I will not go into detail about this aspect of nonprofits' impact, except to observe that this impact may have little to do with their nonprofit status, but much to do with the fact that they are delivering services that someone is paying for. (I said "may" because there may be differences of some social significance in the numbers, levels, or working conditions of employees; I have not looked at literature on such matters.) It is also possible that there are ownership-related differences in the use of local suppliers of goods and services.

Community Benefit Services

If the provision of basic services to paying patients were all that was involved in health care, the question of the contribution of the nonprofit sector would be relatively uninteresting. However, health care has three characteristics that magnify the potential significance of ownership.

First, health care is characterized by substantial informational asymmetries—between patients and providers, between third-party payers and providers, and between payers and patients. Patients and payers have had little choice in many instances but to trust. Alternatives to trust have been developing in the HMO performance measurement movement being led by large purchasers of managed care services, but health care is still an industry characterized by exploitable vulnerabilities and by the necessity for trust. Trustworthiness is therefore desirable and beneficial to the operation of the system; conversely, policies and practices that betray trust or that engender distrust have a societal cost.

Hansmann (1980) suggested that nonprofit organizations play a role in facilitating economic exchange in fields that are characterized by informational asymmetries, and there is some evidence that nonprofits are indeed more trustworthy in several types of health care organizations (Mark, 1996; Weisbrod & Schlesinger, 1986; Gray, 1991).

Second, there is far from a perfect fit between the need for services and the ability to pay for them: 40 million people lack health insurance (and millions more have inadequate insurance); there are public goods involved that will be undersupplied in the commercial market; there are a variety of idiosyncrasies in what third-party payers will and will not pay for; and some government programs (most notably Medicaid) pay less than full cost for their beneficiaries. In other words, many aspects of health care are not adequately covered by existing payment mechanisms.

Third, health care organizations often have great community significance, not merely because they are large employers that provide important services, but because they are part of what makes a community a community. They may have great symbolic importance because they provide help to people whose needs are great. Their boards of trustees are often made up of prominent citizens, and the organizations are often an outlet for community charitable and voluntary activities. Ideally, they take a leadership role in finding ways to address community needs.

Such "community benefit" aspects of nonprofit health care have become important and controversial. "Community benefit" is the Internal Revenue Service criterion for exempting nonprofit health care organizations from paying taxes, and health care is heavily populated by tax-paying for-profit organizations in addition to nonprofits. If charity care were the sole measure of community benefit for tax-exempt organizations, some nonprofits would fail the test (U.S. General Accounting Office, 1990).

A strong case can be made for a broader view of the impact of nonprofit health care organizations and, thus, of the meaning and measurement of community benefit. Table 11.1 shows a more comprehensive set of measures derived from tax law, economic theories of nonprofits, and the work of scholars and hospital associations regarding community benefit (Schlesinger, Gray, & Bradley, 1996). The table is based on thirty different dimensions including activities that create positive externalities (for example, contracting with essential community providers or reporting bad clinical practices to appropriate authorities), minimize negative externalities (for example, shifting the burdens of

Table 11.1. Illustrative Forms of Community Benefits
for Managed Care Organizations

Form of benefit	Specific outcomes/involvements
Positive externalities	Uncompensated care
	Contract with essential community providers
	Connections to functional settings: schools; workplace
	Subsidized Premiums
	Special programs for high-risk enrollees
	Reports of bad clinical practices to hospitals/state medical boards
	Profiling to identify cases that endanger well-being of patients
Negative externalities	Extent of cost shifting to providers
	Extent of cost/burden shifting to family
	Disaffiliation of low-quality providers without reporting their bad practices
Public goods: Information creation	Developing ways of allocating resources more effectively
	Violence identification programs
	Affiliations with research programs/universities
	Involvement with research protocols to improve managed care or clinical practices
	Grant funding from foundations or government agencies
Public goods: Information dissemination	Affiliation with teaching programs
	Health education programs for enrollees
	Provider education regarding appropriateness of care
	Provider education regarding quality of care issues
	Dissemination of review criteria from the utilization review
Trust and information asymmetries	No confidentiality clauses in physician contracts
	Disclosure requirements
	Limits on intensity of financial incentives
	Accuracy of marketing materials
	Warns patients about bad quality practices
	Effectiveness of grievance procedures and oversight
Community involvement	Community needs assessment
	Community health planning/goal development
	Community influence on policies and practices
	Adaptation of utilization review to local norms of treatment

Note. The community benefit activities that are feasible for a managed care organization will vary depending on whether it has its own provider network.
Source: Adapted from "Charity and Community: The Role of Nonprofit Ownership in a Managed Health Care System," by M. Schlesinger, B. Gray, & E. Bradley, Journal of Health Politics, Policy, and Law, 21, 697–751.

cost containment to providers or patients' families), provide public goods (for example, being involved in research and educational activities), minimize exploitation of informational asymmetries, and entail various other forms of community involvement.

This list of possible community benefits was developed for an analysis of the significance of ownership form for one particular type of health care organization—utilization review firms from the managed care field—but it illustrates the breadth with which one might think of community benefit and nonprofits' impact. Other types of health care organizations might have different impacts or benefits.

EVIDENCE ON COMMUNITY BENEFITS

The research base for assessing the overall community benefits of different types of health care organizations has serious inadequacies, and a full summary of available information is beyond the scope of this paper. Researchers have given most attention to hospitals and to service to the poor and uninsured. Much research has focused on comparisons of nonprofit and for-profit hospitals, but in recent years interest has grown in the performance of nonprofits in relation to the magnitude of the benefits they receive via tax exemptions.

Much of our knowledge about hospital services for the poor and uninsured is in the form of accounting data about uncompensated care, generally defined as deductions from gross revenues for bad debt and charity. The imperfections of uncompensated care as a measure of service to the "poor and uninsured" are obvious. Many of the poor are not uninsured, and the bad debt component of uncompensated care does not arise only from service to the poor.

American Hospital Association surveys based on national uncompensated care numbers show only slightly higher levels of uncompensated care in nonprofit than in for-profit hospitals, a pattern that has been quite persistent for many years (Ashby, 1991). Uncompensated care data for 1994 showed nonprofits at 4.5 percent of revenues and for-profits at 4.0 percent (Prospective Payment Assessment Commission, 1996). Public hospitals provide much higher levels of uncompensated care than either nonprofits or for-profits do and clearly play an important role in caring for the poor and uninsured. Many of these institutions receive direct government subsidies for this purpose, which enhances their ability to provide such services (Ashby, 1991).

The picture of comparable nonprofit/for-profit behavior based on national uncompensated care numbers is widely cited as evidence that for-profits and nonprofits are not really different. But this picture may be misleading because it ignores (a) problems regarding the source of the data and (b) state-level differences (Gray, 1991; Lewin, Eckles, & Miller, 1988).

The data come from unaudited self-reports from hospitals surveyed annually by the American Hospital Association and reflect substantial problems with missing data.. Moreover, the amount of a hospital's bad debt and charity is influenced by the magnitude of its charges, and many studies have shown that for-profit hospitals have higher charges than nonprofits (Gray, 1991; Lewin, Eckles, & Miller, 1988).

A clue to the extent to which underlying differences in service to the uninsured may be concealed by numbers related to uncompensated care comes from two studies done in the early 1980s. Rowland's (1984) analysis of data from a 1981 survey by the Office for Civil Rights showed that 6 percent of patients admitted to for-profit hospitals were uninsured, compared with 7.9 percent in nonprofit hospitals and 16.8 percent in public hospitals. Frank, Salkever, and Mullan (1990) analyzed data from the National Hospital Discharge Survey and found that about 4 percent of discharges from for-profit hospitals were uninsured, compared with about 6 percent of discharges from nonprofit hospitals and 11 percent from public hospitals. Both studies found a similar pattern in services to Medicaid patients, but fewer differences in magnitude.

National data likely mute ownership differences. Nonprofit hospitals are found in large numbers in all states, including many that have few uninsured residents and, therefore, proportionately low levels of need for hospitalization among the uninsured. For-profits are concentrated in states with growing populations and friendly regulatory environments; many of these states also have relatively high numbers of uninsured people (Mullner & Hadley, 1984; Watt, Renn, Hahn, Derson, & Schramm, 1986). In such states, nonprofits tend to provide much higher levels of uncompensated care than for-profits do; this is true for Texas, Tennessee, Virginia, and Florida, where nonprofits provide substantially more (in some cases twice as much) uncompensated care than for-profits do (Gray, 1991; Lewin, Eckles, & Miller, 1988). Studies from California, however, show similarly low amounts of uncompensated care in for-profit and nonprofit hospitals, perhaps because of the large numbers of government-subsidized public hospitals in that state (Pattison, 1986; Sofaer, Rundall, & Zellers, 1990). An inference that can be drawn from this pattern is that nonprofits may be more responsive to unmet needs for medical care than for-profits are; where the demand for uncompensated care is low, nonprofits may concentrate on other forms of community benefit or simply charge lower prices.

Nonprofit/for-profit differences in uncompensated care could be due either to differences in the presence of such patients or to differences in willingness to serve. Both factors may be involved. Norton and Staiger (1994) found that ownership differences in uncompensated care were largely explained by for-profits having acquired or located hospitals in relatively high-income areas. For-profit hospitals are also more likely than nonprofits to pressure physicians to turn away uninsured and Medicaid patients (Schlesinger, Bentkover,

Blumenthal, Musacchio, & Willer, 1987), and physicians report conflict over the treatment of indigents more often in for-profit than in nonprofit hospitals (Burns, Anderson, & Shortell, 1990). Finally, for-profit hospitals have been substantially overrepresented among hospitals charged by the Department of Health and Human Services with violating the 1986 "antidumping" legislation, which forbade hospitals from denying treatment to emergency patients and women in labor (Stieber & Wolfe, 1993, 1994). (The 1994 report found that while 14 percent of community hospitals were for-profit, 29 percent of the hospitals cited for violations were for-profit.)

Nonprofit hospitals' uncompensated care could also be compared with the value of their tax exemptions. The argument is sometimes made that the value of a hospital's community benefit activities, particularly uncompensated care, should be at least equivalent to the amount of the "subsidy" that it enjoys by virtue of its tax exemptions (Simon, 1987). The U.S. General Accounting Office conducted a study of California and New York hospitals in 1990 and found that about 20 percent were providing less uncompensated care than the value of their federal tax exemptions; when the narrower definition of "charity care" was adopted, almost 30 percent of New York nonprofit hospitals and almost 60 percent of California nonprofits provided less than the value of their federal tax exemption (U.S. General Accounting Office, 1990). Federal legislation was subsequently proposed, but not passed, to link exemptions to an uncompensated care requirement. Such linkages have been made in a few states.

A wide variety of indicators suggests that nonprofits have substantial advantages from a broadly defined community benefit standpoint. For example, local governance is much more typical among nonprofit hospitals than among for-profits; nonprofit hospitals are more likely to be located in urban areas with large numbers of poor and uninsured; nonprofit hospitals and HMOs are much more involved in research and education than for-profits are; nonprofit hospitals offer a greater array of services including some that typically lose money; and nonprofits are much less likely than for-profits to undergo recurrent changes of ownership and control (Institute of Medicine, 1986; Gray, 1991; Alexander, Lewis, & Morrisey, 1985; Norton & Staiger, 1994; LeBlanc & Hurley, 1995; Prospective Payment Assessment Commission, 1995; Luft & Greenlick, 1996; Veloski, Barzansky, Nash, Bastacky, & Stevens, 1996).

The advantage of a broad definition of community benefit is that it more fully captures the benefits that might be provided by nonprofit organizations and that might be at stake, for example, when organizations consider converting to for-profit status (Gray, 1997). The disadvantage of the broad definition is that it is not based on a common metric that can be quantified and compared across organizations or sectors.

CONCLUSION

A wealth of information exists about the activities of health care organizations, particularly about the services for which they receive payment. From the standpoint of research and public policy regarding nonprofits, however, this is not the most interesting information. Much more important are the ways that nonprofits might differ from for-profit organizations in the same field and the extent to which the community benefit activities of health care organizations justify the benefits they receive via their tax-exempt status. Significant opportunities exist for research regarding (a) the ways that complex organizational structures affect the information reported about nonprofit organizational performance, (b) the broad array of possible community benefits provided by nonprofits, and (c) the trustworthiness and quality of these institutions.

REFERENCES

Alexander, J., Lewis, B., & Morrisey, M. (1985). Acquisition strategies of multihospital systems. *Health Affairs, 4,* 49–66.
American Hospital Association. (1994). *Hospital statistics.* Chicago: Author.
American Hospital Association. (1995). *Hospital statistics.* Chicago: Author.
Ashby, J. (1991). *The trend and distribution of hospital uncompensated care costs, 1980–1989* (p. 13). Washington, DC: Prospective Payment Assessment Commission.
Burns, L. R., Andersen, R. M., & Shortell, S. M.. (1990). The effect of hospital control strategies on physician satisfaction and physician–hospital conflict. *Health Services Research, 25,* 527–558.
Federation of American Health Systems. (1995). *Directory of the Federation of American Health Systems.* Washington, DC: Author.
Frank, R., Salkever, D., & Mullan, F. (1990). Hospital ownership and the care of uninsured and Medicaid patients: Findings from the national hospital discharge survey, 1979–1984. *Health Policy, 14,* 1–11.
Gray, B. H. (1991). *The profit motive and patient care: The changing accountability of doctors and hospitals.* Cambridge, MA: Harvard University Press.
Gray, B. H. (1993). A puzzlement: Health-related organizations in the *Nonprofit Almanac 1992–1993. Voluntas, 4,* 210–220.
Gray, B. H. (1997). Conversions of HMOs and hospitals: What's at stake? *Health Affairs, 16,* 29–47.
Hansmann, H. (1980). The role of nonprofit enterprise. *Yale Law Journal, 89,* 835-901.
Hodgkinson, V. A., & Weitzman, M. S. (1996). *Nonprofit almanac 1996–1997: Dimensions of the independent sector.* San Francisco: Jossey-Bass.
Institute of Medicine. (1986). *For-profit enterprise in health care.* Washington, DC: National Academy Press.
LeBlanc, A. J., & Hurley, R. E. (1995). Adoption of HIV-related services among urban US hospitals: 1988 and 1991. *Medical Care, 33,* 881–891.
Lewin, L. S., Eckles, T. J., & Miller, L. (1988). Setting the record straight: The provision of

uncompensated care by not-for-profit hospitals. *New England Journal of Medicine, 318,* 1212–1215.

Luft, H. S., & Greenlick, M. S. (1996). The contribution of group- and staff-model HMOs to American medicine. *The Milbank Quarterly, 74,* 445–467.

Mark, T. (1996). Psychiatric hospital ownership and performance: Do nonprofit organizations offer advantages in markets characterized by asymmetric information? *Journal of Human Resources, 31,* 631–649.

Marmor, T., Schlesinger, M., & Smithey, R. (1987). Nonprofit organizations and health care. In W. W. Powell (Ed.), *The nonprofit sector: A research handbook* (pp. 221–239). New Haven, CT: Yale University Press.

Mullner, R., & Hadley, J. (1984). Interstate variations in the growth of chain-owned proprietary hospitals, 1973–1982. *Inquiry, 21,* 144–151.

Norton, E. C., & Staiger, D.O. (1994). How hospital ownership affects access to care for the uninsured. *Rand Journal of Economics, 25,* 171–185.

Pattison, R. V. (1986). Response to financial incentives among investor-owned and not-for-profit hospitals: An analysis based on California data, 1978–1982. In *For-profit enterprise in health care.* Washington, DC: National Academy Press.

Prospective Payment Assessment Commission. (1995). *Comparison of HMOs across payer types.* Staff Report. Washington, DC: Author.

Prospective Payment Assessment Commission. (1996). *Medicare and the American health care system: Report to the Congress.* Washington, DC: Author.

Rowland, D. (1984). Hospital care for the uninsured: An analysis of the role of proprietary hospitals. Paper prepared for the annual meeting of the American Public Health Association.

Schlesinger, M., Bentkover, J., Blumenthal, D., Musacchio, R., & Willer, J. (1987). The privatization of health care and physicians' perceptions of access to hospital services. *The Milbank Quarterly, 65,* 25–58.

Schlesinger, M., Gray, B., & Bradley, E. (1996). Charity and community: The role of nonprofit ownership in a managed health care system. *Journal of Health Politics, Policy, and Law, 21,* 697–751.

Simon, J. G. (1987). The tax treatment of nonprofit organizations. In W. W. Powell (Ed.), *The nonprofit sector: A research handbook.* New Haven, CT: Yale University Press.

Sofaer, S., Rundall, T. G., & Zellers, W. L. (1990). Policy changes affecting deductions from revenue in California hospitals, 1981–1986. *Hospital and Health Services Administration, 35,* 191–206.

Stieber, J., & Wolfe, S. M. (1993). *Patient dumping continues in hospital emergency rooms: An updated report on the Department of Health and Human Services' enforcement of the federal Patient Dumping Law.* Washington, DC: Public Citizen's Health Research Group.

Stieber, J., & Wolfe, S. M. (1994). *Update on 'patient dumping' violations.* Washington DC: Public Citizen's Health Research Group.

U.S. General Accounting Office. (1990). *Nonprofit hospitals: Better standards needed for tax exemption.* Washington: Author.

Veloski, J., Barzansky, B., Nash, D. B., Bastacky, S., & Stevens, D. P. (1996). Medical student education in managed care settings: Beyond HMOs. *JAMA, 276,* 667–671.

Watt, J. M., Renn, S. C., Hahn, J. S., Derzon, R. A., & Schramm, C. J. (1986). The effects of ownership and multihospital system membership on hospital functional strategies and economic performance. In B. H. Gray (Ed.), *For-profit enterprise in health care* (pp. 260–289). Washington, DC: National Academy Press.

Weisbrod, B., & Schlesinger, M. (1986). Ownership form and behavior in regulated markets with asymmetric information. In S. Rose-Ackerman (Ed.), *The nonprofit sector: Economic theory and public policy* (pp. 133–151). New York: Oxford University Press.

Chapter 12

Revealing the Implicit
Searching for Measures of the Impact of the Arts

MARGARET JANE WYSZOMIRSKI

In 1781, George Washington wrote that "the arts and sciences [are] essential to the prosperity of the state and to the ornament and happiness of human life" (Independent Commission, 1990, p.7). In 1965, President Lyndon Johnson asserted that the arts were "part of the pursuit of American greatness" (Independent Commission, 1990, p. 9). Both comments illustrate how national political leaders have voiced an implicit belief that the arts have an impact on the society and people of the nation. Indeed, we could assert that both the concept and the logic of concern for societal impact are fundamental precepts of public policy. From the perspective of public officials and policy analysts, attention to the public interest(s) served and to the public benefits derived from publicly supported or authorized activities is natural.

Some economists seek to operationalize this concern by theorizing that the arts constitute "public goods" or "merit goods." Such terms carry the connotation that the arts are, by definition, a societally desirable thing and that the general public is encompassed within their positive effects. Other economists argue that the arts might more accurately be considered "toll goods" or "club goods." According to this argument, arts activities are seen, for the most part,

MARGARET JANE WYSZOMIRSKI • Director, Arts Policy and Administration Program, Ohio State University, Columbus, Ohio 43210.

Measuring the Impact of the Nonprofit Sector, edited by Patrice Flynn and Virginia A. Hodgkinson, New York, Kluwer Academic/Plenum Publishers, 2002.

as providing individual and private benefits. These individual benefits go to those who are willing to pay the necessary "toll" (e.g., ticket prices) or who hold membership in the "club" (e.g., donor or guild members of a particular arts/cultural organization such as a museum or orchestra).

In practice, although both the public goods argument and the toll goods argument carry some logical weight, neither is fully persuasive on its own with regard to the arts and culture. Consequently, from a public policy perspective, multiple measures and categories of impact are needed to demonstrate the societal effects of the activities of nonprofit arts/cultural organizations. Such a multifaceted approach is apparent in this 1988 comment by Vice President George Bush: "The arts...contain the signposts of civilization and provide the symbols and vocabularies of our national identity. They contribute to a community's morale and thus improve its quality of life and contribute to its economic development" (Independent Commission, 1990, p. 11).

A MULTIFACETED CHALLENGE

Measuring the impact of nonprofit arts and cultural organizations is an effort both related to and distinct from efforts to devise valid and informative approaches to evaluation and assessment. Both evaluation/assessment studies and impact analysis can be multidimensional, having many and various units of measurement. At the risk of oversimplification, we might argue that evaluation and assessment generally concern the operations and program activities of nonprofit cultural organizations. The results of such studies are frequently used to inform and guide institutional strategic planning, administrative decision making, organizational management and structure, and program planning and adaptation. In other words, evaluation and assessment efforts have tended to focus either on the organizational operations or on the success or appropriateness of programmatic activities. Thus, evaluation and assessment efforts can be regarded as useful organizational tools for management, development, and reporting.

Impact analysis takes a step beyond assessment and evaluation. It also speaks to a different, and predominantly external, audience. Essentially, impact analysis concerns political and policy purposes. It focuses on questions such as which activities merit public attention and resources and why, or on how effectively, efficiently, and equitably public interests are being addressed. While evaluation and assessment studies can inform impact analyses, they are insufficient in themselves to measure (and convincingly convey) impact.

Comprehensive impact analysis (like policy evaluation) is likely to have many dimensions. It may:

- involve substantive, procedural, and political standards of measurement
- calculate both benefits and costs
- concern both direct and indirect effects
- allow for the possibility of negative as well as positive effects
- recognize both intended and unintended consequences

Few policy areas have developed the full array of such impact analyses. Nonetheless, examples of each of these dimensions abound in other areas of policy debate and analysis.

In the case of the arts, none of these elements have been well developed. Rather, studies often presume an effect, whether positive or negative, and then seek to document that presumption. Few question or confirm the original presumption. Seldom are both positives and negatives combined with costs and benefits into a net assessment of impact. Although many surmise impact from indicators of activity, information on incidence (i.e., who benefits and how) and activity (i.e., how much of what occurs where and under what conditions) is often limited, uneven, and incomplete. Effect or impact is seldom regarded as multidimensional. Assessments of impact are frequently unreliable, nongeneralizable, or inferential. Outputs, outcomes, and impacts are often confused and seldom systematically distinguished or related to inputs. Thus, devising impact measurements for the nonprofit arts that will be informative and persuasive in the policy realm constitutes a fairly sophisticated and urgent challenge.

From an artistic viewpoint, however, the policy concern for measuring societal impact might seem unnecessary, perhaps almost alien. For those concerned with artistic excellence or aesthetic power, "measures" are likely to be categorical (e.g., validated by peer judgment) or else inferred from venue (e.g., occurring in professional nonprofit organizations). Similarly, creativity is likely to be measured nominally (e.g., it is new or innovative) or inferred from location (e.g., it is more likely to occur in spaces other than museums). To the extent that outcomes such as excellence, creativity, and aesthetic effect are notoriously difficult to characterize, attempts to measure the impact of the arts strike many in the arts community as a futile and suspect effort that cannot capture the true value of this "public good."

Furthermore, those who believe in the value of art for art's sake cannot fathom the utility (much less the necessity) of searching for societal impact. This intrinsic perspective is essentially ahistorical, which, in turn, obscures our awareness of possible long-term impacts, such as the significant geographical redistribution of artistic activities and opportunities that has occurred nationally over the past 30 years.

Indeed, artists (and, to some extent, arts patrons) tend to mean something quite different when they refer to the impact of the arts. Impact on the individual often takes the form of anecdotes about the transforming, cathartic, and inspirational effects of the arts. Arts organizations and national service associations gather information about their number, size, finances, activities, and reach, and infer something about impact from these dimensions of output. Public arts agencies as well as private foundations present annual information on the organizations, individuals, and activities they support and display these as indications of public access, geographic and demographic distribution, and artistic merit. Critics of contemporary cultural fare point to the corrosive effect that violence on television has on children and the desensitizing effect it has on society at large. Each of these examples is an effort to demonstrate the implicit belief that the arts have an impact both on society collectively and on citizens individually.

Historically, many in the arts community have regarded measurement efforts with skepticism and calls for impact analysis with suspicion. At times, such calls have been caricatured as coming from outsiders who don't really understand the arts or who lack the credentials to make fully informed judgments. At other times, these calls are simply considered to be politically motivated. Recently, however, such attitudes have shown signs of giving way to an interest in performance measurement, particularly among state arts agencies (SAAs). Indeed, at present, "four out of five state arts councils are now affected by statewide performance measurement mandates" (Barsdate & National Assembly of State Arts Agencies [NASAA], 1996, p.9). Even more important, this new concern with performance measurement is regarded not only as a matter of administrative compliance but also as an asset to agency planning and efficient management. Furthermore, state arts agencies have recognized that "demonstrating accountability and documenting how SAA programs serve the public can help to improve legislative confidence . . . " (Barsdate & NASAA, 1996, p. 9).

TWO CATEGORIES OF INFORMATION

The past 30 years have seen the advent of direct public support for the arts at the national level, the expansion of public funding at the state and local levels, and a significant proliferation of nonprofit arts/cultural organizations and activities throughout the country. Concurrently, the issue of measuring the impact of the arts, of arts organizations, and of arts programming has gained greater currency. To be sure, various efforts have been undertaken to develop better, more comprehensive, and more useful information about the arts. These efforts might be divided into two general categories: those concerned with the

development of field status information and those concerned with documenting specific aspects of societal impact.

Field Status Information

Until well into the 1970s, scholars, policy makers, and other arts funders
bemoaned the dearth of data on nonprofit arts organizations. In their seminal
work, *Performing Arts: The Economic Dilemma*, economists Baumol and Bowen
(1966) had to assemble their own data from primary materials. Although the
Ford Foundation collected and published extensive data in *The Finances of the
Performing Arts* covering the years between 1966 and 1971, and then for fiscal
years 1972 through 1974 (which was not published), such efforts only scratched
the surface. During the past 30 years, the number of nonprofit arts organizations has grown exponentially, and the number of national arts service organizations (ASOs)—whose memberships include many of these organizations—
has expanded apace. Today there are ASOs for virtually every field and art form,
from the American Association of Museums, the Theater Communications
Group, and the American Symphony Orchestra League to Dance USA, the National Association of Artists Organizations, and the National Alliance of Media
Arts Centers. In addition, there are associations of funders such as the Business
Committee for the Arts, the National Assemblies of State and of Local Arts
Agencies, and Grantmakers in the Arts. While few of these groups include all
of the organizations in their field or art form, each does represent a significant
portion of them, particularly of the larger institutions.

Most ASOs conduct periodic membership surveys and undertake special
research projects on activities or issues of importance to the field. Many of
these associations compile data on various output measures (e.g., expenditures,
attendance, number and kind of performances) as well as numerous input factors (e.g., revenue, employment, field size). Most ASOs now have such information for at least the last decade; some have data that cover a period as long as
30 years.

In general, ASOs have compiled membership data on:

- the number, location, and programming of member organizations
- levels and categories of expenditures, revenues, and other financial information
- personnel figures and salaries
- audience and attendance figures; and, sometimes
- board characteristics, activities, and practices

In 1980, the National Endowment for the Arts (NEA) sponsored a research project designed to "assemble, assess, edit and analyze available data sets" on arts organizations; the study also augmented existing data sets. The result was the report "Growth of Arts and Cultural Organizations in the Decade of the 1970s" (Schwarz & Peters, 1983). Subsequently, a comprehensive sampling of such materials was compiled by Westat, Inc. for the National Endowment for the Arts as the *1989 Sourcebook of Arts Statistics* (NEA & Westat, Inc., 1990) and its *1992 Addendum* (NEA & Westat, Inc., 1992).

Information on the status of arts organizations is also collected at the state and local levels. The prevalence of community cultural planning in cities and counties throughout the country has yielded local inventories of cultural organizations and activities. State arts agencies or state arts advocacy groups frequently compile such inventories as part of economic impact studies, and considerable information can also be extracted from the National Information System that SAAs use to report on their grant-making activities. In addition, foundations in Chicago, Philadelphia, and Cleveland have sponsored studies that collect information about arts organizations and activities in their communities in an effort to assess and plan their own funding policies and priorities. However, there is little effort to make such data collection efforts comparable to one another from one community to another.

Information concerning cultural nonprofits has also been collected by other kinds of. organizations. The *Foundation Grants Index* details foundation giving to the arts. *Arts Funding: A Report of Foundation* and *Corporate Grantmaking Trends* and its updates (Weber & Renz, 1993; Renz, 1995; Renz & Lawrence, 1998; and Renz, Atlas, & Kendzior, 1999) provide perhaps the most useful compilation and analysis of such information along with a survey of grant makers on their future intentions and priorities. Independent Sector also gathers and reports information on giving and volunteering related to nonprofit arts organizations (Independent Sector, 1994). The President's Committee on the Arts and Humanities published a report that compiled information from these and other sources into an overview of patterns and trends in private giving to the arts and humanities (Cobb & President's Committee on the Arts and the Humanities, 1996). Although less comprehensive than the coverage of ASO data, such grant-maker information is likely to provide insight into the effect of funders on nonprofit arts organizations rather than on the impact of arts organizations on society.

Perhaps a more useful source of information on impact might be obtained from the increasingly sophisticated program and project evaluations that funders conduct on their grantees. However, these are also likely to exhibit a lack of comparability, since each project evaluation tends to be tailored to either a particular foundation program or to a specific grantee project. Nonetheless, program/project evaluation may be a mechanism for developing and gathering some useful indications of the outcomes of arts programming and projects.

Clearly, more information is being gathered and has been amassed by more groups about nonprofit arts organizations than ever before. However, managers, policy makers, and scholars still confront basic flaws and gaps in this information. The ASO data suffer from the same failings that characterize the arts policy community more generally: it is fragmented, incomplete, and uncoordinated (Wyszomirski, 1995, p. 13). While there is "lots of information...[it]is scattered, not comparable, and not very policy relevant" (DiMaggio & Kaple, 1996, p. 13) With such data, even accurate descriptions of scale, distribution, and dimensions are problematic. Answering more complicated questions about cause and effect, about impact and societal value, is largely out of reach.

Indeed, a concern with data collection may have obscured the development of impact measures that might result from analyses that interrelate discrete pieces of information. For example, more analytical attention to time would clarify various redistributional effects. Artistic production and attendance patterns have been redistributed from a concentration in a few urban (and, especially, coastal) areas to a more equitable national pattern. Expansion and redistribution within the arts have also occurred, with the result that a middle range of organizations has been developed between the established (and often endowed) institutions and the voluntary/community arts groups. Another redistribution of resources has given rise to new kinds of arts organizations, such as alternative spaces, media arts centers, statewide arts and arts education advocacy associations, and even arts service organizations at national, state, and local levels.

Alternatively, by giving greater attention to relating inputs to outputs, we might find that existing information could reveal outcome or impact effects. For example, calculating potential ticket costs on the basis of production expenses and contrasting these to actual ticket prices would reveal the "hidden" redistributive impact of charitable contributions to nonprofit arts organizations. Additionally, existing data might be used to devise cost-benefit ratios for common output indicators such as audience attendance, production, and per client services.

One such attempt at devising a rudimentary indicator of impact used scale and distribution of field activities as a measure of reach. In 1992, the Alliance for the Arts surveyed 100 nonprofit cultural institutions in New York City to ascertain what exhibits, performances, or direct services they provided to other cities and institutions across the United States. The survey was intended to demonstrate the "living connection between a work of art, homegrown in New York and enjoyed in the heartland . . . " (Alliance for the Arts & Mayor's Advisory Commission for Cultural Affairs, 1992).

While successive surveys provide information about trends and patterns in the finances, personnel, and programming of nonprofit arts organizations, these are more likely to suggest how each field within the sector has been affected by external funders, patrons, and environmental conditions, rather than what impact these organizations may have had on a specific community or on society at large.

Indeed, it is probably fair to say that although the amount of information available on the status and dimensions of nonprofit arts organizations has expanded greatly in the past 20 years, little of this information is directly relevant to measuring their societal impact. Furthermore, the emphasis of such efforts has been on gathering information rather than on interpreting or making analytical use of the information. Although not sufficient as a tool for measuring the impact of the arts, comprehensive, reliable, and accessible data on the status of nonprofit arts organizations are essential to impact analysis because these data provide information on the universe from which samples can be drawn and interpreted.

A number of possible next steps suggest themselves if the condition and usefulness of field status information are to be improved. One step could focus on improving the comparability of existing information and finding ways to cross-match separate data sets into a more comprehensive database. In their report, DiMaggio and Kaple (1996) call for such a "unified data base." A key to accomplishing this "unification" may entail the use of a tracer element that reliably identifies each nonprofit arts organization across different data sets. A likely tracer element is a nonprofit organization's tax exempt identification number (EIN) and the classification system embodied in the National Taxonomy of Exempt Entities (NTEE) (Wyszomirski & Standley, 1996). The EIN number could become the equivalent of an organization's social security number, thus ensuring that information from different data sets does, indeed, pertain to the same organization when cross-matching is undertaken. However, efforts would need to be undertaken by all data collectors to include EIN number as a data field. A second step might involve the development of a compatible, if not common, template for collecting information and establishing more consistent reporting standards, a move that would facilitate comparability and cross-matching. Third, a coordinated information-gathering effort could be encouraged at the local level. If a common survey instrument were developed and used by local communities, then each local study could become a building block in a national database. Finally, a fourth step might entail an effort to both identify the likely universe of nonprofit arts and cultural organizations and compare it to the apparent universe as reflected in the membership and information gathered by arts service organizations. Such an effort is part of the National and Local Profiles of the Cultural Support Project underway as a partnership of Americans for the Arts and the Ohio State University (Filicko & Lafferty, 1999).

Alone, each of the existing data sets is incomplete and inadequate. Some measures of their incompleteness will become clearer when the results of the Profiles of Cultural Support Project become available. Together, the various data sets will certainly provide a better information base on the status of nonprofit arts organizations. Such a base would, in turn, prove invaluable to efforts to develop indicators and measures of the impact of arts organizations on society.

Documenting Specific Aspects of Impact

At least four possible impact factors have been the subject of various studies and research: public surveys, economic impact studies, education effect studies, and social utility studies. In the past 20 years, not only have the incidence and accumulation of such information increased, but some of these approaches have been refined and systematized as follows.

Public Surveys

Public surveys come in at least three varieties: audience surveys, public participation surveys, and public opinion surveys. It has become increasingly common for individual arts organizations to survey their audiences in order to know who is in their audience and how they can be better reached. In 1977, an NEA research report found that good audience research was scarce (DiMaggio, Useem, & Brown, 1977). By 1985, the agency's research division had published a manual on how to survey one's audience. It did that as part of an effort to raise awareness of standards regarding audience survey information (NEA, 1985). These efforts occurred following a dramatic expansion of public support for the arts at the federal and state levels, thus spurring an interest in better understanding the public that was directly benefiting from these programs. Publication of the manual also followed a period of increased professionalization of marketing within larger nonprofit arts organizations and among arts consultants. In some fields, such as museums, there is even an affinity group specifically concerned with audience studies.

Of course, for the purposes of measuring impact, certain limitations and qualifications must be noted about audience survey information. Like field status data, audience surveys measure activity rather than impact, unless reach is accepted as an indicator of impact. Only occasionally do audience surveys collect information about client satisfaction—an indicator commonly used in measuring outcomes for other types of nonprofit activity, in gauging policy impact, and in assessing commercial marketing efforts. Audience surveys do collect information about a public, but capture only that part of society that attends a particular artistic event or institution. Such surveys have become increasingly adept at understanding the demographic profile of an organization's audience and are useful as a device for targeting marketing appeals. However, many still lack important information concerning audience attitudes, taste preferences, and other values and lifestyle variables that could help explain behavioral differences between people with similar demographic characteristics. Although some arts organizations have augmented audience surveys with focus group studies, the results of institutionally conducted audience surveys or focus groups are seldom accessible to those outside the sponsoring organization. Recently, some ASOs have begun exploring the possibility of field-wide audience studies. For example, Opera America commissioned ArtsMarket Consulting to conduct a series of focus groups around the country to ascertain what barriers kept people from attending opera, especially if they exhibited an interest in the art form (Stevens, 1996a). The results of the study then inform new marketing, advertising, and development strategies among the participating opera companies and provoked new thinking among others.

Public participation studies take a broader view than audience surveys because participation studies draw a sample that includes both arts attendees (audience members) and nonattendees. Building such information resources is a long process. It took nearly two decades of committed, consistent effort by NEA's Research Division, the assistance of the U.S. Census Bureau, and the involvement of many independent scholars and consultants to develop national time-series data on public participation in the arts (Survey on Public Participation in the Arts/SPPA). As a result of these efforts, however, there is now reliable, basic, national data on public participation in the arts, across the 15 years between 1982 to 1997, as well as a series of special analyses using these data to examine participation patterns and changes in particular art forms and the effects of specific cross-cutting factors (NEA & Jack Faucett Associates with John P. Robinson, 1993). Furthermore, 12 communities in various parts of the country have conducted their own arts participation surveys using questionnaires compatible with SPPA. Once again, such participation data are useful as indicators of reach rather than of impact. However, the participation studies do provide a national baseline and some intriguing suggestions about possible barriers to public participation, about the impact of media and technology on arts participation, and about the role of education. In other words, arts participation studies not only inform us about who participates in what kinds of arts activities, but are also suggestive about the impact of various social and technological factors on the arts and the audiences of arts organizations.

Public opinion studies concerning the arts are a third form of public surveys. Most of these questions fall into a relatively small set of categories: participation and attitudes about participation; private giving and volunteering; education, classes, and children; funding, both public and private; the role of government; obscenity, pornography, and artistic expression; and the arts as a profession/occupation. There are also questions about specific artists and artworks as well as about international comparisons and exchanges. Although most survey questions focus on actions, preferences, attitudes, and general knowledge, others can be revealing about intentions, expectations, and assumed impact. As the author of a comprehensive overview of 50 years of such surveys observed, these surveys seem to indicate that " . . . Americans . . . see the usefulness of exposure to the arts but they are not convinced that that is reason enough to support them financially. . . " and do not "have a consensus on what 'cultural' means" (Filicko, 1996, p. 241). While using public opinion polls to develop a direct measure of the impact of the arts may be daunting, Filicko suggests that opinion polls might be used more explicitly to measure the perception of impact or expectations about the impact of the arts.

Economic Impact Studies

Perhaps the most developed and pervasively used measure of the societal impact of the arts is the economic impact study. According to one researcher, at least 34 states and more than 100 cities, regions, and institutions have used economic impact studies during the past 25 years as an advocacy, planning, or information tool (Radich, 1987, 1993). Derived from techniques and methods used to conduct economic impact studies of higher education, the methodology of cultural economic impact studies was refined—again, through the interaction of scholars, consultants, state arts agencies, and the Research Division of NEA—over a period of 5 to 7 years. Economic impact studies were particularly effective as advocacy tools with local and state officials, spurring increases in public funding for the arts from the late 1970s well into the 1980s. They are also effective in measuring the economic impact of special events (such as festivals) or of specific institutions (such as Lincoln Center, or even individual museums or performing arts organizations). Economic impact studies have often been linked to cultural tourism for measuring the economic impact of special exhibitions, festivals, or performances and of cultural organizations as destination attractions. Unfortunately, consistent methodologies are seldom used from one study to another or even over time in the same state, county, or institution. Studies concerned mainly with assessing the impact of cultural tourism may have greater economic validity if they really are designed to measure the influx of new and external money rather than the direction of funds already in the local economy.

Economic impact studies are used both prospectively and retrospectively. That is, they can be designed to estimate the likely economic impact of cultural activities as a way of gaining support for such activities, or they can be used to demonstrate the actual economic impact that has been derived from these events. For example, it is now common practice for major art museums to routinely conduct economic impact studies of major exhibitions (Smith, 1993). However, the limitations, distortions, and exaggerations of such economic impact studies have become better known with their use, and some skepticism has developed about methodological issues such as what constitutes an appropriate multiplier, what can and should be counted as induced or indirect benefits, and whether other activities might produce similar or greater economic impacts.

One can see evidence of an effort to develop a common and comparable approach to measuring the economic impact of nonprofit arts organizations in a set of 33 community studies that provide a basis from which to extrapolate a national impact (National Assembly of Local Arts Agencies [NALAA], 1993). The national figures arising from these studies, conducted by NALAA, have been widely used in federal and national advocacy activities, while the 33 local studies provide communities with a basis for comparison. In addition, the NALAA studies not only provide information on overall economic impact but also include figures on local and state revenue generated through such arts activities. However, these studies have received little scholarly or methodological review even though they are likely to be an important building block for future assessments of the economic impact of nonprofit arts organizations.

Among the most elaborate and sophisticated of economic impact studies are a pair of studies conducted by the Port Authority of New York and New Jersey (Port Authority of New York & New Jersey, 1983, 1993). In 1994, the state of California also conducted an extensive and innovative study of the economic impact of its arts and cultural industry (California Arts Council, 1994). However, the New York and California studies were not restricted to the activities and impact of nonprofit arts organizations but surveyed, albeit selectively, the economic impact of cultural activities in the for-profit sector as well. Thus, the New York study included such for-profit activity as art galleries and auction houses, commercial theater, and motion picture and television production. In California, the study included the motion picture and television industry, automobile design, and the manufacture of musical instruments. It also tried to capture a measure of the economic and community impact of individual artists.

Economic impact studies of the arts could be improved in a number of ways. For example, most such studies currently present their findings in terms of gross benefits rather than net impact. Thus, findings tend to inherently over-estimate impact while masking both the community investment in the arts and the dividends that accrue to the community. Indeed, a new, and perhaps modified, generation of economic impact studies of the arts might be prompted by the emerging tendency to portray patronage, particularly public support, as a form of public investment in community assets and national cultural resources (NEA, 1992). Another way of getting at an attitudinal dimension of economic value can be found in the contingency valuation approach, such as has been used in a 1998 report on the economic impact of the arts in Kentucky (Thompson, Berger, & Allen, 1998). By implication, an investment carries expectations of payoffs or dividends, hence, economic impacts. Perhaps it is time for a field-wide effort to reevaluate and revamp this methodology; to standardize methods and data collection protocols; and to find ways to integrate additional indicators of such impacts as increased property values, added value to human capital development, produced enhancements to quality of life, and new contributions to community cohesion and engagement. Of course, to do so would indeed reinvent economic impact models. While it might assign economic value to social, personal, and community phenomena, it would no longer be capturing a strictly economic impact. Rather it would use economic (or other quantifiable) indicators to identify and measure a variety of societal impacts.

The most ambitious of the state or regional economic impact studies have another conceptual dimension. They are trying to develop an operational definition of the "cultural industry" or "cultural industries" in the American context, borrowing and adapting ideas from analytic techniques used in other countries (such as Canada) or in UNESCO (United Nations Educational, Scientific and Cultural Organization) reports. Economic impact studies are most effective for well-defined, subnational locales. For example, both California and New York/New Jersey are regions that have unusually high concentrations of artistically engaged workers, cultural activity, and cultural organizations and firms, and thus readily lend themselves to impact analysis. Studies that reach beyond the state/regional scope may approach the outer limits for valid economic impact analyses. There are conceptual problems in trying to extend economic impact approaches to the national level, so this effort would seem to hold little potential as a national measure of the impact of nonprofit arts organizations on society. Conversely, developing a conceptually and methodologically valid definition and a set of measures concerning American cultural industries might further our understanding of the interaction and interrelationship between nonprofit culture organizations and commercial activities in entertainment, leisure, recreation, and publishing (Chartrand, 2000). Such understanding might then provide valuable insights for policy makers as well as organizational planners. However, it would shift the focus from the nonprofit sector per se to intersectoral and cross-sectoral concerns.

Education Effect Studies

Over the past decade, increased attention to arts education has been propelled both by the national education reform agenda and by those specifically concerned with the arts and with arts education. These two forces have dovetailed through a multifaceted process of local action and attention to policy, so that the arts have won themselves a place on the education agenda. Drawing on a long educational tradition of concern with evaluation and outcomes, the educational impact or effect of the arts has been the subject of considerable research and assessment. A wide variety of methods, both quantitative and qualitative, have been employed to measure the educational effect of the arts (Welch & Greene, 1995). These methods include both broad-based and targeted program evaluations, research compilations and syntheses, public opinion and attitude surveys, and information on status and activity dimensions. Educational impact studies have looked at both short-term and long-term effects.

Studies of the educational impact of the arts and of arts education yield a complex set of indicators. Impact has been found in

- student achievement, as seen in standardized test scores and in grades and in a range of subjects
- improved student motivation, engagement in the learning process, and in self-discipline
- better attendance statistics
- the acquisition of both content knowledge and skills, such as communication (written and oral), critical thinking, imagination and creativity, and social interaction
- higher self-esteem
- increased cultural awareness
- the establishment of positive long-term attitudes toward arts participation and support

Ten years ago, there was little evidence of the educational impact of the arts beyond anecdote. Today there is a wealth and variety of impact evidence and analysis. However, because of this abundance, communicating the scale, scope, and significance of these impacts to a general public and to policy makers is difficult and cumbersome. Here, a priority would seem to be finding ways to synthesize and track these impacts over time and in relation to both positive and negative inputs.

Social Utility Impacts

This is actually something of a catch-all category that includes efforts to ascertain the impacts that the arts might have on health and medical treatment; on dealing with at-risk youth; in rehabilitating drug users and criminal offenders; in improving the quality of life and of products through design; in fostering community revitalization and integration; and on a host of other social utilities. A 1996 report of the President's Committee on the Arts and the Humanities and NALAA is illustrative (Weitz, 1996). The report, "Coming Up Taller: Arts and Humanities Programs for Children and Youth at Risk," documents a number of effects that cultural programs can have, including improving student achievement; expanding strategic alliances within a community; creating a safe place for learning; encouraging voluntary participation; improving cognitive learning and interest in learning; and increasing student motivation, resiliency, and organization. Alternatively, a 1994 California economic impact study included a case study of automobile design studios—and in the process provided an example of how product design was influenced by the arts (California Arts Council, 1994).

Still, the process of measuring the social utility impacts of the arts is in the preliminary stages. Several kinds of impacts or effects have been identified and numerous information-gathering efforts are under way to collect anecdotes and cases. However, it would seem that we are just approaching the point at which such anecdotes might be transformed into possible indicators so that methods might be devised to use these indicators to measure the social impact of the arts.

THE TASK AHEAD

Devising measures of the impact of the nonprofit arts on society is a complex, subtle task. Finding systematic, valid, and significant ways to document what is often regarded as implicit will itself require ingenuity and a multiyear, broad-based effort. It is likely to require a shift in focus and a specificity that may challenge the nonprofit arts. The shift in focus will be two-pronged: there will be a shift from gathering information about how social, political, and economic factors impact the arts to one concerned with how the arts impact society; at the same time, there will be a shift from information gathering to a greater emphasis on analysis and evaluation. The effort is also likely to require greater specificity along a complex matrix of dimensions that will require cross-cutting analysis and synthesis.

For example, there are many potential types and many possible targets of impact. Impact may be economic in character and be assessed using a number of possible indicators. Impact could also be educational, medical, political, technological, or social. What measure might be devised to capture the effect the arts have in communicating and embodying personal, community, and national identity or in reinforcing political values such as freedom of expression? Ironically, an entire dimension of impact—the artistic or aesthetic impact, which must include preservation, creative, performing/exhibiting, and appreciation components—is often so implicit that it is seldom measured. An important part of improving, assessing, and demonstrating the impact of the nonprofit arts on society will lie in devising specific measures for each of these types of impacts.

In addition, there are many possible targets of such impact. Individuals may be affected, as may organizations, fields, and professions. The scale of impact may be local, national, or even international. The impact may be immediate, long-term, or historical. Thus, another task involves adapting the measures of type of impact to different targets and time frames of impact. Even if all this is done, we may find ourselves with improved but nonetheless fragmented information that paints a composite picture incomprehensible to most people. Therefore, the ultimate goal for finding measures of the arts' impact on society may involve the design of a set of indexes that can effectively present all this information to a nonspecialist audience. Exploratory work on at least one aspect of indexing has been undertaken by a major arts consulting firm; it focuses on the development of a market demand index that can be used comparatively across communities or states and that is likely to be useful in cultural planning activities (Stevens, 1996b).

The concept of indexes, while new to the nonprofit arts, is well established in the American politico-economy. The economy takes for granted the sophisticated market research and economic statistics that are reflected in a Dow Jones Index, the gross national product, and the Consumer Price Index. We are equally familiar with the wind-chill factor, the humidity index, crime rate statistics, and education report cards. A lack of similar common parlance for cultural indexes helps perpetuate the virtual invisibility of the impact of the arts. Given the complexity of the task involved, a set of indexes is likely to be needed, perhaps one for organizational "health," another for economic impact, one for educational impact, and another for community effect. Maybe all of these can be combined into one grand index. Certainly, much remains to be done, if the implicit impact of the arts on society is to be revealed.

REFERENCES

Alliance for the Arts & Mayor's Advisory Commission for Cultural Affairs. (1992, March 27). *New York City's contribution to America's cultural life.* (Report to the Congressional Arts Caucus). New York: Alliance for the Arts.

Barsdate, K. J., & National Assembly of State Arts Agencies. (1996). *A state arts agency performance measurement toolkit.* Washington, DC: National Assembly of State Arts Agencies.

Baumol, W. J., & Bowen, W. G. (1966). *Performing arts: The economic dilemma.* Cambridge, MA: MIT Press.

California Arts Council. (1994). *The arts: A competitive advantage for California.* (Prepared by Policy Economics Group. KPMG Peat Marwick). Sacramento, CA: Author.

Chartrand, H. H. (2000). Towards an American arts industry. In J. M. Cherbo and M. J. Wyszomirski (Eds.), *The public life of the arts in America.* New Brunswick, NJ: Rutgers University Press.

Cobb, N. K., and President's Committee on the Arts and the Humanities. (1996). *Looking ahead: Private sector giving to the arts and the humanities.* Washington, DC: President's Committee on the Arts and the Humanities.

DiMaggio, P., & Kaple, D. (1996). Information on arts organizations: Some new opportunities. *Newsletter of Grantmakers in the Arts,* 7(2), 2–16.

DiMaggio, P., Useem, M., & Brown, P. (1977). *Audience studies of the performing arts and museums: A critical review* (NEA Research Report No. 9). Washington, DC: National Endowment for the Arts.

Filicko, T. (1996). In what spirit Americans cultivate the arts: Public opinion and the arts. *Journal of Arts Management, Law and Society,* 26(3), 221–246.

Filicko, T., & Lafferty, S. A. (1999). *Defining the arts and cultural universe: Early lessons from the profiles project.* Columbus, OH: Arts Policy and Administration Program, Occasional Paper #7.

Independent Commission. (1990, September). *A report to the Congress on the National Endowment for the Arts.* Washington, DC: Author.

Independent Sector. (1994). *Giving and volunteering in the United States.* Washington, DC: Author.

National Assembly of Local Arts Agencies. (1993). *Arts in the local economy.* Washington, DC: Author.

National Endowment for the Arts. (1985). *Surveying your arts audience (A research division manual).* Washington, DC: Author.

National Endowment for the Arts. (1992). *The arts in America, 1992: A report to the President and to the Congress.* Washington, DC: Author.

National Endowment for the Arts, & Jack Faucett Associates with John P. Robinson. (1993). *Arts participation in America: 1982–1992* (NEA Research Report No. 27). Washington, DC: National Endowment for the Arts.

National Endowment for the Arts & Westat, Inc. (1990, April). *A sourcebook of arts statistics: 1989.* Washington, DC: National Endowment for the Arts.

National Endowment for the Arts & Westat, Inc. (1992, May). *1992 addendum to the 1989 sourcebook of arts statistics.* Washington, DC: National Endowment for the Arts.

Port Authority of New York & New Jersey. (1983). *The arts as an industry.* New York: Author.

Port Authority of New York & New Jersey. (1993, October). *The arts as an industry: Their economic importance to the New York–New Jersey region.* New York: Author.

Radich, A. J. (Ed.). (1987, May). *Economic impact of the arts: A sourcebook.* Denver, CO: National Conference of State Legislatures.

Radich, A. J. (1993). *Twenty years of economic impact studies of the arts: An overview.* Unpublished research report sponsored by the NEA Research Division.

Renz, L. (1995). *Arts funding revisited.* New York: The Foundation Center.

Renz, L., & Lawrence, S. (1998). *Arts funding: An update on foundation trends* (3rd ed.). New York: The Foundation Center in cooperation with Grantmakers in the Arts.

Renz, L., Atlas, C., & Kendzior, J. (1999). *Arts funding 2000: Funder perspectives on current and future trends.* New York: The Foundation Center in cooperation with Grantmakers in the Arts.

Schwarz, S., & Peters, M. G. (1983). *Growth of arts and cultural organizations in the decade of the 1970s.* Rockville, MD: Informatics General Corporation.

Smith, J. K. (1993). *The economic impact of major exhibitions at the Metropolitan Museum of Art, the Museum of Modern Art, the Solomon R. Guggenheim Museum: Fall and winter 1992–93.* New York: Arts Research Center.

Stevens, L. (1996a). *Motivating opera attendance: Comparative qualitative research in 10 U.S./Canadian cities.* Marion, MA: ArtsMarket Consulting Inc.

Stevens, L. (1996b). *Too much product for the marketplace.* Paper presented at the Annual Conference on Social Theory, Politics, and the Arts, Montreal, Quebec.

Thompson, E. C., Berger, M. C., & Allen, S. (1998). *Arts and the Kentucky economy.* Louisville, KY: University of Kentucky Center for Business and Economic Research.

Weber, N., & Renz, L. (1993). *Arts funding: A report on foundation and corporate grantmaking trends.* New York: The Foundation Center.

Weitz, J. H. (1996, April). *Coming up taller: Arts and humanities programs for children and youth at risk.* Washington, DC: President's Committee on the Arts and Humanities and the National Assembly of Local Arts Agencies.

Welch, N., & Greene, A. (1995, June). *Schools, communities, and the arts: A research compendium.* Washington DC: National Endowment for the Arts and the Kennedy Center Education Department.

Wyszomirski, M. J. (1995, Autumn). Policy communities and policy influence: Securing a government role in cultural policy for the 21st century. *Newsletter of Grantmakers in the Arts,* 6(2).

Wyszomirski, M. J., & Standley, A. P. (1996, November). *NTEE/arts, culture and humanities: A preliminary profile and a draft manual* (Report prepared for the Aspen Institute and the National Center for Charitable Statistics). Cleveland, OH: Mandel Center for Nonprofit Organizations.

Chapter 13

The Emerging Status of Outcome Measurement in the Nonprofit Human Service Sector

Martha Taylor Greenway

Determining the separate and distinct contribution of the nonprofit human services sector is fraught with difficulty for a number of reasons. For one, such agencies are, more often than not, also recipients of government funding, generally a mixture of federal and state dollars from a federally legislated program. Consider, for instance, United Way—supported agencies as a microcosm of the nonprofit human services sector: government funding represents 45.7 percent of their total revenue. Thus, the distinction between public human services and private nonprofit is blurred from the outset.

Another reason for the difficulty is that the ultimate purpose of the nonprofit human services sector is to improve the condition of people. But people are affected by an infinite array of experiences, opportunities, organizations, and other people. Even the synergistic effects of these combinations of factors change as individuals move through time and across geographic boundaries. To specifically identify the contribution of any particular organization, or sector of organizations, toward measurable improvement in the lives of individuals is tricky business indeed.

MARTHA TAYLOR GREENWAY • Executive Director, Planning, Research, and Policy, Fulton County Schools, Atlanta, Georgia 30315.

Measuring the Impact of the Nonprofit Sector, edited by Patrice Flynn and Virginia A. Hodgkinson, New York, Kluwer Academic/Plenum Publishers, 2002.

Nonetheless, providers of human services increasingly realize that they must document the impacts of their programs on those who participate or risk losing in the competition for increasingly limited resources. Those agencies that successfully complete the assessment process often find that there are additional benefits, such as improving program performance, motivating staff, and recruiting high-caliber volunteers (Hatry, Van Houten, Plantz, & Greenway, 1996).

In the discussion here, I use the term "outcome" as opposed to "impact" because of the considerable disagreement in the human services sector about what impact means. Usages of "impact" range from an evaluation design—to control for non-program factors that may have caused the results (the definition used in the federal government)—to the effects of service interventions on community-level issues (a common lay use within the human services system).

Outcomes, as defined in *Measuring Program Outcomes: A Practical Approach* (Hatry et al., 1996), are benefits participants receive during or after their involvement with a program. Outcomes may relate to knowledge, attitudes, skills, behavior, values, condition, or status. Outcomes are distinct from outputs, which are defined as measures of the volume of a program's activities, such as the number of *units* of service, or number of people served.

Program outcomes are the results that accrue to participants in an individual program. *Community outcomes* are the cumulative results of a multiplicity of programs, policies, citizen efforts, and environmental factors upon the status of a certain issue, such as infant death rates. (Although the term "outcome" is slightly less ambiguous than "impact," definitions of the former are by no means universally agreed upon.)

CURRENT APPROACHES TO MEASURING OUTCOMES: SELECTED FINDINGS

Current efforts of nonprofit human services organizations to assess their outcomes fall into several broad categories. In the following pages, we will discuss these categories and consider examples of the types of efforts each category might include.

National Studies Using Experimental or Quasiexperimental Designs to Attribute Participant Outcomes to Program Activities

This type of study is conducted almost exclusively within national human services organizations, with their local affiliates serving as study sites. Such studies are generally financed by corporate or private foundations, often as part of a program grant. Examples of this type of study include the following:

1. The Child Welfare League of America (1995) has designed a study to profile child and youth participants in programs with various types of settings and services and to determine related outcomes. The League will track short-term outcomes, such as placements into less intensive settings, family reunification, educational achievement, and behavioral problems; and longer-term outcomes, such as employment, contacts with the juvenile and criminal justice system, and use of alcohol and drugs. It will assess measures at various intervals prior to service; at one-year intervals during service; at the end of service, and at 6 months, one year, and two years after service. Baseline assessments have been completed for more than 2,000 children and youth living in residential group care and therapeutic foster care. Analyses of outcome data will begin soon (Curtis & Norris, 2000).

2. Girls Incorporated evaluated the Friendly PEERsuasion Program. This program is intended to help middle-school girls learn about and practice making their own decisions, to resist peer pressure without losing friends, to find adult role models, and to become role models for younger children. The study assessed attitudes toward substance abuse, relationships with peers who used harmful substances, and the onset of use of harmful substances (cigarettes, alcohol, and drugs) (Jacobs, Nicholson, Plotch, & Weiss, 1993). It was conducted across four sites and involved a control group as well as pre- and posttesting. The assessment showed that the program reduced the incidence of drinking among participants and delayed the age at which they began drinking. Participants in the experimental group were also more likely to leave situations in which peers were using harmful substances and had less favorable attitudes toward drinking alcohol.

3. Another study of a Girls Incorporated program examined the effects of four, age-targeted program components on sexual activity, use of birth control, and pregnancy (Nicholson, Postrada, & Weiss, 1991). The three-year study was conducted at four sites and included 750 girls aged 12–17. Generally, the study found that the program reduced the incidence of intercourse, increased use of contraceptives for girls who were sexually active, and decreased the incidence of pregnancy.

4. Big Brothers Big Sisters of America evaluated an elementary-school-based, intergenerational-linkages program (Peterson, 1994). The program, conducted at eight local sites, matched 20 at-risk, elementary school children with 20 adults over age 55. The evaluation found an

increase in grades across all school subjects and increases in social and emotional growth (noted by the parent/guardian, the volunteer, and the teacher).

5. Public/Private Ventures, a private research and evaluation group, also evaluated the Big Brothers Big Sisters program (Tierney, Grossman, & Resch, 1995). At eight sites, this comparative study of 10- to 16-year-olds randomly assigned half of the 959 youth to an experimental group and the other half to a waiting list as a control group. Members of the experimental group were matched with mentors and the two groups were compared after 18 months. The study found that those with mentors were less likely to start using drugs or alcohol, were less likely to hit someone, had improved school attendance and performance, and had better peer and family relationships.

6. Education Resources Group (1996) conducted a study of a program to establish partnerships between local Girl Scout councils and science and technology museums around the country as a way to promote science interest among girls. The evaluation found that participants reported more positive attitudes toward science and continued an interest in science while in Scouting. Participants also reported remembering the specific science projects they worked on—even six or seven years after participating.

National Surveys of Local Program Participants to Assess Current or Retrospective Perceptions

In this assessment model, a national organization directly surveys a representative group of program participants from across the country.

1. The American Red Cross conducted client satisfaction surveys in nine State Service Councils and 78 chapters (Silva, 1995). Some services included assessments of service effectiveness. The chapters collaborated to collect data on customer satisfaction with major Red Cross services including: disaster services, emergency communications, first aid and cardiopulmonary resuscitation (CPR), lifeguard training and HIV/AIDS prevention education. Subjects for the study were drawn from participant lists at the chapters providing the services. Questions covered referral sources, service quality, satisfaction, and basic demographic information.

2. Louis Harris and Associates has conducted two studies for the Girl Scouts of the USA that fall into this category. The first study was conducted with a nationally representative sample of 1,284 junior, cadet,

and senior Girl Scouts; an over-sample of 463 girls from non-White racial and ethnic groups; and a comparison group of a national cross section of American girls (Brown & Conn, 1990). The evaluation found that Girl Scouts had better grades than the comparison group; were more actively involved in extracurricular activities; and were less likely to say that they would cheat on a test, engage in sexual activity, and drink alcohol. In the other Harris study, former Girl Scouts, who were named in *Who's Who of American Women* as adults, were asked about the impact of Scouting on their lives (Harris & Setlow, 1991). Some 82 percent said that Girl Scouting had had a positive effect on their ability to work with other people at the time; 80 percent said it had positively affected their self-confidence at the time. Some 69 percent said it had affected their moral values during their formative days, and 60 percent said it influenced their current moral values.

3. Louis Harris and Associates has also conducted two similar studies for the Boy Scouts of America. The first showed that men who are in Scouting for many years maintain higher ethical standards, attain higher educational levels, and show less antisocial behavior than do those with no Scouting background. The second studied a national random sample of 3,000 individuals, including parents and members of Cub Scouts, Boy Scouts, and Venturers for one program year. Results showed 95 percent of parents believed their Cub Scouts learned moral and ethical values in the program; and 88 percent of Boy Scouts said that Scouting taught them skills they would not have learned elsewhere.

National Assistance to Local Human Services Affiliates

Another emerging approach is for national organizations or trade groups to provide nonprofit human services agencies with the resources and models to monitor their own outcomes. This approach suggests that individual program managers regularly monitor the proportion of participants who benefit from the program. Such approaches do not expect local organizations to prove that their programs, alone, caused outcomes—that would require experimental designs using control groups. Clearly, one of the limitations to experimental types of studies is that they are impossible to maintain over time and they are too expensive and intrusive to be conducted in each program locality.

1. Several national human services organizations or associations have developed outcome-monitoring approaches for their affiliates. Ideally, a national experimental study is conducted that links an intervention to specific outcomes, and then monitoring tools are developed for local

sites. Big Brothers Big Sisters of America has developed such products for their affiliates, building on results of the Public/Private Ventures study cited earlier. *Program-Based Outcome Evaluation* helps local affiliates perform ongoing assessment of their impact on youth development (Big Brothers Big Sisters, 1998). The manual describes an overview of assessing outcomes, implementation, and ensuring quality data. Affiliates survey five key stakeholders in the mentoring relationship—the youth, the adult volunteer, the parent, the teacher, and the case manager—on 18 core indicators which can be adapted to local needs.

2. In 1997, Girl Scouts of the USA and SPEC Associates produced an *Outcome Procedures Manual* based on a national study of how well local Councils met the four main program goals. This manual provides councils with tools to help them mirror the national study, including sample surveys and guidance on implementation and sampling issues. Girl Scouts also offers Councils an Excel data entry disk, which is currently being revised, to facilitate analysis of local data and to produce graphs and charts that mirror the national study. New outcome measurement tools are in development, such as toolkits on resident camping and on the quality of the troop and group experience. Girl Scouts of the USA develops these tools through a three-way collaboration between their research staff, SPEC Associates, and local council staff.

3. Girls Incorporated has published *Assess for Success*, a manual that provides an overview of outcome measurement concepts, as well as instructions and data collection instruments (Frederick & Nicholson, 1991). Data collection is directed toward observing participants' behavior as well as surveying them and their parents about their success in meeting program goals. The instruments are specific to various program components and are age-appropriate so that even younger girls participating in the program can express their perceptions.

4. Boy Scouts of America has produced a *Guide to Outcome Funding for United Way* (1996). It was developed primarily in response to local United Ways' increasing requests for funded agencies to document program outcomes. This report includes definitions of outcomes versus outputs and examples of how outcomes of various Boy Scout programs can be defined.

5. Boys and Girls Clubs of America, along with Policy Studies Associates, created the *Outcome Measurement Toolkit*. Local Clubs conduct a standardized survey of youth participants to measure whether their programs are effective. Boys and Girls Clubs of America provides training on the Toolkit, offers an internet site for local clubs to enter surveys, and calculates results.

6. *Measuring Program Outcomes: A Practical Approach*, published by United Way of America (Hatry et al., 1996), is designed for any nonprofit human services agency that wants to develop an outcome measurement system. It includes a step-by-step process for identifying outcomes, indicators, and data collection methods as well as for reporting and using data. It does not include program-specific outcome indicators or data collection methods. In addition, many local human services agencies have developed sound outcome-monitoring approaches using local resources. *Measuring Program Outcomes: A Practical Approach* includes quotations and vignettes from more than 50 such organizations.

National Certification That Requires Outcome Measurement

Certification and accrediting bodies are increasingly reviewing how affiliates measure outcomes. One emerging force in this area is the funding of programs of nonprofit human services agencies through third-party insurance companies using a managed care provider. Agencies such as affiliates of Catholic Charities and the Alliance for Children and Families are facing this issue in the counseling and home health areas. In some cases, these *outcome* measures are being dictated by the managed care company—generally on the basis of little more than intuition about what the desired outcome might be. At this point, no standard, managed-care outcome measures have been promulgated for human services although several accrediting bodies have adopted standards for outcome measurement.

1. The Council on Quality and Leadership in Supports for People with Disabilities has defined outcome measures for services provided by its affiliate organizations and has published *Personal Outcome Measures* (2000). This manual describes the specific desired outcomes based on 3,000 interviews with people receiving services. It suggests how accredited agencies can assess these outcomes within their organizations and describes the Council's independent quality-review process for these outcome measures.
2. The Council on Accreditation for Children and Family Services evaluates agencies based on their compliance with nationally endorsed best practice standards—with client outcomes as a necessary component. Its *Standards for Behavioral Health Care Services and Community Support and Education Services* (1997) establishes performance measures and requires that agencies maintain data on program quality and client service quality. These standards are currently being revised to give agencies more flexibility in deciding what measures should be tracked. The

Council neither dictates how agencies should collect data nor endorses specific measurement tools.

3. The National Results Council has created a scorecard system for employment and training programs to enable stakeholders to compare results achieved by organizations based on national benchmarks for rehabilitation services. Using customized software to analyze client data, the Council adjusts for local conditions and provides feedback on program performance with state and national comparisons. Quarterly reports to participating agencies provide information to promote exchanging best practices.

Locally Developed Experimental Evaluations That Become National Models

This approach is rare. It occurs when a particularly sophisticated and resourceful local program manager develops an experimental design within a program, which then is replicated across the country.

An evaluation of the Families and Schools Together (FAST) program, developed by a Family Service affiliate in Madison, Wisconsin, used an experimental design and a random control group to show that the program improved parents' assessments of children's behavior, and children's maternal acceptance, self-competence, and peer acceptance (McDonald, 1995). The program was then implemented throughout Wisconsin and the outcomes were monitored via pre- and postmeasurement. Families participating in the program showed significant improvements in family functioning, and children in these families showed significant improvements in behavior. The program has been replicated nationally. All sites use the same outcome assessment tools, which are collected and analyzed nationally, and each site receives an individual report comparing its performance to national norms.

COMMON INDICATORS OF OUTPUTS AND OUTCOMES: POTENTIAL AND LIMITATIONS

Generally, output measures fall into one of two categories: products delivered or people served. Each is a typical measure of volume.

For example, measures of products delivered might be numbers of classes offered or of counseling sessions held; days of care provided or of camping offered; or how many brochures were distributed, public awareness messages aired, or the hours of tutoring.

Measures of people served reflect the unduplicated count of people who receive service over a given period of time. Obtaining an unduplicated count is not always possible. In programs where participants are anonymous (e.g., crisis hot lines or information and referral programs), or where interaction is limited and names are not given (e.g., at food pantries), an unduplicated count may not be possible.

With this exception, there are no intrinsic limitations to the currently used output measures. Their basic limitation is that they are not outcome measures. All they tell us is how much effort has been generated for how many people. They tell us nothing about whether this effort has made any difference.

I would add to these two basic types of output measures the following two, which are often put in separate categories: measures of participant satisfaction with the service and measures of participant characteristics.

Participant satisfaction can include perceptions of service accessibility; physical and cultural accessibility, timeliness of service delivery, staff courtesy, physical condition of facilities, and overall satisfaction with the service provider.

Participant characteristics include basic demographics such as age, income level, race/ethnicity, gender, marital status, area of residence, and source of referral. These characteristics are unique to each program and are determined by its service methodology and its funding and licensing requirements.

Participant satisfaction and participant characteristics are not outcome measures. They are necessary, however, for interpreting and acting on outcome data because they reveal why desired outcomes may not be achieved and whether programs have greater success with certain types of participants. Such information can explain why overall outcomes may be lower than for similar programs, or lower than expected, and can help program operators modify programs accordingly.

In considering outcomes, either at the program level or the community level, it is useful to recognize that outcomes are hierarchical—they often occur in a sequence, generally separated by time and participants' level of involvement with a program or service system. For example, an individual program seeking to increase the rate of healthy births may provide nutritional counseling to pregnant teens. The outcome of this action would be increased knowledge. This increased knowledge may result in a subsequent outcome of changed behavior. For instance, the pregnant teens may actually eat the proper foods; take a prenatal vitamin each day; and avoid cigarettes, drugs, and alcohol. These actions may, in turn, have the longer term outcome of producing healthy babies—babies who weigh more than 5.5 pounds and who are free of the effects of alcohol and drugs.

There are an infinite number of possible outcome measures in human services, some of which are shorter term, others of which are longer term. What may be a longer-term measure for one program—such as school achievement for a mentoring program—may be a short-term measure for another—such as school achievement for a job training and placement program.

Outcome measures usually fall into measures of values, attitudes, knowledge, skills, behavior, and conditions. A sample value outcome would be the belief that cheating on a test is wrong. An attitude outcome would be the recognition that school achievement is necessary to future success. A knowledge outcome would be a pregnant woman's ability to recite her daily nutritional requirements. A skill outcome would be the ability to read at the sixth-grade level. A behavior outcome would be use of verbal, rather than physical, means to resolve conflict. An outcome of condition would be residence in a permanent, independent setting.

Such outcome information is of tremendous benefit. The United Way of America's research on outcome measurement development (Hatry et al., 1996) revealed that human services agencies that successfully measured program outcomes were generally better able to achieve focus and clarity to guide their work. Understanding their current level of outcome achievement provides a barometer for assessing their progress, improving programs, and directing their future activities. Such information is a powerful motivator for staff, who can now observe the progress they are making with participants in a consistent, tangible manner. It is a powerful recruitment tool for volunteers, who have many other choices for spending their time. It helps position the agency in the community as a successful organization, which, in turn, increases visibility and financial support.

When funders and policy makers consider outcomes, they are most often interested in change in conditions. However, many individual programs are not able to track such outcomes. This is particularly true of early intervention or developmental programs, especially those dealing with children and youth. These programs can track knowledge, behavior, and skills that are commonly related to changes in certain conditions. For example, school achievement can be assumed to contribute to the condition of graduation. Focused, academically designed, longitudinal studies have demonstrated that the presence of certain positive influences and resources relate to lower rates of adolescent pregnancy, criminal arrests, and suicide, but few youth development organizations can track these longer term conditions for their participants.

The absence of comparable benchmarks also plagues the human services sector. For most program areas, there is no clear target for what *good* performance looks like. If a program working to move homeless families toward self-sufficiency places 20 percent of them in independent, self-supported living situations within a year, is this outcome abysmal or tremendous?

Another limitation to the outcome measures we have discussed is their scope—they focus on program success rather than community-level outcomes. For example, an individual program may have improved the health outcomes of babies born to teen participants, but that result alone will not necessarily effect community-level change on the outcome of healthy births. The number of babies affected by this program may be a statistical drop in the bucket when compared with the number of babies born in a given community.

Additionally, community outcomes are driven by more than the outcomes of individual human services programs. They are driven by collaborative efforts across programs and sectors that address such issues as physical and economic access to service and cultural sensitivity to participants. Community outcomes are affected by public policy, economic conditions, and the informal support systems of churches, families, neighbors, and civic groups.

One of the travesties that occurs in most examinations of community outcomes for human services is that they ignore the multitude of factors affecting outcomes and try to link inputs to a specific program strategy that has longer term, community outcomes. This action ignores the possible benefits that these strategies have on outcomes for individual program participants. Such outcomes may not be of sufficient scale to affect community outcomes, yet they may contribute to community outcomes (for instance, improving school attendance and increasing time spent on homework, which contribute to improved test scores and graduation rates). Alternatively, they may be countered by negative outcomes resulting from policies or economic factors in the community.

INDICATORS AND DATA SYSTEMS REQUIRED TO MEASURE OUTCOMES

Much work needs to be done to improve outcome measurement in human services. Much is being accomplished at the program level, and I believe that the state of the art will advance rapidly. The need is great for a means to share indicators and successful measurement methods. Currently, most nonprofit human services agencies are working in isolation on this task. It is unwise to adopt common outcomes for programs that deal with similar issues because the appropriate outcomes for each program are dictated by multiple factors including target population, service methodology, available resources, and the organization's overall mission. Nonetheless, it does not make sense for every program to start from scratch, especially in some of the areas that are more difficult to measure. In particular, organizations that are not supported by a national group could benefit from sharing information on successful outcome measurement approaches.

Ultimately, systems could evolve that provide both outcome measurement approaches and results. This would help to identify effective practices and to establish some comparative outcome measures among programs.

At the community level, we require systems that enable us to draw connections among outcome measures for individual programs and among community factors such as public policies, economic factors, and outcomes of informal service delivery systems and collaborative efforts. We need to first establish theories of change that tie all of these elements together into a comprehensive whole that can be practically expected to have the scope and influence required to affect community issues. Then we need to align the achievements of individual programs with the outcomes that we theorize are required for community change. This effort will build the bridge between individual program outcome measurement and community *milestone* or *benchmark* indicators, such as those developed in Portland, Oregon (Portland-Multnomah Progress Board, 1996).

IMPORTANT RESEARCH QUESTIONS

The following important questions remain as the nonprofit human service field moves forward in the implementation of outcome measurement. What else is known about effective, nonprofit human services outcomes from experimental or quasi-experimental studies? With this information, an outcome monitoring approach could be more confidently instituted as a basis for measuring human services outcomes. Yet, it is my impression that a lot of that knowledge is locked away in foundation files or consultant's closets. A review of knowledge that goes beyond the published data would be extremely beneficial.

What nonprofit human services organizations are monitoring their program outcomes now, and what are their results? This information would help identify and promote exchange of effective practices, outcome measurement approaches, and benchmarks. What is an appropriate theoretical framework for developing and monitoring systems of outcomes in communities and what methods can be utilized to gather and analyze outcome data about systems of outcomes?

Emerging efforts are underway to tackle these essential questions. However, unlike previous efforts that have been achieved largely by individual, nonprofit organizations working independently, these questions must be answered through collaboration, transfer of information, and willingness to openly compare and contrast outcomes among organizations. This, in turn, requires a culture that values use of outcome measurement for purposes of improvement rather than for purposes of accountability or sanction. Even if these behaviors and values are established, addressing these research questions will require dedication of time and effort. Hopefully, the perceived benefit of the answers to these questions will be great enough to outweigh these constraints.

REFERENCES

Big Brothers Big Sisters of America. (1998). *Program-based outcome evaluation (POE): A casework management approach to measuring outcomes in mentoring programs.* Philadelphia, PA: Author.

Boy Scouts of America. (1996). *Guide to outcome funding for United Way.* Dallas, TX: Author.

Brown, S., & Conn, M. (1990). *Girl Scouts: Who we are, what we think.* New York: Girl Scouts of the USA.

Child Welfare League of America. (1995). *The odyssey project: A descriptive and prospective study of children in residential treatment, group homes, and therapeutic foster care.* Washington, DC: Author.

Council on Accreditation for Children and Family Services. (1997). *Standards for behavioral health care services and community support and education services.* New York: Author.

Council on Quality and Leadership in Supports for People with Disabilities. (2000). *Personal outcome measures.* Towson, MD: Author.

Curtis, P., & Norris, L. (2000). *The odyssey project: Report #5—the odyssey project at baseline.* Washington, DC: Child Welfare League of America.

Education Resources Group. (1996). *Evaluation and follow-up of the National Science Partnership.* Princeton, NJ: Author.

Frederick, J., & Nicholson, H. (1991). *Assess for success.* Indianapolis, IN: Girls Incorporated.

Girl Scouts of the USA. (1997). *Outcomes procedures manual.* New York: Author.

Harris, L., & Setlow, C. (1991). *Girl Scouts: Its role in the lives of American women of distinction.* New York: Girl Scouts of the USA.

Hatry, H., Van Houten, T., Plantz, M., & Greenway, M. (1996). *Measuring program outcomes: A practical approach.* Alexandria, VA:. United Way of America.

Jacobs, L., Nicholson, H., Plotch, A., & Weiss, F. (1993). *It's my party: Girls choose to be substance free.* Indianapolis, IN: Girls Incorporated.

McDonald, L. (1995). *Evaluation report on the national replication of FAST (Families and Schools Together).* Milwaukee, WI: Family Service America, Inc.

Nicholson, H., Postrada, L., & Weiss, W. (1991). *Truth, trust and technology: New research on preventing adolescent pregnancy.* Indianapolis, IN: Girls Incorporated.

Peterson, D. (1994). *An evaluation of an elementary school based intergenerational linkages program: Mentoring for academic enrichment.* Philadelphia: Big Brothers Big Sisters of America.

Portland-Multnomah Progress Board (1996). *Portland/Multnomah benchmarks.* Portland, OR: Author.

Silva, S. (1995). *Client satisfaction survey results: Nine state survey.* Washington, DC: American Red Cross.

Tierney, J., Grossman, J., & Resch, N. (1995). *Making a difference: An impact study of Big Brothers/ Big Sisters.* Philadelphia: Public/Private Ventures.

Chapter 14

The Religious Dimensions
of Giving and Volunteering

ROBERT WUTHNOW

At present, approximately half of all charitable giving from individual donors in the United States goes to religious organizations, most of which use some of these funds for a wide variety of services to their communities. A substantial share of volunteer time is also donated to these organizations, and religious convictions are one of the primary motivations given for volunteering, prompting religiously involved people to give and volunteer at rates higher than the national average. For these reasons, measurement of religious commitment has become a significant aspect of recent research on the nonprofit sector (Wuthnow & Hodgkinson, 1991). This chapter examines the contribution that research, sponsored in recent years by the Independent Sector, has made to knowledge of the relationships among religion, giving, and volunteering. It then offers a critical assessment of this contribution and suggests ways to measure religious commitment that have proven helpful in other studies and that might be usefully incorporated into future work on the impact of giving and volunteering. Finally, several specific areas are identified in which further research might be especially valuable.

ROBERT WUTHNOW • Professor of Sociology and Director, Center for the Study of Religion, Princeton University, Princeton, New Jersey 08644.

Measuring the Impact of the Nonprofit Sector, edited by Patrice Flynn and Virginia A. Hodgkinson, New York, Kluwer Academic/Plenum Publishers, 2002.

A BRIEF OVERVIEW

As recently as the middle 1980s, little interest had been devoted to exploring the mutual relations between religion and the nonprofit sector. A comprehensive handbook of research on the nonprofit sector published in 1987, for example, contained no entry on the role of religion (Powell, 1987). Similarly, relatively little of the voluminous literature produced by sociologists and psychologists of religion focused on issues of giving or engagement in community service activities. The most prominent exceptions to this pattern were several Gallup surveys conducted during the late 1970s and early 1980s in which individual involvement in charities and service activities was shown to vary with levels of religious involvement, but it was unclear from such surveys whether the questions were simply tapping different ways of being involved in churches and synagogues (Gallup, 1982). It should be pointed out that little existed in the scholarly literature to suggest that religion did anything but promote charitable and philanthropic impulses. Nevertheless, research pinning down these relationships was sparse, and it failed to influence the wider literature that was beginning to focus on the nonprofit sector and its place in modern societies.

This lack of interest is surprising because Western religion has been regarded by historians as one of the principal contributions to the modern spirit of volunteering and philanthropy (Adams, 1986). Jewish and Christian traditions are replete with teachings about care for the poor, obligations to the community, and giving service to the needy. Although these teachings have not always been put into practice, they inspired the first European settlers in North America to establish relief chests and hospitals; to set up missions programs; and eventually to sponsor national benevolent associations, temperance societies, abolitionist organizations, and local congregations devoted to the needs of their members. As important as these efforts were, the tradition of free and competing religious organizations contributed even more to the creation of a public space in American society for the emergence of advocacy groups, fraternal orders, reform societies, and trade unions, all with no coercive powers and with different aims from business. It was from these secondary associations that the nonprofit sector in the contemporary United States emerged. Because of its historic pluralism, religion has continued to thrive in the United States, its combined membership reaching a high point in the 1950s and, since then, declining only modestly as a proportion of the population. With some 300,000 local congregations, American religion continues to be a prominent aspect of civil society in the United States. And with approximately 4 adults in 10 attending religious services in any given week, religious commitment appears to be higher in the United States than in virtually any other industrialized country (Verba, Schlozman, & Brady, 1995, p. 80).

The reasons for the specific disjuncture between researchers interested in religion and those interested in nonprofit organizations during the 1970s and early 1980s probably have more to do with academic specialties and institutional arrangements than with deeper intellectual convictions. Much of the policy-oriented research focusing on religion in these years was carried out by the research divisions of major religious bodies themselves, such as the Presbyterian Church, the Lutheran Church in America, and the Southern Baptist Convention, and much of this research focused on the beliefs and behavior of members of particular denominations. Through the National Council of Churches, annual statistics on financial giving were obtained from a number of denominations. Academic researchers interested in religion were organized in subfields that supported scholarly organizations like the Society for the Scientific Study of Religion, the American Academy of Religion, the Association for Sociology of Religion, and the Religious Research Association, all of which published their own journals. Many of these researchers taught courses in sociology or psychology of religion, looked to a long and outstanding tradition of theoretical thought within their own disciplines, or taught at seminaries or in colleges with confessional roots. Their research dealt frequently with the impact of religion on society, including such topics as race relations, attitudes toward the poor, prejudice, and views of government policies. The study of volunteering, voluntary associations, and nonprofit organizations was scattered during the 1960s and 1970s among researchers interested in such varied topics as secondary associations and mediating structures, formal organizations, game theory, and public policy, and it was often eclipsed by studies of political protests and social movements. As the study of the nonprofit sector began to emerge as a distinct subfield, it grew from these sources, from organizational theorists and economists, and at centers concerned with public management and fund raising and philanthropy. Few researchers on either side were familiar with what was happening on the other side.

Whatever the reasons, efforts to address more systematically the relationships between religion and nonprofits have emerged largely in the past decade, and they have been greatly facilitated by the work of Independent Sector. Under the direction of Virginia Hodgkinson and with input from the Religion Division of the Lilly Endowment (whose vice president was Robert Wood Lynn), deliberate efforts were made in the late 1980s to incorporate religious questions into research being initiated by Independent Sector and to make religious leaders more aware of their growing role the nonprofit sector.

The giving and volunteering surveys that were started in 1988, and conducted every two years thereafter, put religious participation in the wider context of other forms of voluntary participation and financial contributions. It was from these surveys that the magnitude of religion's role in the nonprofit sector became known. Compared with the arts, health, or education, far more giving and volunteering is devoted annually to religious organizations, and this proportion has remained high in recent years despite the view voiced recurrently in the media that religion and civic engagement are declining. Using relatively straightforward measures of participation, the giving and volunteering surveys also show that philanthropic activity and frequency of attendance at religious services are positively related to each other.

In addition, Independent Sector surveys of teenagers show that volunteering for a wide variety of causes is higher among young people who attend church, participate in a youth group, or are church members, than among other youth (Hodgkinson & Weitzman, 1992). As with some other kinds of organizational factors, there is also a contextual effect: young people whose friends are church members are more likely to do volunteer work than are young people whose friends are not church members, whether or not the individual respondent is a church member (my analysis). Independent Sector surveys of congregations have also generated valuable information on the broader social role of these organizations. Congregations overwhelmingly report involvement with such activities as community service, caring for the elderly, and visiting the sick.

CRITICAL ASSESSMENT

The giving and volunteering surveys were initiated after questions about religion had been asked in surveys for nearly half a century, so they were able to benefit from this previous research. Questions regarding religious preference and attendance at religious services have been asked in ways comparable to other surveys. In many surveys, the roughly one-third of the population that attends religious services fairly frequently is different enough from the approximately one-third who seldom or never attend so that crude measures of participation are sufficient. Simple measures of religious belief and motivation, it should be noted, sometimes add little to what can be determined from measures of participation. Put simply, the religiously inclined are more generous than the religiously disinclined. It is worth noting that generosity may also reinforce religious participation, although the causal direction has implicitly been assumed to be the opposite.

The reason for including subjective measures of religious belief in addition to religious participation is to be able to determine whether it is belief or practice that has the strongest impact on philanthropic behavior. In my research (Wuthnow, 1991), I compared people who registered the same level of subjective commitment to religion but who did or did not actually participate in religious services. This comparison showed that (a) participation had the strongest effect and (b) strength of subjective commitment had a positive effect on volunteering only among those who actually participated in a congregation. Although this pattern needs to be examined further, it is an important one because many more people in the United States claim to value religion than actually participate.

The main weakness of the giving and volunteering surveys is that they do not distinguish very well among specific types of religious involvement, and thus do not provide leaders with useful ideas about how to stimulate giving and volunteering, other than by heightening overall levels of religious participation. This lack is troublesome because other research suggests that religiously involved people may be giving a declining share of their family income to charitable causes, may be less loyal than in the past to specific congregations, may not understand stewardship very well, and may be joining congregations that focus on personal happiness instead of service or sacrifice. The difficulty in addressing these issues, of course, is that giving and volunteering surveys are already quite long.

Other research suggests that the inclusion of several simple questions could enhance the value of giving and volunteering surveys for understanding the relationship between religious participation and philanthropic behavior. One is a question about participation in small fellowship groups within congregations, such as Bible study groups or prayer fellowships. By chance, the 1988 Giving and Volunteering survey questions were given to the same respondents who had answered a set of questions (for another sponsor) that included one about small groups. This question proved to be a strong predictor of charitable behavior, even when church attendance and standard demographic factors were controlled (Wuthnow, 1994a, Chapter 11).

In assessing the impact of charitable behavior, it would also be helpful to know if people who do volunteer work in religious organizations make friends, come to understand the value of these organizations, develop a sense of ownership, and thus become more committed to participating in them for longer periods of time. Some qualitative evidence suggests that people who volunteer for service activities at their churches or synagogues find ways to transcend themselves, to receive the personal support they need in times of crisis, and to become stronger individuals and more effective citizens (Wuthnow, 1995).

Another suggestion is to include questions about having heard a stewardship sermon, receiving a pledge card, being asked to serve on a committee, or participating in a class focusing on giving and volunteering. Other research shows that these deliberate activities in churches make a significant difference in philanthropic behavior. People who are asked to volunteer often do so, as do people who are exposed to stewardship sermons and pledge drives (Wuthnow, 1994b).

Questions about religious beliefs and motivations are more difficult to conceptualize. Some observers argue that religion generates guilt, from which giving springs, while others argue that gratitude is a stronger source of motivation. Some attention might be paid to these attitudes. A different picture of motivation that comes from qualitative research emphasizes its connections with narratives. People need to hear stories that encourage good deeds, and they need to see people enact these stories and then have stories of their own to tell. Simple questions about knowing the story of the Good Samaritan or being inspired by the example of Mother Teresa are useful predictors of giving and volunteering. Also, stories are scripts that spark the imagination both to be or to refrain from being generous. Stories heard in religious organizations about people being helped can be positive motivators; stories of corruption can have the opposite effect. Some survey questions have been developed that ask people directly if they would be more or less likely to give under various circumstances, for example, if they had more information about how their church spent its money if the clergy talked more about money or if the clergy preached better sermons. The implication of these studies for measuring the social impact of nonprofit behavior is that charitable practices are processes that cannot be reduced to simple cause–effect models. An important aspect of altruistic behavior is that people develop understandings of it that permit them to continue engaging in it; that is, its impact is to sustain other charitable behavior over a period of time. Personal narratives, role models, and supportive environments help to reproduce philanthropic activities.

For tracking change in the impact of nonprofit activity on religion, three areas of inquiry recommend themselves: size of congregation, length of time in the congregation, and religious orientation (liberal, moderate, or conservative). At present there is much speculation about the possibility of small congregations dying and being replaced by large congregations (including "megachurches" of 5,000 to 10,000 members). It seems likely that change in the average size of congregations will take place, but it is unclear what the effect of such change may be on giving and volunteering. Some observers fear that large congregations will generate more "free riders" who do nothing to help, while other observers believe large congregations can provide more attractive opportunities for service. It is also unclear whether time and money given to large organizations have the same social benefit as similar contributions to small organizations; certainly the majority of the public believes that smaller organizations are preferable.

The duration-of-involvement question is important because some research suggests that people are shopping around and changing churches more often. Again, the implications for giving and volunteering are unclear: switchers may be more motivated to help others through their newfound congregation, but the "repotting" thesis suggests that they may take longer to sink roots and become involved.

The religious orientation question is useful partly because it has been asked in national surveys since 1984 and can thus track trends about polarization in American religion (the question is a six-point scale asking people to identify their own religious views from "very conservative" to "very liberal" [Wuthnow, 1996]). Religious conservatives appear to give more generously than do moderates or liberals; this question is an efficient way of assessing such differences.

Congregational surveys have been of more limited value than the giving and volunteering studies because of low response rates and because cooperating churches have been promised that their denominational identities will not be revealed. The inability to distinguish Catholic and Protestant congregations is especially problematic. Nevertheless, these surveys need to be continued and refined. They are the only national surveys available that make it possible to compare large numbers of congregations as far as service activities are concerned. With data from geographic information systems now available, it should be possible to connect the responses from congregations with information about the communities in which these congregations are located and thus to assess the impact of their activities more directly. Such information could be especially valuable in determining the effects of neighborhood conditions on churches' abilities to carry out their programs. For example, church programs could be compared for low-income and more affluent communities; services could be compared with the needs of local populations, such as the need to reduce crime, poverty, or teen pregnancy, or to serve elderly residents.

Short of an ambitious national survey of congregations, a research effort might be launched to monitor the activities of particular congregations or communities over an extended period of time in order to determine their impact. The effort to study Muncie, Indiana, in the 1980s, as a half-century follow-up to the "Middletown" research conducted there in the 1930s, is a commendable example (Caplow, Bahr, & Chadwick, 1983). Metropolitan areas, such as Indianapolis and Philadelphia, which have developed extensive geographic information systems data for identifying churches and other community agencies, might be targeted for follow-up in the future.

Another need is to develop measures for assessing the changing role of clergy as opinion leaders in the field of philanthropy. Given their prominence in local congregations, it is curious that no periodic surveys are conducted to ask about such topics as stewardship, the poor, or social justice. Asking clergy about the sermons they preach, about giving, about their views toward money, and their understanding of doing God's work could be a valuable addition to such information from laity.

Because research has been especially concerned with monitoring overall trends in giving and volunteering in the U.S. population, little effort has been directed, thus far, to studying special populations in which philanthropy is especially strong. In conjunction with national surveys, special studies might be commissioned among Jews or Mormons, for example, to examine why and in what ways giving and volunteering differs in these communities. Independent scholars might also be encouraged to use standard questions from national surveys to explore patterns in local congregations. The results of such research could provide models that other communities might attempt to employ.

One of the difficulties with replicating the Giving and Volunteering surveys in other studies, and, thus, assessing the impact of charitable behavior on other attitudes and activities, is that the basic questions are overwhelmingly complicated and time-consuming. They cannot be administered by telephone because of the need for hand cards, and the division of giving and volunteering into so many functional areas and for different time periods makes it hard to administer questions in brief interviews. Urgently needed are survey questions that can be asked efficiently. A principal recommendation of this essay is that Independent Sector experiment with such questions in order to see which ones most closely approximate the results of its current surveys.

Another recommendation is that greater attention be devoted to exploring the civic dimension of religion and volunteering. At the moment, religion's positive effect on philanthropy is assumed to lie in organizational and altruistic factors. The quintessential religious altruist is the individual helper who visits the sick or gives money to an organization that makes such visits. Yet most religious teachings recognize the importance of also working to change social conditions that may be unjust. Without duplicating the work of national election studies, some effort should be devoted to questions about such "volunteer" activities as writing petitions, supporting candidates, participating in planning meetings, attending the PTA, and supporting public interest groups. Such issues are of particular value for understanding the changing religious contribution to philanthropy because many religious organizations now appear to be directing more of their energies toward civic action than toward ameliorative programs.

It should be noted that some promising work has already been done in which the effects of religious organizations and a variety of other community organizations are compared in terms of their capacity to generate civic skills, such as knowing how to lead a meeting, understanding democracy, or having information about political resources and community needs. Although most associations had a positive effect on civic skills, this effect was generally much weaker among disadvantaged people than among people of privilege. The single exception was churches. In religious organizations, the learning of civic skills was more egalitarian (Verba et al., 1995).

Overall, the work of Independent Sector has provided more information than has been thoroughly utilized in secondary analysis, so more should be done to exploit the available data. But the data's value could also be enhanced, especially by including some of the short questions that have been suggested here. Most of the research to date has also assumed, implicitly at least, that religious belief and practice were useful as predictors of other kinds of philanthropic behavior. Turning the question around is a matter of urgent importance: to what extent does the nonprofit sector have an impact on religious participation?

The most interesting aspect of this question is whether opportunities for giving and service to secular nonprofit organizations erode the capacity of religious organizations to secure commitment, or whether the two are able to work in harmony. Clergy and lay leaders complain that it is harder to raise money because parishioners are making donations to colleges and universities, and youth pastors often point out the difficulties of evoking involvement in church activities among teenagers because of soccer schedules and mandated community service activities in schools. Some evidence, however, suggests that secular nonprofits have augmented religious activities, if anything. For instance, studies of association memberships generally show that members of virtually all other kinds of associations are also more likely to be church members than are nonmembers. Similarly, a long-term study of public and private education and health care in the United States showed that sectarian colleges and hospitals grew as other private and public organizations grew (Freeland, 1992).

The other issue that bears careful examination is the impact of information about fund raising on the ways in which religious organizations engage in their own stewardship campaigns. Historically, religious organizations have imitated corporations in the ways in which national offices were established, and, in recent decades, religious organizations have responded to government initiatives. It appears that churches and synagogues have also been influenced for some time by the work of fraternal orders, service organizations, and charities. For instance, there was little emphasis on stewardship as a distinct theological concept in many churches until the early twentieth century, when service organizations started to compete with churches. At present, religious fundraising drives are often carried out by the same public relations firms that conduct drives for universities and other secular nonprofits. Some observers argue that these drives are more effective as a result of utilizing such expertise; others argue that the distinctive appeal of religious values may be lost in the process.

As some of these remarks suggest, it is also important to consider the impact of the nonprofit sector on religion in a historical and comparative framework. In a highly secular society such as the United States, a large and semiautonomous nonprofit sector may be a significant resource for religious organizations. Alliances can perhaps be formed to promote the interests of secular and religious nonprofits alike in their relationships with government and business. Religious leaders have jealously guarded separation of church and state as a way of promoting freedom of religious expression, and this tradition may be strengthened as other nonprofits also worry about government incursions. The line between nonprofits and for-profits is often less distinct, but it is often assumed that nonprofits uphold values that cannot (or should not) be reduced to questions of profitability (Weisbrod, 1988). If this assumption is correct, then a healthy nonprofit sector is likely to benefit religion as well.

SUGGESTIONS FOR FURTHER RESEARCH

The foregoing suggests the importance of continuing to monitor involvement in giving and volunteering as a way of tracking changes in crucial aspects of religious and nonsectarian philanthropic behavior. As national surveys are replicated over a period of years, it will be possible to assess more carefully the impact of such factors as changing economic and political conditions as well as the entry and exit of birth cohorts. The paucity of regular trend data provides a compelling argument for continuing to ask basic questions that have been included in these surveys since the late 1980s.

However, changing social conditions, as well as having thoroughly explored some aspects of giving and volunteering, also argue for initiating several kinds of studies that have hitherto been neglected. The most important research question needing to be addressed concerns the changing organizational forms through which giving and volunteering are carried out, including the ways in which these organizations are connected with one another. What I have in mind as examples are partnerships such as interfaith coalitions, community development initiatives that bring public and private nonprofit organizations together, and volunteer organizations that function as referral networks for clients by linking them to a variety of services.

The standard imagery of volunteer organizations emphasizes the stand-alone nonprofit corporation or secondary association that enlists the resources of individuals in order to provide a clearly delineated menu of services. A local religious congregation is one such example. Others might include a local chapter of Rotary or Kiwanis, a scouting troop, or a shelter for abused women and children. Standard ways of asking survey questions reinforce this imagery by dividing the nonprofit sector into functionally specific segments such as religion, education, or youth.

But qualitative research shows that these kinds of organizations are increasingly engaged in diverse partnerships with other organizations and that newer, less clearly defined organizations are also an important part of the voluntary arena. For instance, a community resource center in Houston provides inner-city residents with an array of services, ranging from job training and youth programs to day care and family counseling. It was founded by a large African American church which continues to be a source of volunteers, but it is a separately incorporated entity with its own budget and is connected to many other service agencies in the area. Another example is a violence prevention organization in the Lehigh Valley (Pennsylvania) that came into existence five years ago to fight violence in public schools. It is a skeleton operation consisting of four regular volunteers whose efforts are occasionally multiplied by a hundred (to help with special events) but who work mainly to coordinate flows of information among school administrators, concerned parents, the media, local churches, and the department of human services.

One of the clearest lessons that emerges from examining newer organizations, networks, and alliances is that service activities are successful, not just when they enlist large numbers of volunteers, but when they are smarter in their use of volunteer time, especially in putting together the right people with the right skills at the right times. In the case of the Houston organization, being separately incorporated is beneficial for obtaining funds from government as well as from private donations, but maintaining an interlocking directorate with the church is helpful in recruiting volunteers from its membership. In the violence prevention program, minimal and sporadic volunteer time is used maximally by planning high-profile media events and by utilizing the resources of paid staff at schools and the human services department.

Understanding the impact of nonprofit organizational structures and networks is best accomplished by research that examines the entities directly through participant observation or that surveys directors, coordinators, and other informed sources within these organizations. Such studies are best conducted with the community context clearly in mind so that questions can be asked about relationships with other organizations. A specific strategy would be to develop a preliminary list of all nonprofit organizations in a community, to solicit information from informed sources in these organizations about activities and the numbers of clients and volunteers, and then to repeat the process for organizations identified in the first step.

It is also possible to conceive of including a battery of questions in national giving and volunteering surveys aimed at improving our understanding of the organizational dimension of philanthropic activity. Individual volunteers might be asked to answer questions about the number of other volunteers with whom they actually work, the total number who volunteer for the organization, the number of paid staff with whom they interact, and the range of other organizations they come into contact with through their volunteering.

Such preliminary efforts could provide a basis on which to conduct more intensive research aimed at determining the kinds of interorganizational networks that are most effective and the resources needed to sustain these networks. As in the private for-profit sector, a dynamic mix of large and small organizations, wholly owned subsidiaries and independent suppliers, and specialists as well as generalists is probably key to a strong nonprofit sector. Understanding the complexity of this mix is an essential next step in any overall research agenda.

Clearly, the study of volunteers' relationships with complex organizational networks extends well beyond questions of religion itself. The reason this topic is of special importance to the measurement of religion's role in the voluntary sector is that the organizational character of American religion has been changing dramatically in recent years. Typically, the local congregation and denominational offices or interdenominational federations comprised its structure, but increasingly it is working through special interest groups, parachurch agencies, and semiautonomous partnerships with secular nonprofits. The implications of these changes have not yet been fully explored.

A second high-priority item is research focusing specifically on the increasingly diverse racial, ethnic, and religious character of the American population. This diversity has grown significantly during the past three decades as a result of relaxed U.S. immigration policies, political and economic hardships in many parts of the world, and above-average birth rates among some minority populations. Asian American, Hispanic, and African American populations have increased relative to the size of the White European-American population. Religious diversity in the United States includes larger numbers of Muslims, Hindus, and Buddhists, as well as greater eclecticism in styles of spirituality. The challenge posed by this diversity for research on giving and volunteering is twofold: first, to understand more about the philanthropic practices of new immigrant and other ethnic groups themselves and, second, to learn more about nonprofit organizations devoted to bridging racial and ethnic divisions.

A number of strategies can be identified for addressing these issues. Of course, one is to over sample Hispanics and African Americans, as has been done in some of the previous giving and volunteering surveys. Another is to commission surveys parallel to the national Giving and Volunteering survey in metropolitan areas with highly diverse ethnic populations, such as Los Angeles, Houston, New York City, or Miami. In addition, qualitative research is needed among foundations and leaders of community agencies to determine what is proving most effective in healing tensions among racial and ethnic groups. As a first step, a conference that brings researchers and representatives of various groups and communities together could be enormously valuable.

This research item is of particular importance to questions of religion because the new ethnic diversity offers an opportunity to examine the effects of different religious beliefs and practices on giving and volunteering, thereby also enhancing knowledge about the distinctive ways in which majority religious communities function. In addition, religious organizations remain relatively homogeneous at the local level but are becoming more diverse at regional and national levels. Their financial well-being is thus affected significantly by changing memberships. The new diversity is also likely to affect the economic composition of religious bodies. For example, Catholic parishes are absorbing large numbers of lower income Hispanics and are experiencing tensions involving the expectations of middle-income members; African American churches are facing different ideas of giving as they shift away from traditional mutual-aid models to embrace a more diverse mix of inner-city and suburban members; and Asian American churches are sometimes divided over supporting traditional denominational activities or restricting giving to local ministries.

Finally, at a more narrow level of analysis, research is needed to improve understanding of how individuals develop and maintain a portfolio of charitable interests and activities over the course of their lifetime. Some evidence has been obtained from previous giving and volunteering surveys, including ones conducted among teenagers, to suggest the continuity among parental influences, early socialization, and adult volunteering, as well as between the effects of participation in high school clubs and community service projects. There is also some evidence that giving and volunteering varies with cohorts and over the life cycle as a result of changing family and work demands on time and personal finances. Despite this research, little is known about how individuals actually change, because few studies have tracked people over a period of years.

The more important reason for emphasizing life-course research, however, is that major changes in social conditions are making it harder for Americans to join service organizations that enlist their volunteering over a long period of time or enable them to give in regular, planned ways. These changes include the fact that growing numbers of Americans divorce and remarry, move from community to community, change jobs, undergo major shifts in their careers or lines of work, make new friends in more diverse places, and change their political and religious loyalties. These changes are reinforced both by the general freedom that an affluent market economy provides and by the uncertainties that face businesses, governments, and communities. For many Americans, it becomes neither possible nor desirable to make long-term commitments. In volunteering, they make short-term and sometimes impulsive commitments, and in the future an increasing amount of their overall volunteer time may be concentrated in particular periods, such as teenage or retirement years. The impact of giving and volunteering is likely to be enhanced if ways can be found to integrate these actions effectively with the changing characteristics of individual lifestyles.

The implications for religious organizations is that programs may need to be geared more deliberately toward sporadic, short-term commitments, on the one hand, and particular age groups, on the other hand, in order to be effective. To some extent, religious organizations have much to teach other volunteer agencies because they have long recognized the importance of these life-cycle patterns. However, it is not clear that any organizations have been very effective in encouraging potential volunteers and donors to actually think in these terms.

Research on religious socialization and development does provide clues about the issues that need to be understood. One is the need for giving and volunteering to be seen as a vehicle for personal growth. Many people, in fact, mention personal growth as a motivation for altruistic behavior. An important question to consider more deeply is the following: What kinds of growth are important at different stages of life? Developmental models focusing on faith stages and moral reasoning provide insight into the ways in which people arrive at deeper understandings of their own motives and commitments to service. Another idea reflects the importance of journaling and other forms of storytelling in spiritual development. Altruistic behavior also needs to be a self-reflective process that involves narrative constructions. These stories help reveal ways in which parental models, teachers, pastors, and other significant figures shaped one's views. Finally, many such stories focus on debts incurred to others and thus heighten the need to "pay back" one's family, church, or community.

These last remarks necessitate a concluding observation about the more general issue of methodology. Most foundations and government agencies recognize the value of scholarly research and, for this reason, devote a portion of scarce programmatic funds to the support of such research. Yet there is a wide range of methodological styles from which to choose. These styles have, in fact, been the subject of intense scrutiny within the past decade by researchers, themselves. Some researchers are deeply committed to the value of work that imitates studies in the natural sciences while others are skeptical of such studies. The foregoing suggests that different styles of research are needed to address different kinds of questions. Systematic quantitative data drawn from surveys can be enormously useful, but so can qualitative studies of organizations or of individual biographies and personal narratives. To focus on measurement may be taken as an indication that only quantitative measures are desirable. Yet, quantitative work has always been strongest when shaped by previous research involving participant observation and in-depth interviews, and the results of statistical studies can generally be interpreted more effectively in light of qualitative research. The next generation of research will need to use all of these styles in strategic combinations, and foundation leaders must be prepared to understand, learn from, and support these various research strategies.

REFERENCES

Adams, J. L. (1986). *Voluntary associations.* Chicago: Explorations Press.

Caplow, T., Bahr, H. M., & Chadwick, B. A. (1983). *All faithful people: Change and continuity in Middletown's religion.* Minneapolis: University of Minnesota Press.

Freeland, E. P. (1992). *The dynamics of nonprofit and public organizational growth in health care and higher education: A study of U.S. states, 1910–1980.* Unpublished doctoral dissertation, Department of Sociology, Princeton University, Princeton, NJ.

Gallup, G. (1982). *Religion in America: 1982.* Princeton, NJ: Princeton Religion Research Center.

Hodgkinson, V. A., & Weitzman, M. S. (1992). *Volunteering and giving among American teenagers 12 to 17 years of age: Findings from a national survey.* Washington, DC: Independent Sector.

Powell, W. (Ed.). (1987). *The nonprofit sector: A research handbook.* New Haven, CT: Yale University Press.

Verba, S., Schlozman, K. L., & Brady, H. E. (1995). *Voice and equality: Civic voluntarism in American politics.* Cambridge, MA: Harvard University Press.

Weisbrod, B. A. (1988). *The nonprofit economy.* Cambridge, MA: Harvard University Press.

Wuthnow, R. (1991). *Acts of compassion.* Princeton, NJ: Princeton University Press.

Wuthnow, R. (1994a). *Sharing the journey.* New York: Free Press.

Wuthnow, R. (1994b). *God and Mammon in America.* New York: Free Press.

Wuthnow, R. (1995). *Learning to care.* New York: Oxford University Press.

Wuthnow, R. (1996, August). Restructuring of American religion: Further evidence. *Sociological Inquiry, 66,* 303–329.

Wuthnow, R., & Hodgkinson, V. A. (Eds.). (1991). *Faith and philanthropy.* San Francisco: Jossey-Bass.

Part **V**

Conclusions

The final section reminds us of why it is important to develop a research agenda and precise empirical tools to measure the impact of the nonprofit sector. Paul DiMaggio and Burton Weisbrod present ideas on how to approach the exercise, some pitfalls to avoid, and the potential rewards.

DiMaggio (Chapter 15) is equally cautious about the downside of instrumental rationality, the "sacred cow" of modern culture, which manifests itself in our emphasis on performance assessment, cost-benefit analysis, and the pursuit of efficiency. Defining it as "the systematic attempt to understand and act upon one's understanding of systems of cause and effect," the author warns us that the instrumental rationality approach may be ill-suited to measuring the impact of the nonprofit sector in which goals are heterogeneous. Nonetheless, he concludes that the ritual of applying rational techniques "may move people to self-improvement and cooperative action, thus enhancing the collective capacity of organizations and industries to achieve collective goals."

DiMaggio lists three impediments to impact measurement. First is the lack of a causal model of the relationship between goals and the factors that lead to their achievement. Like firms in the for-profit sector, nonprofit organizations know little about the relationship between indicators and future performance either in the short or long term. Further difficulties are related to the fact that individual organizations have only a modest influence on the social objectives they are designed to address (e.g., eradicating poverty), making it nearly impossible for a single organization to be successful. Conversely, aggregate measures of performance may conceal the heterogeneous nature of the universe of nonprofits pursuing different strategies.

The second impediment reflects the political disincentives for organizations to provide necessary information to conduct sectoral assessments and to test the causal model. Concerns about what the information might "indicate" or how it will be used make organizations reticent to comply to measurement surveys. The third problem addresses institutional constraints on the available information that will vary in quality and structure among nonprofit subsectors. Together, these problems "conspire against us" and limit our ability to measure what we mean to measure or mean to serve as a basis for policymaking.

However, the ritual of trying to calculate the impact of nonprofit subsectors may be fruitful, concludes DiMaggio, because of its power "to bring people together, to define identities, and to move people to seek change . . . [through] a kind of religiously infused social movement." Specifically, the exercise may help the sector clarify its objectives, focus the attention of managers and trustees on their organizations' missions, provide a nonthreatening context in which different parts of the sector coalesce, and generate new and potentially valuable research.

Weisbrod (Chapter 16) provides an insightful overview of the need for carefully developed evaluations of the nonprofit sector as a whole, obstacles in the process, and proposed approaches. The focus of his inquiry is the degree to which the expansion of the nonprofit sector, over the past three decades, is economically efficient and desirable. Weisbrod advises caution when attempting to measure sectoral outputs and outcomes. The danger, he argues, stems from the fact that nonprofit organizations are more likely than for-profit firms to provide outputs that are difficult to value and, hence, to measure. A flawed attempt at measurement would yield a systematic underestimation of nonprofits' social contribution.

Despite the difficulties, Weisbrod argues that the exercise is critical for a number of reasons. First, throughout American history the nonprofit sector has not been granted the justification (or status) held by privately owned, for-profit enterprises. Therefore, when nonprofits clash with private firms, the nonprofit organization "is on the defensive to demonstrate its social value." Solid evidence that nonprofits make a difference and that they perform economically viable functions not afforded by private firms or government would clarify the unique role of nonprofits in society. A second rationale stems from the increased blurring of lines between for-profit and nonprofit activities, which begs the question as to whether nonprofits are acting more like for-profit firms and thus forfeiting their claim to special status and privilege. Solid evidence on the contributions, successes, and uniqueness of the nonprofit sector could help inform the ongoing debate about the organization of society into the three distinct sectors of government, business, and nonprofits.

Chapter 15

Measuring the Impact of the Nonprofit Sector on Society Is Probably Impossible but Possibly Useful

A Sociological Perspective

PAUL DiMAGGIO

Although we often contrast the cool scientific temperament of modernity to the superstition, ignorance, and magical thought of premodern eras, modern culture is notable less for the degree to which ritual and myth are important than for the kinds of myths and rituals that have been substituted for the religious and nationalist orthodoxies of the past (Meyer, 1988). As Weber foresaw in *The Protestant Ethic*, first published in 1904, the most powerful of modern icons is "rationality," the deliberative, instrumental orientation that Weber warned would confine humanity within "an iron cage" until "the last ton of fossilized coal is burnt" (Weber, 1958, p. 181). Impelled by economic competition, sponsored by state bureaucrats and policy elites, supported by an indus-

PAUL DiMAGGIO • Professor, Department of Sociology, Princeton University, Princeton, New Jersey 08544.

Measuring the Impact of the Nonprofit Sector, edited by Patrice Flynn and Virginia A. Hodgkinson, New York, Kluwer Academic/Plenum Publishers, 2002.

try of consultants, techniques aimed at maximizing instrumental rationality—by which I mean the systematic attempt to understand and act on one's understanding of systems of cause and effect—have proliferated (Meyer & Gupta, 1994). Today, the United States is a society in which cost–benefit analysis, performance assessment, and the pursuit of efficiency represent a cultural system that is as much taken for granted and as tightly linked to society's most powerful institutions as was Buddhism in medieval Japan or the divine right of kings in early modern France (Meyer, Boli, & Thomas, 1987; Dobbin, 1994).

This chapter analyzes the practical implications of the quasi-religious—or at least deeply culturally embedded—character of the contemporary emphasis on performance assessment. I should make clear that I am a big fan of instrumental rationality and in my own managerial practice attempt to use information systematically to align actions with goals. The problem is not with the impulse or the basic idea of performance assessment, but with the cultural embedding of that impulse, which animates rational technique with what Roy (1954), the organizational sociologist, long ago referred to as "sentiments of rationality." As I shall argue, the bad thing about sentimental commitments to rationality is that they lead us to expect rational techniques to work in situations to which they are profoundly ill suited. The good thing about the quasi-religious quality of rationality-enhancing techniques such as performance assessment is that even when the techniques fail, the ritual of their application, like any successful ritual, may move people to self-improvement and cooperative action and so enhance the capacity of organizations or industries to achieve collective goals. Thus the verdict of this chapter's title—sectoral performance assessment is impossible but possibly useful.

The first part of the chapter explains why we cannot say very much—at least not very much that should be taken seriously on scientific grounds—about the performance of the nonprofit sector. The reasons are many and include those that make performance assessment hard to apply even in single business organizations (where a focus on profitability makes it easiest), as well as those that result when one tries to assess the performance of fields (such as nonprofit subsectors) in which goals are multiple at the organizational level and heterogeneous for the industry as a whole.

The second part of the chapter explains why the effort to measure the impact of the nonprofit sector (or, more realistically, of nonprofit subsectors) is valuable even if, in a scientific sense, it is doomed and somewhat risky. My conclusion, "one cheer for sectoral performance assessment," is that the effort is worthwhile but for reasons that are somewhat inconsistent with prevailing views and only if one does not expect more than the exercise can deliver.

WHY MEASURING THE IMPACT OF THE NONPROFIT SECTOR IS PROBABLY IMPOSSIBLE

The chief impediments to impact measurement include the fact that we cannot assess impact without having better causal models than we possess, a problem that applies alike to for-profit and nonprofit sectors and consists of several technical entailments; political disincentives for organizations to provide information necessary for sectoral assessment; and institutional constraints on the information it is possible to collect, even if organizations are inclined to provide it. I shall discuss each in turn.

The Lack of a Causal Model

Much policy discussion, especially during political campaigns, is anecdotal. Conclusions about the effectiveness of programs are drawn from isolated but rhetorically striking instances. The electorate hears stories about "welfare cheats" and concludes that the system must be reformed. Or we hear that a job training program has enabled a displaced middle-aged worker to make a new start in life, and our support for such programs increases.

Our opinions about nonprofit organizations and their programs are equally shaped by anecdote and particularity (which is why international relief organizations find it so tempting to downplay systemic explanations, show pictures of hungry but attractive kids, and promise to match donors with particular children in their appeals). I renew my membership in Habitat for Humanity because I am impressed by their philosophy and by the stories they tell of individual and collective transformation, not because I know much about that organization's impact on the urban housing problem or because I can compare the effect on urban problems of a gift to Habitat to that of a gift to some other organization.

Anecdotes (supported by general reputation) are useful triggers for decisions about small individual gifts. But despite their compelling quality, stories are poor guides to public policy. Anecdotes tell us nothing about the overall impact of an organization, or of a nonprofit subsector, on the problems it is trying to solve. An alternative to relying on anecdotes is to make inferences from the analysis of trends in the incidence of some social problems, such as that institutions responsible for solving problems that are getting better are effective and those responsible for solving problems that are getting worse are ineffective. The problem with this strategy is that problems have dynamics of their own and may get better or worse for reasons unrelated or related in unexpected ways to the organizations charged with addressing them. For example, many critics assumed that falling Scholastic Aptitude Test (SAT) scores in the 1970s and 1980s meant that schools were becoming less effective, when the declines actually reflected the fact that more people were taking SATs. Recently, politicians have lauded the police because crime rates were falling, even though at least part of the decline occurred because fewer members of an aging public were in age cohorts most likely to commit many kinds of crimes. Or take an example from a front page of a local paper, which expressed great satisfaction that the town's high school was rated 13th among some 259 in the state on the basis of such measures as college placements, SAT scores, and competitive awards won by its students, but failed to note that the town's parents are so highly educated that one would expect such an outcome on the basis of the students' home backgrounds alone (Szczesny, 1996).

In order to make any confident statements about the effectiveness of an organization or set of organizations, we need what social scientists call a "causal model." Such a model is an account of goals and of the factors that lead to their achievement. It details the processes by which objectives are attained and describes these processes in terms of discrete variables. The variables can be measured, and the relationships of the variables to one another and to desired outcomes can be expressed mathematically.

To assess a subsector's performance, we need a causal model that focuses either on outcomes or on organizational behaviors that we believe will effect desired outcomes. If we focus on outcomes—for example, infant mortality as a basis for evaluating hospitals—we need a causal model to factor out the influence of things other than the treatments hospitals provide before coming to a verdict on hospital effectiveness. (For example, communities with lots of well-nourished, health-conscious mothers will have better infant mortality statistics than communities with lots of drug-addicted mothers, even if hospitals in the latter give better care.) If we focus on behaviors likely to create desired outcomes, then we need a causal model of the relationships between the behaviors and the outcomes themselves.

In fact, we rarely understand the relationship between cause and effect well enough to make confident estimates of the performance of organizations. I note in this chapter a few of the difficulties that beset efforts to do so, beginning with for-profit firms—which should represent the easiest case for performance assessment (and here I rely on the excellent work of Marshall Meyer)—and then discussing two additional layers of complexity inherent in performance assessment of nonprofit subsectors. The first layer is introduced by focusing on aggregates of organizations rather than on single firms; the second by evaluating organizations with multiple and contested goals.

PERFORMANCE INDICATORS IN FOR-PROFIT FIRMS

Performance assessment comes from the for-profit sector, where the presence of a single objective—maximizing profit—simplifies matters greatly. Yet even in the for-profit sector, finding the right performance indicators has proved to be a daunting challenge to companies and their analysts alike. Meyer, who has chronicled this problem (Meyer & Gupta, 1994; Meyer, 1999), reports that corporate performance indicators have been poorly correlated and fluid, and tend to decline in variance (and thus predictive power) over time. Corporations have responded by adopting new indicators (and only sometimes abandoning old ones), so that performance indicators have proliferated, creating a "crowded and disorganized scorecard" (Meyer, 1999). Meyer suggests several reasons for this result:

1. *Unknown effects.* Firms actually know very little about the relationship between indicators and future performance, especially once one gets beyond the accounting measures that financial economists have analyzed so thoroughly to increasingly popular measures of such things as performance quality and human resource management.

2. *Changing effects.* One of Meyer's most striking findings is that the variance of most performance measures (the differences among firms) declines over time (Meyer & Gupta, 1994). Measures call attention to problems, and most companies work at the things they measure, showing improvement over time, either because they learn how to do a better job or because they learn how to improve the measure without improving performance. Because the relationship between indicator and future performance depends on the specific point in the future that one wants to predict, and because relationships between indicators and performance change over time, companies have found self-assessment to be a moving target. Measures on which firms vary little predict performance poorly, leading companies to reach out for new measures.

3. *Different effects for different time frames.* Many strategies involve a decision to accept short-term losses in the interest of maximizing long-term gains. If one compares the short-run effects of several strategies, one will underestimate the value of strategies with the longer term payoffs as compared with those whose benefits are front loaded, even if the former yield the best overall outcome. For this reason, performance measures may be good indicators of short-term performance, but bad indicators of long-term performance, or vice versa. Focusing on short-term performance indicators provides disincentives for organizations to develop long-term strategies. For example, the emphasis of U.S. capital markets on quarterly measures was a common explanation for

the superior performance of Japanese companies during the 1980s (Hayes & Abernathy, 1980). Yet a focus that is too long-term may make performance assessment impossible, as when Marxist or monetarist economic ideologues argue that persistent stagnation reflects transitional difficulties to be overcome by greater commitment to the policies that caused it.

WHY PERFORMANCE ASSESSMENT IS EVEN HARDER AT THE SECTORAL LEVEL

Meyer's work is about efforts to evaluate the performance of single firms. Evaluating the performance of a whole sector or industry is even harder, for reasons noted below.

The Noisy World Problem

Most corporate performance measures aim to predict a company's future performance compared to other firms in its industry. Even if it is difficult to select the right measures, it seems reasonable to assume that what companies do today will have a big impact on how they do tomorrow, relative to similar firms.

By contrast, particular companies have far less influence over the performance of an entire industry or subsector. Industry financial performance is a function of market conditions over which companies have little control (Burt, 1992). It is also likely that nonprofits, no matter how effective, could exert only modest influence on the social objectives they are designed to address. Evaluating this performance requires that we accurately model the effects not simply of industry characteristics, but of the many external influences—processes that may involve families, government at many levels, or even changes in the natural environment—that can affect societal conditions as well. Needless to say, there are few if any areas in which social science modeling has reached this level of precision.

The Heterogeneity Problem

Moreover, aggregate information about performance may conceal trends in a heterogeneous organizational population. If organizations are pursuing different strategies, especially strategies pointed toward different time horizons, then performance assessment at a given time may be a poor measure of likely long-term outcomes. Imagine, for example, a population of nonprofits that includes two subtypes, each devoted to eradicating poverty: (a) volunteer organizations that fight poverty directly by building housing and other infrastructure in poor communities and (b) nonprofits that organize community residents to participate effectively in the political system and thus demand better service from local government. Imagine, as well, that the two strategies are equally efficacious, but that the first strategy tends to yield incremental, linear improvements whereas the latter yields few payoffs in the early years but substantial ones after a takeoff threshold. Finally, let us assume an interdependence between the two strategies, such that each is more effective in the presence of the other. Aggregate outcome measures taken at early points in time will underestimate the effectiveness of the subsector as a whole.

The Small-N Problem

This problem is more strictly methodological. In order to assess performance, one must be able to test the causal model on which one's measures are predicated. If you are working at the organizational level, you can explore the relationship between, say, the professional training of social workers that a family-service organization employs and changes in the behavior of families the organization serves, by comparing the results of otherwise similar organizations that hire different kinds of social workers. By contrast, if you are interested in the effectiveness of the nonprofit family-service sector in the United States, finding the right comparison will be much harder. (You could compare the United States to other countries, but to do so would require truly heroic assumptions about similarities in the factors that influence the well-being of families in countries with very different social structures, religious traditions, and government responsibilities.)

There are solutions to the problem, though none are entirely effective. One can use time-series data to model the effects of changes in industry characteristics on changes in family well-being, with appropriate controls, especially if one can reasonably assume stability in the model predicting measures of well-being over time. Or one can compare metropolitan areas throughout the United States to explore the relationship between characteristics of local nonprofit fields and measures of family quality.

The Ecological Problem

Although it is tempting to seek generalizations about the performance of nonprofit sectors (either locally or nationally), one cannot look at a single sector in isolation from those with which it competes. Nonprofit sectors occupy particular niches in the intersectoral division of labor; their effectiveness is always to some extent a function of the particular niche they occupy, which, in turn, emerges in interaction with the public and for-profit sectors.

Industrial or Spatial Variation in Niches

As Weisbrod (1990) demonstrated, nonprofits in different industries serve different niches, in some cases (e.g., charitable agencies that aid families in crisis) providing a safety net for poor members of their community, in other cases (e.g., prep schools) providing services of particularly high quality to well-off consumers who demand more than the median voter is willing to pay government to provide. In some cases, subsectors in the same industry occupy different niches in different regions, depending on the role of government and the private sector. (For example, in some areas nonprofit day-care centers serve children whose parents are too poor to afford for-profit providers whereas, in others, they serve children whose parents want higher quality services than government centers provide. Clearly, where nonprofits in different areas are performing different functions for different client groups, no set of performance indicators will fit the industry as a whole. A technical implication is that if we are to assess the effect of the nonprofit sector on particular outcomes, we must include in our models measures of related activity by government and for-profit organizations and specify those models so that they can capture the possibility that the performance of the nonprofit sector is contingent (positively or negatively) upon the level and type of activity in other sectors.

Opportunity Costs and Counterfactuals

An ecological perspective also calls attention to opportunity costs. Even if we find that nonprofit organizations in a given subsector are reasonably effective in addressing a particular problem, we must ask: Would an alternative use of the funds yield even better outcomes? For example, studies that document the economic impact of nonprofit arts organizations on local communities rarely ask whether alternative forms of investment would have even greater impact. (One study that did ask this question concluded that Times Square might contribute more to New York's economy as a red-light district than as an arts center [Netzer, 1978].) Critics of the current health care system acknowledge the ability of doctors to treat many illnesses effectively but contend that a redistribution of funds from treatment facilities to public health would yield a healthier population. Moderate advocacy organizations take pride in winning legislative concessions that support their cause, while radical organizations accuse moderates of covering for opponents who would otherwise have to face the public's wrath.

Such reasoning involves the use of counterfactuals—assumptions about states of the world that have not been observed—and counterfactual reasoning is always a dicey business. The conclusion one reaches often rides on the type of counterfactual one employs. One kind of counterfactual, which tends to make nonprofits look ineffective, compares current practice with the results of synoptic analyses, the conclusions of which would be enacted by a philosopher-king. Another, which tends to make nonprofits look better, relies on assumptions about individual choices and pragmatic political conditions. Synoptic reasoning might lead a health care expert to recommend eliminating deductibility for gifts to nonprofit hospitals and investing the additional tax revenues in public health programs. Pragmatic reasoning might lead an expert to oppose such a change on the grounds that hospitals would suffer and the additional tax revenues would probably be spent on defense, tax cuts, or deficit reduction rather than on public health.

MULTIPLE GOALS JUST MAKE THINGS WORSE

So far we have talked about organizations and industries with single objectives: maximizing profits, helping families, delivering health care, or ameliorating poverty. The most distinctive and universal characteristic of real nonprofits, however, is that they have more than one objective. Nonprofits are chronically multiple-goal, multiple-constituency organizations that attempt to pursue several worthy objectives at once. And because such objectives are usually linked closely either to delicate issues of internal politics or to relations with stakeholders (including donors), explicit strategic ordering of objectives at a concrete enough level to inform action is rare (DiMaggio, 1992; DiMaggio & Anheier, 1990; Kanter & Summers, 1987). Instead, most nonprofit managers deal with disagreements about goals by papering them over with inspiring but vague mission statements; by attending to different goals in sequence without making explicit long-term trade-offs; by segregating members of the organization or parts of its environment that are likely to disagree; and by maintaining a portfolio of objectives, their investments in which depend at least in part on opportunity and accident.[1]

The problem of goal ambiguity is exacerbated because some goals are more legitimate than others and easier to articulate in the language of contemporary U.S. organizational culture. In particular, it is more legitimate to express goals in technical terms (serve an additional 3000 meals per week) than as moral imperatives (end hunger in the community), and easier to describe numerical goals (increase attendance among underserved publics) than qualitative ones (make the audience's experience more meaningful). Because many people are motivated to work in the nonprofit sector precisely by qualitative goals and moral convictions, these linguistic conventions are more consistent with the technical need for numerical indicators in performance assessment than with the way many nonprofit staff and managers seem to think and talk about their work.

Assessing the extent to which organizations meet their objectives is difficult, to say the least, when those organizations have many objectives, when
those objectives are actively concealed or difficult to articulate, and when trade-
offs do not derive from a stable objective function but rather emerge in real
time out of politics and serendipity. It is not hopeless, however, because one
can build goal dissensus into the assessment by using an approach developed
by Guttentag (Guttentag, 1973; Edwards, Guttentag, & Singer, 1983) for program evaluation. The core of the strategy is to use interview techniques to
identify legitimate stakeholders, construct an objective function for each group,
and find measures of progress toward each objective. The output of the assessment, then, is not a single yardstick of success, but rather a series of outcomes
weighted to correspond to the objective function of each stakeholder group,
permitting assessment of the extent to which the organization effectively addresses the priority of each.

As usual, however, aggregation—thinking about the effectiveness of a
subsector rather than a single organization—complicates matters even more.
Meyer (1999) recommends that firms use performance indicators that measure
progress toward strategic objectives. Because firms can formulate strategies,
but fields (at least fields as large and uncoordinated as most nonprofit subsectors)
cannot, this approach is useful at the aggregate level only insofar as most of the
organizations in a particular field have similar objectives. (This dilemma is a
special case of the "heterogeneity problem" noted earlier.)

The great temptation, of course, is to impose a collective objective on the
basis of what the analyst believes the nonprofits *should* accomplish. The value
of this approach depends on where the analysts get their performance criteria.
Certainly the analysts' own values should not be the source of such criteria.
Nor, less obviously, can even a well-defended account of "society's values" (a
dubious notion, at best) provide a yardstick, for a central rationale for policies
supporting the nonprofit sector is that it keeps alive values that "society" would
not nurture through government or the market (Douglas, 1983). An approach,
such as Guttentag's, that acknowledges goal diversity and brings it to the center of the analytic method is preferable. But one will nonetheless end up assessing the subsector's performance on the basis of goals that are not the ones that
at least some participants think they are pursuing.

BAD THINGS HAPPEN TO GOOD MEASURES

Even if one can identify theoretically defensible performance indicators
for nonprofit subsectors, it may be impossible to make them work in practice.
Too often, we think of collecting data on performance as a technical matter to

be addressed with expertise on survey design and administration. It is this, to be sure, but performance data collection is also an extended game between researcher and respondent in which the former seeks compliance and the latter seeks advantage, providing or withholding information to shape public perceptions and to provide leverage over the content of the questionnaire. Unfortunately, researchers focus too exclusively on the technical and not enough on the game-like aspects of data systems (Starr, 1987).

With respect to the latter, two processes are ubiquitous. The first is that organizations often try to decouple indicators from the behaviors they are meant to indicate. The second is that organizations resist releasing accurate information.

The Flamingo Problem

In *Alice and Wonderland*, Lewis Carroll has Alice, his heroine, play a croquet game in which flamingos are mallets and hedgehogs are balls. Because both mallets and balls moved of their own accord, Alice found the game very difficult to play. Like Alice's flamingo mallets, performance indicators often develop lives of their own, and their meanings change as they are measured. This problem is ubiquitous and well documented in single firms (see, for example, Cyert & March, 1963). The problem is even more severe when data are collected by outside agencies without active sponsorship by the firms' management.

Two things happen when a data collection system adds a new item. First, new data are collected. Second, the reporting organizations are given an incentive to attend to the behavior or outcome being measured. Ideally, such attention leads to improved practice and thus to improved scores on the indicator. But given the inertia that characterizes many organizations, it is equally probable that the organization will figure out how to game the system. Asked to produce information on administrative costs, nonprofits will adopt functional accounting systems that permit them to write off administrative salaries to program areas they oversee. Evaluated on the basis of clients treated, counseling organizations may replace psychoanalysts with social workers oriented to short-term therapies or substitute clients with short-term life-transition problems for patients in need of long-term treatment. After a while, what started out as a fine performance indicator becomes far less closely connected to the phenomenon it was intended to measure.

Power and Ambiguity

As I have noted, nonprofit managers often find ambiguity and secrecy useful tools in negotiating the conflicting demands of varying constituencies. Managers rarely see it as in their interest to release information on organizational processes and outcomes if they do not have to. Managers in many fields recognize that information is a collective good and work with service organizations or trade associations to produce standard statistical series. But in so doing, they highlight information that is useful for purposes of advocacy and avoid data that could be used by industry critics.

When regulators demand data useful for performance assessment, as in the health care industry (Gray, 1991), organizations will produce it in some form, especially if noncompliance subjects them to civil or criminal penalties. When data collectors are unable to employ coercion, they must negotiate each item with nonprofits or with the service organizations that represent them. Rarely do they have the upper hand. Weiss and Gruber's (1987) superb study of federal education statistics documents one instance of this. In order to gain compliance from state education departments and local school districts, federal data agencies made so many compromises that the Common Core of Data they collected was virtually irrelevant to the decade's education policy debates.

The Capacity Problem

Even when nonprofit organizations are willing to release information relevant to performance assessment, they may lack the capacity to do so. Staff members of arts service organizations with active data collection programs, interviewed for a study of data resources on arts organizations, told us of the difficulties they had gathering reliable financial and program information, of the need to limit the questions asked in order to get acceptable response rates, and of the hours they spend on the phone correcting responses that are inconsistent or obviously incorrect.

The capacity to provide reliable information is a function of size: hard-pressed, small organizations with poor management information systems are particularly unlikely to have the staff capacity necessary to respond to requests for information. But even large organizations with sophisticated information systems may define items differently, providing incomparable responses that render aggregation misleading. According to our respondents, this is the case even for financial data, where uniform accounting standards should guarantee comparability. Apparently, large accounting firms with many nonprofit arts clients (primarily those in Los Angeles, New York, or Chicago) understand the standards and use them correctly, but firms without large arts clienteles ordinarily do not (Kaple, Morris, Rivkin-Fish, & DiMaggio, 1996).

Looking under the Lamppost

To a great extent, we are prisoners of existing institutional arrangements, which make it easier to collect data that reinforce—rather than challenge—

current forms of organizing and that make it easier to gather information about typical—rather than unusual—nonprofit organizations. Put another way, the more probing the questions we want to ask and the more inclusive the population of nonprofit organizations we want to address, the more we will have to spend to measure a sector's impact. For the foreseeable future, cost considerations are likely to require that we depend largely on existing data to assess national impact. (Locally based research may hold greater potential for cost-efficient innovation.) If we must depend on data that are already collected, or even collect new data in a cost-efficient manner, we are put in the position of someone who has lost a wallet and begins to look for it under the lamppost because "that's where the light is best."

Variations in Data Availability across Sectors

The availability of data is itself a function of the way in which nonprofit subsectors are organized. Data quality and structure reflect several aspects of industry structure.

1. *Organizational size distributions.* Other things being equal, industries with relatively few large organizations will produce better data than industries with many small organizations. The arts sector, for example, produces poor data in part because it consists of a very large number of very small organizations, as well as a relatively small number of large institutions (Bowen, Nygren, Turner, & Duffy, 1994, p. 123). In contrast, the university sector, with fewer organizations of larger size, produces higher quality information.

2. *Regulatory patterns.* Other things being equal, regulated industries produce more and better data than do unregulated industries. As Netzer (1977) noted, "the best Federal government economic statistics are those for particular sectors that have long been 'clients' of the Federal government, with major, well-established Federal agencies devoted to their welfare" (pp. 1–2). Information about universities and hospitals is relatively plentiful because these institutions have been heavily funded by government (directly and indirectly), which has consequently had sufficient leverage to impose more complex reporting requirements. In contrast, the arts depend on dispersed gifts from many donors and institutions that lack the capacity to organize in order to make demands for information on the field as a whole.

3. *Nature of government's role.* Comparability among nonprofit sectors depends on definitions of function embedded in data collection systems that, in turn, depend on the division of labor among government agencies concerned with a nonprofit subsector. Where many agencies compete for jurisdiction, as in education and health, data sources are diverse and fragmented (Scott & Meyer, 1983); unified responsibility may yield more unified data. Data on arts organi-

zations reflect the division of labor in support for the arts in the American federal system: a strong division of labor between federal government and states, centralized responsibility for the arts at each level, and a generally cooperative and politically interdependent relationship between agencies and the organizations they support. Such a structure has led to a mediation strategy whereby the National Endowment for the Arts (NEA) rarely collected data from arts organizations (or even used information acquired through the application process), instead working through discipline-based service organizations and state arts agencies. The result is a data system that reflects the needs of service organizations and grants accounting rather than those of policy makers and policy analysts (Kaple et al., 1996).

Institutional Boundaries

The intimate relationship between the organization of activity and the organization of information makes it difficult to ask some questions that are crucial for sectoral performance assessment. Institutional boundaries have particularly significant implications for the types of organizations whose activities we can compare.

Institutional Boundaries among Sectors

As I argued earlier, it is virtually impossible to say much about the impact of the nonprofit sector on a problem without good information about allied efforts by government agencies and for-profit firms. A causal model that describes the U.S. health care system in terms of the characteristics of nonprofit hospitals would clearly be misleading without including comparable information about public and proprietary institutions, for example.

Yet the number of industries in which comparable data are collected from providers of different kinds are relatively few: hospitals, colleges and universities, and in some states day-care centers and nursing homes. (Even in some of these cases, lower response rates from for-profit firms—such as company foundations in the Foundation Center database or proprietary hospitals in the American Hospital Association data series—cause additional problems.) In other industries, we are less accustomed to thinking about nonprofits and for-profits as being in the same business. In the arts, for example, data on jazz quintets or jazz nightclubs are never collected alongside information on chamber groups or chamber-music presenters, although the functions are quite similar. And although there are many for-profit museums, we cannot compare them to nonprofit museums because the government agency and service organization responsible for compiling information on museums arbitrarily includes nonpropriety charter as part of the definition of "museum" (DiMaggio, 1987).

Such differences in the availability of information probably lead researchers to underestimate the distinctiveness of the nonprofit sector. The reason for this underestimation is that the same shared regulatory and competitive environment that leads to the collection of comparable data on organizations in different sectors also exerts pressures on those organizations to become more similar to one another. For example, public and nonprofit technical colleges are supported by the same federal agencies and accredited by the same private associations, so we have data that permit easy comparison. In contrast, proprietary trade schools are regulated and accredited by different bodies, so we have little information for comparing them to their public and nonprofit counterparts. Technical training programs within corporations are unregulated and unaccredited, so we know virtually nothing about them. Such disparities thwart efforts to estimate the impact of nonprofit technical education on society, to say the least.

Weak Institutionalization and Data Comparability

Organizations in strongly institutionalized fields tend to become similar to one another in structure and function as a result of common environmental pressures and common cultural definitions (DiMaggio & Powell, 1983). Where institutional pressures are weaker, internal variation is greater and comparable data are therefore more difficult to come by. Chamber ensembles, for example, may be organized as freestanding nonprofit organizations, subunits of symphony orchestras, components of universities, or proprietary partnerships. An ensemble's organizational form will have a big effect on how it keeps track of and reports staffing, expenditures, and revenues. Local arts agencies are equally diverse in structure and also diverse in the programs they pursue, again making comparisons difficult. In contrast, colleges or hospitals are strongly institutionalized, tend to be organized in similar fashions and do similar things, and therefore generate comparable data.

Invisible Organizations

Particularly in periods of social and institutional change, large numbers of organizations in forms that are weakly institutionalized may be effectively invisible from the standpoint of data collection. Several factors make it easier to collect data on organizational forms that are well institutionalized, as opposed to organizations that do not fit into well-established institutional definitions. First, it is easier to recognize an organization that fits an established institutional form. Cognitive psychologists have demonstrated that we use prototypes and schemata to recognize and interpret new information (Zerubavel, 1997). Institutions work the same way, but are even more powerful because they are bolstered by concrete arrangements that standardize categories in reality as well as in our minds. Institutionalization shapes our perception of the kinds of organizations that are numerous and important. It influences the ease with which one can find and count organizations. Strongly institutionalized fields tend to have service organizations or accrediting institutions that compile lists and identify population boundaries. Because organizations in well-institutionalized fields are more similar than those in less institutionalized fields, it is easier to design appropriate data collection instruments for the former. All of these things lower the cost of surveying highly institutionalized organizations and raise the costs of studying less well-institutionalized forms. Large organizations in well-institutionalized forms are cheaper to find, easier to recognize, easier to classify, cheaper to contact, and can be surveyed with less complicated instruments. The result is powerful pressure toward bias against new and emerging organizations, including neighborhood-based nonprofits and unincorporated voluntary associations, in most data collection systems (Kaple et al., 1996, Chapter 1).

WHY MEASURING IMPACT IS PROBABLY USEFUL

I have argued that measuring the impact of the nonprofit sector—or even of nonprofit subsectors—is impossible, at least by social science standards of measurement. The issue is not whether we can perform technical analyses and emit numerical estimates (we can), but whether such estimates can be taken to measure what they are meant to measure and can responsibly be taken as even partial bases for policy making (they cannot). Our inability to perform scientifically valid sectoral impact studies is overdetermined: Technical considerations, sectoral and organizational politics, respondent capacity, and institutional factors all conspire against us.

Why, then, do we study the subject? In part, because it would be desirable to measure the performance of nonprofit subsectors in order to make better policy (insofar as policy making is responsive to knowledge), and researchers have risen to the challenge.

But there is perhaps more to it than that. To be sure, impact assessment at the level of nonprofit subsectors (as distinct from organizational performance assessment, which is feasible and productive, if difficult) will never yield to scientific technique. It will always be a kind of cultural ritual. But to call something a ritual is not to say that it is without value. Indeed, it is precisely because of the symbolic power of rational technique in contemporary culture that efforts to calculate the impact of nonprofit subsectors may be fruitful. For like religious rituals, secular rituals—even rituals of rationality—have the power to bring people together, to define identities, and to move people to seek change. If we view the drive toward aggregate performance measurement not as a misguided search for a technical fix but as a kind of religiously infused social movement, its value may be clarified.

Performance Assessment as Legitimating Ritual

Organizations frequently use rituals to symbolize their commitment to prevailing values (Meyer, Boli, & Rowan, 1977). During the progressive era, nonprofit organizations staffed by professionals routinely declared their commitment to the value of measurement, often using the language of scientific management, with far less substance behind it than we have today. (See, for example, Rea's [1932] effort to assess the impact of art museums, measured as number of people served, with the aid of a series of incorrectly conducted regression analyses.) Such work reinforced a commitment to systematic, rational action on behalf of collective social goals that distinguished the progressive approach from that of voluntary associations that preceded it.

What is striking about nonprofit discourse in the 1910s and 1920s is the fusion of substantive and instrumental rationality. Leaders in the nonprofit community combined strong policy commitments with a genuine faith in planning and coordination that put them in step with the values of the corporate and public sectors of the time.

During the 1950s and 1960s, the nonprofit sector's focus on substantive rationality—the orientation of action to valued ends—was undiminished, but the emphasis on instrumental rationality seems to have declined. In a sense, the sector may have fallen culturally out of step, first, with the corporate world, whose appetite for technical management systems was intensified by the expansion of high-speed computing capacity and by the emergence of takeover markets and international competition; and, by the late 1980s, with government, which sought in zero-based budgeting, performance assessment, and total quality management a means of doing more with less and winning back the public's trust in the bargain (Gore, 1993).

From this perspective, impact assessment and related techniques are legitimating rituals that underscore the sector's commitment to prevailing rational values. As with other forms of business-based management techniques, performance assessment serves both as a symbol of the sector's legitimacy and a signal to outsiders that nonprofits are prepared to take responsibility for their own affairs (Feldman & March, 1981). Such signals may help combat skepticism and gain political and economic support.

Performance Assessment As Transformative Ritual

A more important consequence of performance assessment and related techniques may be to provoke change processes that improve nonprofit organizations and enhance their contribution. This aspiration may seem inconsistent with my argument that sectoral impact analysis cannot yield scientifically valid estimates of impact on which policy changes can be based. But it is only inconsistent if we think that decisions about policy and strategy are based directly on the results of formal research. In fact, many policy studies tell us that research enters into policy making indirectly, in combination with more influential factors such as politics, anecdote, and intuition (Lindblom & Cohen, 1979; Lindblom, 1990). If this is the case, we can look to impact analysis to serve as a catalyst for improving the quality of discourse about nonprofit organizations even if it provides no clear implications for action.

Research as Part of an Extended Conversation

Perhaps the most important function of research of this kind is to push forward an ongoing conversation about the nonprofit sector and its appropriate role. As Cohen and Garrett (1975) observed about education policy research, good research is much less likely to resolve an argument than it is to make it more interesting and more sophisticated. Efforts at impact assessment may do this in several ways:

1. *Clarifying objectives.* I noted earlier that nonprofit organizations experience endemic goal diversity, which managers often do their best to elide, deny, or conceal. If nothing else, meaningful efforts to assess the impact of nonprofit sectors will encourage explicit debate over the purposes that nonprofit organizations should serve. Such debate, at the very least, may clarify the choices that policy makers and managers face.

2. *Focusing attention.* Many studies of policy research and applied organizational research report that much research is done not to solve problems but to focus subordinates' attention (Langley, 1989; DiMaggio & Useem, 1980). Systematic efforts at impact analysis can become an occasion to focus the attention of nonprofit managers and trustees on their organizations' missions. Even if the process fails to come up with effective performance indicators, calling attention to performance may yield other benefits.

3. *Negotiating shared identities.* The very heterogeneity that makes it impossible to assess the impact of the nonprofit sector as a whole has also been an impediment to the collective pursuit of legislative and other sectoral goals. Particularly within local communities, conversations about impact assessment

may provide a relatively unthreatening context in which representatives of different parts of the nonprofit sector—large institutional service providers and small neighborhood organizations, organizations that serve the poor and those that serve the rich, advocacy organizations and parts of the establishment—can transcend long-standing tensions and construct new shared identities (Sabel, 1994).

4. *Generating research.* Large-scale interest in impact assessment is likely to generate new research initiatives that may significantly expand our understanding of nonprofit organizations. For example, systematic research using the methods of organizational ecology to estimate competitive relationships among nonprofit, proprietary, and government firms in the same industry are a natural framework for testing the leading theories of the intersectoral division of labor, as well as a necessary concomitant of serious impact analysis.

Shaking Up the System

Some students of organizational change have suggested that managers are attracted to large-scale rational techniques such as total quality management, performance assessment, or internal price systems not because they believe these methods will "work" in any simple sense, but because the techniques offer points of leverage from which to shake up calcified management systems and perhaps transform them into more productive arrangements. For example, Eccles and White (1988) report that corporate executives recognize that transfer pricing systems cannot create efficient internal markets, but use them anyway as a means of gaining greater information about and leverage over the cost structures of the divisions they oversee. Similarly, Winter (1994) argues that total quality management is useful not because the particular techniques it entails are especially efficacious, but because when implemented well it creates a sense of excitement and shared mission that can propel long-term change. Like other systems of rational technical analysis, impact assessment can focus attention and energy in ways that facilitate collective change efforts that might otherwise never occur. Such efforts are unlikely to reflect directly any particular research findings. Instead, they may arise out of social interactions that the effort entails, interactions heightened in intensity by the quasi-religious quality of the quest for rationality.

Impact Assessment in Different Contexts

We may speculate that the results of efforts at subsectoral impact assessment will vary among nonprofit industries with different characteristics. Begin by distinguishing nonprofit subsectors across two dimensions: one, homogeneity versus heterogeneity, referring to structural features such as size, sponsorship, and organizational form; the other, low shared mission versus high shared mission, referring to organizational goals.

Figure 15.1 arrays these two dimensions as dichotomies, in tabular form, in order to describe intuitions that could serve as the basis for more elaborate hypotheses. Quadrant A includes industries in which nonprofits are structurally homogeneous but lack any kind of shared mission. An example might be small nonprofit organizations created for primarily commercial purposes, which some commentators have called "pseudo-nonprofits." Such organizations will have little reason to make common cause and much reason to conceal information. Attempts at impact analysis in such fields are likely to succumb to passive resistance.

Quadrant B includes subsectors that consist of heterogeneous organizations with diverse missions. An example might be the environmental sector, which includes large membership organizations and small membership groups and spans the political spectrum from free-market conservative to radical green. This quadrant also seems an unpromising one for impact analysis, as any effort to identify collective purposes is likely to dissolve into conflict.

The potential utility of impact analysis rises in quadrant C, which consists of homogeneous organizations that share strong missions: Community-based theater companies and women's health clinics might appear in this quadrant. The presence of a shared mission should make it easy to arrive at common goals and achievement indicators. But the very homogeneity of such organizations, tied to strong policy commitments, may make participation in research difficult. For one thing, participants may have little experience in reflexive managerial thought because a strong culture substitutes for explicit planning and policy making. For another, the strength of shared identities may discour-

	Structural Features	
	Homogeneous	**Heterogeneous**
Weak Shared Mission	A. Incentives to conceal, local focus. *Passive-resistance trap*	B. Segmentation, *Conflict trap*
Strong Shared Mission	C. Strong culture. *Self-censorship trap*	D. Strong capacity for exchange and growth.

Figure 15.1. Industry types and impact-assessment outcomes.

age critical talk, lest the speaker be perceived as disloyal. To be effective in such subsectors, impact analysis projects must be sensitive to such considerations.

Impact analysis may hold great promise for subsectors in quadrant D, which consists of organizations with strong shared missions but heterogeneous forms: Museums, universities, and many kinds of religious nonprofits fit into this sector. Shared mission should permit agreement regarding the impact ultimately desired. At the same time, structural diversity may promote a more sophisticated and reflexive discussion about measurable indicators of short-term progress toward shared goals.

These remarks are almost entirely speculative. The important point is that if, as I suggest, we regard impact analysis as ritual rather than science, then we should expect certain kinds of nonprofit subsectors to be better candidates than others for taking advantage of the ritual's therapeutic potential.

CONCLUSION

Perhaps the most fitting conclusion to this essay is "One cheer for impact analysis." If the effort to estimate the nonprofit sector's impact on society is regarded as a scientific enterprise, I argue that it is doomed to fail. In contrast, if we treat it as a ritual that can both legitimize and, under the right conditions, transform nonprofit fields, then it may be well worth pursuing.

I say "one cheer" rather than "two cheers" because the enterprise is not without risk. Precisely because there is no accessible method that will separate fact from value and yield scientifically reliable information, such efforts could easily be politicized by the sector's adversaries. Even if the process is not commandeered by hostile forces, risks remain. Readily measurable indicators will tend to drive out less easily measurable ones—for example, those that gather information about organizational vitality and the quality of services delivered to clients. This "confusion of performance measures with performance outcomes" (M. Meyer, 1999) may lead researchers to focus attention on the wrong outcomes or the wrong indicators, over the wrong time horizon.

On balance, however, the potential of impact analysis for enhancing the reflexivity of the nonprofit sector, for encouraging dialogue between researchers and practitioners, and for creating more sophisticated ways of thinking about the sector and its goals strikes me as making the quest worthwhile. True, assessing the sector's impact is, strictly speaking, impossible. But then, alchemists made significant contributions to modern chemistry, even though they never succeeded in turning lead into gold.

NOTE

1. In an insightful article on art museums, economists Frey and Pommerehne (1980, p. 232) went so far as to assert that the museum director's major responsibility is to ensure "that the production function connected with the museum services is actively hidden . . . and cannot easily be detected."

REFERENCES

Bowen, W. G., Nygren, T. I., Turner, S. E., & Duffy, E. A. (1994). *The charitable nonprofits.* San Francisco: Jossey-Bass.

Burt, R. L. (1992). The social structure of competition. In N. Nohria & R. G. Eccles (Eds.), *Networks and organizations: Structure, form, and action* (pp. 57–91). Boston: Harvard Business School Press.

Cohen, D. K., & Garrett, M. (1975). Reforming educational policy with applied social research. *Harvard Educational Review, 45,* 17–41.

Cyert, R. M., & March, J. G. (1963). *A behavioral theory of the firm.* Englewood Cliffs, NJ: Prentice-Hall.

DiMaggio, P. (1987). Nonprofit organizations in the production and distribution of culture. In W. W. Powell (Ed.), *The nonprofit sector: A research handbook* (pp. 195–220). New Haven, CT: Yale University Press.

DiMaggio, P. (1992). Notes on the relationship between art museums and their publics. In M. Feldstein (Ed.), *The economics of art museums* (pp. 39–49). Chicago: University of Chicago Press.

DiMaggio, P., & Anheier, H. K. (1990). The sociology of nonprofit organizations and sectors. *Annual Review of Sociology, 16,* 137–159.

DiMaggio, P., & Powell, W. W. (1983). The iron cage revisited: Institutional isomorphism and collective rationality in organizational fields. *American Sociological Review, 48,* 147–160.

DiMaggio, P., & Useem, M. (1980). Small-scale policy research in the arts. *Policy Analysis, 6,* 187–210.

Dobbin, F. (1994). Cultural models of organization: The social construction of rational organizing principles. In D. Crane (Ed.), *The sociology of culture: Emerging theoretical perspectives.* Cambridge, MA: Blackwell.

Douglas, J. (1983). *Why charity?* Beverly Hills, CA: Sage.

Eccles, R., & White, H. C. (1988). Price and authority in inter-profit-center transactions [Supplementary special issue]. *American Journal of Sociology, 94,* S17–S51.

Edwards, W., Guttentag, M., & Singer, K. (1983). A decision theoretic approach to evaluation research. In E. Struening & M. B. Brewer (Eds.), *Handbook of evaluation research* (University ed., pp. 139–179). Beverly Hills, CA: Sage.

Feldman, M., & March, J. G. (1981). Information in organizations as signal and symbol. *Administrative Science Quarterly, 26,* 171–186.

Frey, B. S., & Pommerehne, W. W. (1980). Economic analysis of the museum. In W. S. Hendon, J. L. Shanahan, & A. J. MacDonald (Eds.), *Economic policy for the arts* (pp. 248–259). Cambridge, MA: Abt Books.

Gore, A. (1993). *From red tape to results: Creating a government that works better and costs less. Report of the National Performance Review.* Washington, DC: U.S. Government Printing Office.

Gray, B. H. (1991). Data bases in health care. *Nonprofit Management and Leadership, 2*, 89–96.

Guttentag, M. (1973). Subjectivity and its uses in evaluation research. *Evaluation, 1*, 60–65.

Hayes, R. H., & Abernathy, W. (1980). Managing our way to economic decline. *Harvard Business Review* (July-August), 67–87.

Kanter, R. M., & Summers, D. V. (1987). Doing well while doing good: Dilemmas of performance measurement in nonprofit organizations and the need for a multiple constituency approach. In W. W. Powell (Ed.), *The nonprofit sector: A research handbook* (pp. 154–166). New Haven, CT: Yale University Press.

Kaple, D., Morris, L., Rivkin-Fish, Z., & DiMaggio, P. (1996). *Data on arts organizations: A review and needs assessment, with design implications.* Report to Research Division, National Endowment for the Arts. Princeton: Princeton University Center for Arts and Cultural Policy Studies, Working Paper #1.

Langley, A. (1989). In search of rationality: The purposes behind the use of formal analyses in organizations. *Administrative Science Quarterly, 34*, 598–631.

Lindblom, E. E. (1990). *Inquiry and change: The troubled attempt to understand and shape society.* New Haven, CT: Yale University Press.

Lindblom, E. E., & Cohen, D. E. (1979). *Usable knowledge.* New Haven, CT: Yale University Press.

Meyer, J. W. (1988). Society without culture: A nineteenth-century legacy. In F. O. Ramirez & J. Boli (Eds.), *Rethinking the nineteenth century: Contradictions and movements* (pp. 193–202). Beverly Hills, CA: Sage.

Meyer, J. W., Boli, J., & Rowan, B. (1977). Institutionalized organizations: Formal structure as myth and ceremony. *American Journal of Sociology, 83*, 340–363.

Meyer, J. W., Boli, J., & Thomas, G. M. (1987). Ontology and rationalization in the Western cultural account. In G. M. Thomas, J. W. Meyer, F. O. Ramirez, & J. Boli (Eds.), *Institutional structure: Constituting state, society and the individual* (pp. 12–38). Beverly Hills, CA: Sage.

Meyer, M. (1999). *Finding Performance: The New Discipline in Management.* Boston: Harvard Business School Press.

Meyer, M., & Gupta, V. (1994). The performance paradox. *Research in Organizational Behavior, 16*, 309–369.

Netzer, D. (1977). *Final report on a feasibility study for an economic data program on the condition of arts and cultural organizations.* Report to Research Division, National Endowment for the Arts. New York: New York University Graduate School of Public Administration.

Netzer, D. (1978). The worm in the apple. *New York Affairs, 4*, 40–48.

Rea, P. M. (1932). *The Museum and the community: A study of social laws and consequences.* Lancaster, PA: Science Press.

Roy, D. (1954). Efficiency and 'the fix.' *American Journal of Sociology, 60*, 155–166.

Sabel, C. (1994). Learning by monitoring: The institutions of economic development. In N. Smelser & R. Swedberg (Eds.), *The handbook of economic sociology* (pp. 137–165). Princeton, NJ: Princeton University Press and Russell Sage Foundation.

Scott, W. R., & Meyer, J. W. (1983). The organization of societal sectors. In J. W. Meyer & W. R. Scott (Eds.), *Organizational environments: Ritual and rationality* (pp. 129–153). Beverly Hills, CA: Sage.

Szczesny, D. J. (1996, August 23). Area schools best in state, survey says. *Princeton Packet*, pp. 1, 13A.

Starr, P. (1987). The sociology of official statistics. In W. Alonso & P. Starr (Eds.), *The politics of numbers* (pp. 7–57). New York: Russell Sage Foundation.

Weber, M. (1958). *The Protestant ethic and the spirit of capitalism.* New York: Scribner's. (Original work published in 1904–1905.)

Weisbrod, B. A. (1990). *The nonprofit economy*. Cambridge, MA: Harvard University Press.

Weiss, J., & Gruber, J. (1987). The managed irrelevance of federal education statistics. In W. Alonso & P. Starr (Eds.), *The politics of numbers* (pp. 363–391). New York: Russell Sage Foundation.

Winter, S. (1994). Organizing for continuous improvement: Evolutionary theory meets the quality revolution. In J. A. C. Baum & J. V. Singh (Eds.), *Evolutionary Dynamics of Organizations*, New York: Oxford University Press.

Zerubavel, E. (1997). *Social Mindscapes*. Cambridge: Harvard University Press.

Chapter 16

An Agenda for Quantitative Evaluation of the Nonprofit Sector
Need, Obstacles, and Approaches

Burton A. Weisbrod

The nonprofit sector is growing rapidly. The number of nonprofit organizations has tripled, from 309,000 in 1967, to nearly one million today. Total revenues, less than 6 percent of the gross national product in 1975, exceeded 10 percent in 1990 (Herman, 1995). Between 1980 and 1990, the number of employees paid by nonprofits grew by 41 percent, more than double the national rate (Salamon & Anheier, 1995).

It is natural to ask whether such expansion is efficient. Does society need nonprofits, and if it does, where in the economic system are they most useful? How are they different from, and better than, private firms and government? In what ways and to what extent do nonprofits strengthen these other economic sectors, or weaken them? Such questions highlight the need to evaluate the effects of nonprofit organizations in our mixed economy. Serious questions are arising about the efficiency and, more generally, the "desirability" of current public policy that encourages formation of nonprofit organizations, particularly the 501(c)(3) nonprofits that receive the principal public subsidies and that are the focus of this chapter.[1]

Burton A. Weisbrod • John Evans Professor of Economics and Faculty Fellow, Institute for Policy Research, and Chair, Philanthropy, Voluntarism, and Nonprofite Organizations Program, Northwestern University, Evanston, Illinois 60208.

Measuring the Impact of the Nonprofit Sector, edited by Patrice Flynn and Virginia A. Hodgkinson, New York, Kluwer Academic/Plenum Publishers, 2002.

Good evaluation is tricky business. If measuring the nonprofit sector's benefits and costs, advantages and disadvantages, is not done well, it will likely lead to erroneous decisions. Done well, it will likely be expensive and time consuming.

Posing the question as to whether the nonprofit is a desirable institutional form is not the appropriate starting point for designing an evaluation strategy. More significant are the questions of which economic activities should nonprofits be encouraged to provide, how much encouragement is warranted, and in what forms? That is, the principal issues of public policy toward the nonprofit sector involve not its existence, but whether its size and scope should be expanded or contracted. The contemporary debate over the desirability of a full tax credit for charitable donations—but only to antipoverty programs, as proposed by candidate Robert Dole during the 1996 presidential campaign—illustrates the issue of identifying the appropriate domain for nonprofits' subsidized activity. Currently, most tax-exempt contributions go to nonprofits that would be excluded from the tax credit proposal because they are not primarily oriented to the poor: colleges, hospitals, museums, symphony orchestras, arts groups, disaster-relief agencies, public radio and television, and philanthropies fostering medical research.

Pressure is growing from a number of sources to rein in the expanding nonprofit economy. Local governments see the expansion of tax-exempt nonprofits as taking more property off the tax roles. Private enterprise often sees nonprofit sector growth as generating "unfair competition." The nonprofit sector, under attack from both governments and private enterprise and amidst growing, if anecdotal, evidence of fraud, corruption, and seemingly excessive executive salaries, is finding its motives and behavior under increasing scrutiny.

From this weakening base of support, it is but a short additional step to the point at which government imposes greater regulatory scrutiny on nonprofits and more restrictions on their entry and activities. Even if the base of support for nonprofits is not weakening, it is clear that the political forces intent on slowing, if not reversing, nonprofits' expansion have already had some success. At the state government level, property tax exemptions have been withdrawn from some nonprofits in states such as Utah and Pennsylvania, and further restrictions have been considered by the legislature of Maine and appeared as a referendum on the fall 1996 ballot in Colorado (which was defeated). At the federal level, Congress has recently passed legislation that institutes a variety of new penalties for inappropriate behavior by nonprofits.

These types of political action run far ahead of understanding. Evidence—particularly quantitative evidence—is greatly needed on the effects, favorable and unfavorable, of nonprofits playing a larger, smaller, or different role in economic, social, and political life. It is needed not only for the nonprofit sector as a whole, but even more important, for particular activities and industries. Evidence is also needed on the effects of various regulatory changes that would make it easier or harder for the nonprofit sector to expand into new revenue-producing realms.

MEASURING OUTPUTS AND OUTCOMES: ISSUES AND CAUTIONS

Quantitative evaluation of the role of nonprofits can be helpful, but it can also be incomplete, biased, and, hence, misleading. Interpreting evidence about the effectiveness of nonprofit organizations is hazardous. The danger is that easily measured outputs or outcomes will be measured while others remain unmeasured and, in effect, valued at zero. Resources will then be misallocated, with too few going to the provision of such subtle outputs as tender loving care in a nursing home, appreciation of art and music, and education in cultural values. This is an important matter because nonprofits are more likely than private firms to be providing outputs that are difficult to measure and value.

If nonprofit and private firms in the same industry differ in their relative provision of what I have termed elsewhere "Type I" (easy to monitor) and "Type II" (costly to monitor) dimensions of services, with nonprofits providing relatively more Type II outputs, the evaluation process would systematically underestimate the social contribution of nonprofits (Weisbrod, 1988). Measuring nonprofits' social contribution would be biased and counterproductive. Consider day-care centers, for example. If they are evaluated in terms of their costs per child-day, a Type I measure, while nonprofit and for-profit caregivers differ in their sensitivity to special needs in subtle forms that at least some parents cannot easily monitor and assess, a Type II measure, then centers that provide the most sensitivity will be undervalued. If nonprofits engage in more of such activities, their social contribution will be underestimated. Although evidence on Type II outputs is inherently difficult to obtain, it is vital.

Implicit in these cautions about the dangers of quantification when some consequences are potentially important but difficult to measure, is an underlying assumption about the goal of assessment. What, exactly, is the purpose of evaluation and measurement? It should be easy to answer this question: Would some, or even all, resources now flowing into nonprofit organizations be "better" utilized elsewhere in the economy? The answer, of course, hinges on what nonprofits do with resources that is different from what other types of organizations, such as private enterprises and governments, would do with them. Shortcomings of nonprofits, while real, are not determining since all forms of institutions are imperfect.

WHY IS IT IMPORTANT TO EVALUATE
THE NONPROFIT SECTOR'S ROLE?

Difficult as it may be to measure the advantages and disadvantages of non-profit organizations in any industry, doing so is an essential ingredient of public policy. However, it is also critical to nonprofits, themselves, lest the uncertainty of their social contribution continue. Even their access to donations hinges on their ability to convey to prospective donors the validity of claims to be different and "better."

The pressure to evaluate the nonprofit sector has no counterpart in the private enterprise sector. Why is it important to evaluate the contribution of nonprofits but not private enterprise? The answer, I suggest, is that there is both an extensive foundation of economic theory justifying a decentralized, privately owned economic system and an enormous body of experience with it. In the case of the nonprofit sector, the experience is long but far less extensive, and the theoretic justification is newer and has generated less consensus; the intellectual base for private enterprise, as initially set forth by Adam Smith in 1776, does not yet have a well-accepted counterpart for nonprofits. Thus, when the nonprofit sector clashes with private enterprise, it is the "upstart" nonprofit sector that is on the defensive to demonstrate its social value. Perhaps such asymmetry is unwarranted, but I suggest it exists.

The nonprofit sector's position in the court of public opinion is weakened further by the seemingly growing frequency of scandals—the conviction of a former president of United Way of America for defrauding the charity of $1 million "to fund a luxurious lifestyle" (Walsh, 1996); and the formal charges that an organization, Feed America, illegally solicited contributions for victims of the Oklahoma City federal office bombing that occurred on April 19, 1995 (Swarns, 1996). Even the case of a nonprofit organization executive (the president and chief executive officer of the nonprofit United Way of America) who *declined* a departure "gift" of $292,500 from board members raised questions of propriety (Sinclair, 1996). Evidence of nonprofit sector executives receiving compensation that many people regard as unseemly—for example, the $523,000 compensation package of the president of Adelphi University (Lambert, 1996)— has further fueled the demand for accountability (Herzlinger, 1996).

VALUING OUTPUTS AND OUTCOMES

Another problem confronts serious evaluation of the nonprofit sector: How do we place value on the sector's various advantages and disadvantages? Unless the variety of consequences can be aggregated in terms of one metric—dollars or other—the evaluation process will lead to evidence that cannot be compared. How should a value be attached to the harm that private firms claim is caused by nonprofits' "unfair competition"? How should a value be attached to the benefits from nonprofit hospitals' greater services to the poor (Kuttner, 1996), to the research on the causes of cancer or heart disease, or to museums' preservation of artistic and cultural values? The appropriate conclusion is not that evaluation of the nonprofit sector should be foregone because some important forms of effects are not easily measured or valued. Instead, great caution is necessary in interpreting findings, lest, as noted above, what is easily measured and valued receives undue weight while consequences that are more difficult to value, or even to measure in non-monetary terms, are overlooked.

Placing values on "outputs" (meaning all outcomes) is fundamentally more complex for nonprofit sector activities than for private enterprise activities. The reason is that nonprofit activities, like many government services, are basically justified by their "public" or "collective" goods character—that is, goods and services that provide benefits to persons regardless of whether the beneficiaries pay. The value of these benefits is underestimated by the prices consumers actually pay. Examples include such nonprofit services as basic scientific research at universities; museums' preservation of art, culture, and history; "public" radio and television programming; and hospitals' community education activities. Even services to the poor, such as shelter to the homeless, while provided to specific people, have an important degree of collectiveness because the nonpoor also benefit from assistance to the poor.

Valuing benefits from such collective goods is extremely difficult and requires information on the total willingness of all persons to pay for the good ("willingness" encompasses ability to pay). The national income and product accounting system finesses this difficult problem by valuing government services at their cost—a method that is obviously useless for evaluating the economic efficiency of the services. In the private enterprise market, where private-type, rather than collective-type, goods are exchanged, consumers' willingness to pay is manifest in actual prices paid for goods purchased. In collective-goods markets, however, the fact that even nonpayers can derive utility generates free-ride behavior. The result is that voluntary payments understate actual benefits—perhaps enormously. In the case of public radio, for example, only some 10 percent of listeners contribute financially to the stations; it would be erroneous to measure the value of these nonprofit radio services by this level of contribution. One challenge is to determine how to value the benefits to the 90 percent who do not contribute. Even the 10 percent who pay something are likely to understate their valuation of the services. Similar reasoning applies to most nonprofit activities, which benefit many persons who do not pay. Estimating the value of those benefits is difficult, as it is with most government services.

This undervaluation problem for nonprofit sector activities takes yet another form. Insofar as nonprofits pursue non-profit-maximizing goals that encompass avoidance of opportunistic behavior, including antisocial activities such as polluting or taking advantage of underinformed consumers, their outputs will, again, be undervalued relative to those of private firms. It would be erroneous, for instance, to conclude that patients entering hospices are well informed about the optimal time to enter the facility. Because they are vulnerable, the prices they or their insurers pay are questionable as unbiased measures of well-informed valuations. This conclusion is implicit in the concern expressed in a recent study. The authors speculate that " . . . because evaluating newly admitted patients is expensive, and because payment is made on a per-diem basis, . . . [for-profit hospices] may encourage early enrollment of patients as a way to recoup the high up-front costs associated with admission." The longer stays in for-profit hospices, averaging 52 days till death, compared with 32 days at nonprofits, have a number of possible interpretations. The authors suggest that for-profit hospices may admit patients inappropriately early and may refuse to admit patients who are near death (Christakis and Escarce, 1996, p. 177). The germane question to the nonprofit evaluation process is whether nonprofit facilities behave differently from private firms, taking less advantage of underinformed consumers. This illustrates the importance of measuring and valuing nonprofit sector outputs that consumers find difficult to assess.

Attaching a value to nonprofit outputs is challenging but not impossible. Estimating the value of collective goods has received increasing attention via research on "contingent valuation" (*Symposium on Contingent Valuation*, 1994). This approach involves surveying individuals' willingness to pay for services that they are not currently receiving—for example, cleaner air and standby ambulance services. The contingent valuation approach has potential when willingness to pay is a socially acceptable criterion for valuing output, but it also confronts a sizeable hurdle. This hurdle is the hypothetical character of the questions and the need for respondents to sometimes indicate their willingness to pay for services with which they may have little or no experience, such as treatment for a particular illness, an increment of education, less-polluted air, or the opportunity to deal with a nonprofit service provider. Even when the service being evaluated is not hypothetical, but is familiar to the respondent, as with public radio listeners who are not paying but who know what service they are receiving, the difficulty of getting respondents to reveal their true valuations, assuming they know them, can be great. This demand-revelation problem, important for valuing output, is a general difficulty with collective goods—how to get consumers to reveal their true willingness to pay, without overstating it, when their answers do not affect their access to the goods.

The contingent valuation approach is far less useful when the valuation problem results from consumers' low-income status rather than from consumers' unrevealed benefits. The social value of food and shelter for the homeless cannot be measured meaningfully by the willingness of people in abject poverty to pay. Some other basis for valuation is necessary to determine whether the nonprofit sector's allocation of resources to such programs passes a social benefit–cost test. That might be the willingness of the nonpoor to pay for services to the poor, or the amount that poor would pay if they had a "socially acceptable" level of income.

A serious valuation problem exists for services that nonprofits provide free even to the nonpoor. The mission of nonprofits often encompasses making services widely available to all "deserving" students, to all who "need" hospital care, to all who could benefit from visiting a museum. Nonprofits recognize not only that charging higher prices can restrict access, but also that they cannot easily determine how high a price a specific consumer can be charged without the person turning away. Many universities deal with this informational problem by requiring parental income tax returns before the level of scholarship aid (reduction in price from the gross tuition fee) is fixed. Museums seek to avoid pricing consumers out of the market by waiving admission fees for school children and by having a weekly free-admission day for everyone. Surely, the social value of the museum services to the nonpaying attendees is not zero. Such price-discrimination policies, while imperfect, are means for balancing the organization's goal of maximizing output for the intended beneficiaries, against the constraining effect of its budget. Charging (higher) admission fees may generate much-needed revenue, but, in the process, it is likely to exclude some intended beneficiaries from the market (Steinberg & Weisbrod, 1996). The effectiveness of nonprofits in balancing the benefits of added revenue against the costs of excluding intended beneficiaries is another element of the nonprofit sector evaluation process.

The value of volunteer labor services must also be factored into a long-range process of valuing nonprofit activities. The uncompensated time of the millions of volunteer workers does not have zero value to either the organizations (largely nonprofits) or to the volunteers themselves.[2] Independent Sector has valued volunteer services at the average nonagricultural wage in the economy, plus fringe benefits; the actual value to users, however, may be substantially more or less and is an appropriate subject of research.

The overall objective of efforts to evaluate alternative levels of nonprofit activities should be to determine whether the combination of forces often claimed to operate in the nonprofit sector—*goals* that are essentially public serving and *constraints* mandating that profits be used only to purchase inputs—lead to decisions that are socially preferred to those of private firms or government. Assertions will not do. Evidence is needed to either support or condemn nonprofits' current but changing role.

WHAT KINDS OF EVIDENCE ARE NEEDED FOR EVALUATION?

To evaluate performance in the nonprofit sector, we must first specify criteria and then develop evidence about each. For measurement to proceed, there must be clarity regarding what to measure. It is a challenge, to say the least, to document or to refute the claim that "major differences between for-profit and not-for-profit health care plans lie in purpose, values, attitude . . . " (Nudelman & Andrews, 1996, p. 1057).

The list of criteria for gauging nonprofit organization performance is lengthy. Supporters of nonprofits claim benefits that include (a) efficiency and output quality, particularly in dimensions that are difficult for consumers to observe (Hansmann, 1980; Ben-Ner, 1986; Weisbrod, 1988); (b) access by consumers regardless of ability to pay (Schlesinger, 1997); (c) provision of collective goods that complement those of government (Weisbrod, 1975); (d) encouragement of altruistic values such as the opportunity to volunteer (Wuthnow, 1995); (e) alternatives to government in the social welfare area (Sills, 1968); and (f) preserving national identity (Schuster, 1994). Critics allege inefficiency and unresponsiveness (Alchian & Demsetz, 1972). Both may be right, but quantitative evidence requires that such criteria be made operational. How does one measure, let alone assign monetary value to, nonprofits' alleged contribution to the "integration of subgroups into the national society" and "distributing power, in which the power of the sovereign state is balanced by the power of dispersed associations" (Pearce, 1993, p. 27)?

In short, while nonprofits provide many private-type services familiar to us all, and these are susceptible to quantification, measurement, and valuation, they also claim to offer less conventional outputs that are major hurdles for the would-be evaluator. The social justification for the nonprofit sector is that it is more than a provider of private goods and services, that it is a provider of collective goods, an expression of socially oriented motivations, a mechanism for shaping and adding variety to the political system. Measurement and valuation of such benefits are unquestionably problematical.

There is another side to the assessment of the net social value of nonprofits. Whatever benefits they may contribute, nonprofits also impose a variety of costs. The costs are in the form of public subsidies that affect the way resources are used. Because buildings and real estate owned by charitable nonprofits are typically exempt from local property taxes, nonprofits have a greater incentive than private firms to locate in high-cost urban areas. Because nonprofits benefit from subsidized postal rates, they have the incentive to use the mail rather than alternative means of communication. Because of these and other public subsidies, as well as apparently greater access to volunteer labor, nonprofits find it profitable to compete with private firms in many markets, thereby imposing costs and raising charges of unfair competition. More generally, the impact of nonprofits' activities on other sectors of the economy is an important, but understudied, element of a full appraisal of nonprofits' overall contributions.

Nonprofits claim to pursue a wider range of goals than do for-profits. This leads to the testable prediction that nonprofits do not supply precisely the same output quality, style, and distribution of services as for-profit and government providers. It is important to understand and to measure such differences. Unless that is done, the results will be mismeasurement of differential costs per unit of "output" among sectors, differential "productivity," which depends on the measurement of output, and differential prices, which also reflect the definition of a "unit" of output.

HOW DOES THE GROWTH OF THE NONPROFIT SECTOR AFFECT OTHER PARTS OF THE ECONOMY?

Nonprofits are entwined with the rest of the economy in ways that appear to be in flux (Weisbrod, 1997). Confronted with seemingly growing revenue "needs" but declining government support, the nonprofit sector is reaching out for new sources of revenue.

The most promising strategy for nonprofits is finding new goods and services that they can sell profitably in order to finance their socially preferred collective activities (James, 1983; Schiff & Weisbrod, 1991).[3] This is occurring and, as it does, nonprofits are increasingly competing with private firms thereby attracting growing political attention.

The drive for new markets is also fostering increased *cooperation* between nonprofits and private firms. Public recognition of the alliances between nonprofits and private enterprises and between nonprofits and government has been scant and there is even less measurement and evaluation of these relationships. Whatever the specific form of entanglement between nonprofits and the rest of the economy, however, problems and stresses emerge. Measurement of the effects of the expanded realm of nonprofit sector activity is essential to thorough evaluation.

When nonprofits enter new markets, what are the consequences for private enterprise, for government, and for the nonprofit sector, itself? The following brief review focuses both on nonprofit activities that compete with the private and public sectors and on those that involve cooperation with them.

Effects on the Private Sector

Nonprofits are competing increasingly with for-profit firms in an amazing variety of forms and encountering resistance in the process (U.S. Small Business Administration, 1983; Emshwiller, 1995). The following examples are anecdotal; there has not been systematic measurement:

- The nonprofit Metropolitan Museum of Art operates 16 museum shops in the United States and 21 abroad, in addition to its catalog of items for sale (Cronin, 1995).
- The nonprofit Duke University Medical Center established a business unit to "compete with private sector companies that run trials for drug and medical-device companies" (Winslow, 1995).
- Nonprofit food banks established to feed the poor are building food dehydrating plants that compete with private firms (Lewin, 1994).
- Nonprofit churches are running tours in competition with for-profit travel agencies (Brannigan, 1995).

At the same time that nonprofits are moving into activities that have previously been the domain of for-profit firms, private firms are expanding into traditionally nonprofit areas. Thus, private health clubs have entered an industry long the preserve of the nonprofit YMCAs and YWCAs in the United States, and for-profit amusement parks "are encroaching on [nonprofit] museum turf by adding educational aspects to their entertainment products" (Becker, 1995).

The "growing commercialism" of nonprofits is also taking forms in which nonprofits and private firms join forces. Between 1980–1981, and 1987–1988, for example, private industry support for university research in the United States more than doubled in real terms (as it also has in France, Germany, Japan, and the United Kingdom) (Webster, 1994). Virtually every major U.S. university has joined forces in some manner with large multinational firms, mostly pharmaceutical and chemical firms (Blumenthal, Causino, Campbell, & Louis, 1996): Harvard University has contracted with the German chemical company, Hoechst A.G.; Washington University with Monsanto Chemical Company; and Northwestern University with Dow Chemical.

Alliances are also occurring in athletics. Pennsylvania State University signed a $2.6 million, 3-year contract with Nike not only to advertise its athletic shoes but also to display Nike's "swoosh" logo prominently on its football team's jerseys—as have at least eight other universities. Reebok has lucrative contracts with additional universities such as Michigan State, Northwestern, and Texas. The risk, as one observer put it, is "sweetening the pot of temptation and feeding the argument that college football and basketball players . . . should get paid for enriching their schools" (Thurow, 1995). The key question, within the evaluation context, is whether such contracts are affecting the attainment of nonprofits' missions.

Examining the causes for the apparent mushrooming of these symbiotic relationships is beyond the scope of this paper (see Weisbrod, 1997, for more on this topic). The consequences, however, are relevant to our discussion here. Since the principal source of the tightening relationships among sectors is their differential tax treatment, the result of the interaction can be increased revenue to both parties but negative overall economic effects. Because nonprofits receive many subsidies, they can, if they are clever, convert those benefits into something that is saleable in private markets.

The point is this: it is increasingly difficult to evaluate the social contribution of nonprofits in the modern world where barriers between nonprofit and for-profit firms are crumbling. Whether nonprofits collaborate with private firms or compete with them, evaluations must answer this critical question: *Are nonprofits acting increasingly more like private firms, and in so doing, forfeiting their claim to special status and privilege?*

Effects on Government

Growth of the nonprofit sector is also affecting governments. When nonprofits expand, governments lose tax revenue, at least relative to a situation in which the same tax base was in the private, taxed sector. The U.S. Treasury Department reported that 10 percent of all property in the country was held by tax-exempt nonprofits in 1977 (Arenson, 1995), and the figure is surely higher today. In 1993, Syracuse, New York, found that 59 percent of its real estate was tax exempt; in Buffalo, New York, the figure was 34 percent (Glaberson, 1996).

Governments have responded to the erosion of their tax base: Cities are withholding zoning approval and building permits for new buildings for nonprofits unless the university, hospital, or symphony orchestra agrees to pay a "voluntary" tax. Lawmakers are even searching for reasons to withdraw tax-exempt status altogether, as has been done for some nonprofit hospitals in Utah and at least one nonprofit college in Pennsylvania. These and other ramifications of nonprofit sector growth, such as the tightening of antitrust law enforcement against nonprofits ("MIT Wins a New Trial in Price-Fixing Case," 1993) are elements of a full evaluation of the sector and its expanding scope.

However, the search for revenue by nonprofits is sometimes beneficial to government rather than harmful. For example, nonprofits have joined with 36 state governments to market specialty car license plates that advertise arts organizations, universities, environmental groups, and garden clubs. UCLA is collaborating with the state of California to sell a license plate that finances student scholarships (Herman, 1995). Such cooperative ventures between nonprofits and governments appear to be rare but are increasing rapidly. Measuring their effects should also be part of a comprehensive evaluation of the nonprofit sector.

Effects on Nonprofits Themselves

Tension is growing inside the nonprofit sector, too. As nonprofit activities become increasingly commercial, they are doing things not customarily identified with the genteel approaches of benevolent organizations. Charities are bringing lawsuits for breach of contract against people who pledge donations but do not fulfill their commitment (Schmitt, 1995). Universities are sending recruiters (some might term them "salespeople") around the world in search of tuition-paying students (Hancock & Roberts, 1994). Nonprofit organizations are developing for-profit subsidiaries. At Northwestern University's Institute for Learning Sciences, for instance, a for-profit firm has been started to market a customized computer program that allows users to hold conversations with experts in a field—and the director of the Institute is also the acting president of the new corporation (*PARKprogress*, 1995).

There is absolutely nothing illegal with such arrangements, but they do blur the distinctions between nonprofits and private firms and they need to be assessed (Young, 1994; Kramer, 1995). In the case of university–industry cooperation in research, the key question is whether the direction of university research, researchers' interpretation of findings, and the dissemination of findings are being affected. A new study of nearly 200 firms engaged in collaborative research with universities disclosed numerous agreements to keep research results secret, even beyond the time required to file for a patent (Blumenthal et al., 1996). Was the IRS justified in claiming that, in some arrangements, the nonprofit partner was sacrificing the interests of charity and hence violating the tax code requirement that it be "operated exclusively for. . .charitable purposes" (Simon, 1987, p. 93)?

WHAT EVIDENCE IS THERE THAT NONPROFITS BEHAVE DIFFERENTLY FROM FOR-PROFITS AND GOVERNMENT ORGANIZATIONS?

The final question to be examined is whether nonprofits perform economically valuable functions that private firms or government do not. The strength of the evidence, as well as its shortcomings, highlight the directions that future research on output measurement can take. The list of criteria for gauging the performance of nonprofits, as illustrated above, is lengthy. This section focuses on a few—efficiency and quality of output, particularly in Type II dimensions, methods used to control access to services, and volunteering. Following are some of the types of data that can be used and what they measure.

Efficiency, Output Quality, and Trustworthiness

Use of sedatives in nursing homes as an indicator of quality is difficult for consumers to monitor. Family members cannot easily determine whether a patient is being sedated to address a medical need or to reduce the labor costs associated with caring for more active patients. According to one study, the use of sedatives for apparently similar medical needs was 4 times higher at for-profit facilities (12.5 units per month) than at church-related nonprofit facilities (3.0 units per month) (Svarstad & Bond, 1984). We do not know, however, whether the for-profit firms provided too much sedation or the nonprofits, too little.

The Survey of Institutionalized Persons (SIP) collected evidence on hard-to-monitor aspects of service quality at nursing homes and at facilities for the mentally handicapped. The proxy measures used for output quality are (a) the amount of labor inputs per 100 patients and (b) consumer satisfaction with services.[4] Here are some highlights of SIP, which illustrate both the feasibility of measuring an organization's behavior and the difficulty of developing operational measures of hard-to-monitor (Type II) outputs (Weisbrod, 1998):

1. *Labor inputs are indirect measures of quality.* Church-related nonprofit facilities in both industries provide more labor inputs per 100 beds than do for-profit facilities. Among nursing homes, for example, church-related facilities employ significantly more nurses, dietitians, maintenance workers, and volunteers. These homes used five full-time registered nurses per 100 beds, nearly double the 2.6 at proprietary homes; their 2.4 full-time dietitians were four times the number at a proprietary home (0.6); and 41 persons volunteer at least once per month compared with 24 at a for-profit home of the same size.

2. *Consumer satisfaction is another measure of quality.* SIP asked family members about their satisfaction—overall and separately—with buildings and grounds, rooms and furnishings, staff, social activities, and treatment services. The findings are strong. Among both nursing homes and facilities for the mentally handicapped, *satisfaction was consistently highest at church-related nonprofit facilities and lowest at for-profit facilities,* the differential being around 17 percentage points. *Nonchurch nonprofits, however, are indistinguishable from for-profit facilities.* There is much room for debate over the interpretation of data on satisfaction; nonetheless, in an important sense such satisfaction is precisely the socially desired goal of all economic activity—at least if consumers are well informed about the services they are obtaining. This qualifier is important, as one of the justifications consumers give for preferring nonprofits is their alleged superiority in markets where consumers are poorly informed.

Access to Services: Pricing Policies and Waiting Lists

Nonprofit organizations may be socially valuable not only because of the outputs they produce but also because of the ways in which they distribute them. Society often has distributional goals that are inconsistent with unbridled private market behavior (for example, the sale of human organs has been prohibited in a number of countries).

SIP examined patient access in two ways: (a) the organization's pricing practices—its price-cost margin (the difference between its charges and its average cost)—and (b) its use of a waiting list. The findings are that nonprofit and for-profit organizations use quite different ways to distribute their services in both industries. First, price-cost margins differ materially; other things equal, churches and other nonprofits have profit margins that are significantly smaller than those of proprietary facilities—an average $80 per month smaller at facilities for the mentally handicapped and $120 per month smaller at nursing homes (12 percent to 20 percent of the average costs in the two industries, of approximately $600 per month).

Second, waiting lists are also used differentially to control access. In both industries, church-related facilities are far more likely than other nonprofits to have a waiting list—92 percent for church-run nursing homes compared with 65 percent for other nonprofit-run homes, and 92 percent versus 60 percent among facilities for the mentally handicapped.

Opportunities to Volunteer

One performance measure noted above was the opportunity for people who wished to volunteer to help others. I have already noted the greater use of volunteers by nonprofit facilities in both industries. This is also the case in the child day care industry; in a recent survey, 14 percent of parents with children in for-profit centers reported that they volunteer, compared with 51 percent of parents at church-related nonprofits (Mauser, 1993, Chapter 6).

Managerial Compensation

Another way to shed light on the behavior of nonprofit organizations relative to other forms of institutions is to examine the ways they compensate and, hence, motivate their top executives. A number of studies have found lower wages in nonprofit organizations; some workers appear willing to work for less pay at an organization engaged in public-serving activities. In nonprofit "public interest" law firms, lawyers receive some 15 percent less pay than they could have received in private enterprise, given their experience, gender, law school class rank, and law school quality (Weisbrod, 1983). There has been debate, however, over whether this difference is attributable to a sorting of lower productivity lawyers to nonprofits (Goddeeris, 1988). In the hospital industry, top management in non-profits was also found to receive 15 percent to 20 percent less pay than their for-profit counterparts, after adjusting for the greater complexity of corresponding jobs at the lower-paying nonprofit hospitals (Roomkin & Weisbrod, 1999). Not every study has found this pattern, however (Preston, 1988), and so the issue of whether pay differentials reflect greater willingness to work for a nonprofit, because of its activities, or differences in worker productivity, is not resolved.

Some new evidence highlights the *structure* of executive compensation. Roomkin and Weisbrod (1999) found, in a study of 1,268 hospitals in 1992, that nonprofits actually paid higher base salaries to their chief executives, but that for-profit hospitals paid far higher bonuses, based on performance, leading to about 15 percent higher total compensation. By placing greater reliance on bonuses, for-profit hospitals tend to attract managers who are less risk averse, that is, more willing to make decisions involving greater risk but also greater rewards.

POLICY IMPLICATIONS AND DIRECTIONS FOR FUTURE RESEARCH ON MEASUREMENT

The growth of the nonprofit sector is thrusting it into the central debate over the organization of society. Until now, the sector has benefited from being small and largely out of sight. Success has changed this, with growing demands for accountability. Success has its price! For the nonprofit sector, the price is increased scrutiny and demand for evidence that its social contribution is not merely positive but great enough to justify its privileged status.

The call for measurement of nonprofits' contribution to society is part of a wider demand for evidence of the benefits from programs that depend on public funding. Thus, government science agencies have been mandated to develop quantitative measures of their scientific achievements. The problem is "to find useful measures of progress that will satisfy Congress without trivializing the science they fund" (Mervis, 1996). When the National Oceanic and Atmospheric Administration provides statistical evidence of its improved ability to predict tornadoes, it captures the attention of critics. The nonprofit sector needs comparable evidence of "success."

NOTES

1. This paper addresses the challenge of measuring the social value of the nonprofit sector as a whole and in particular, industries and market segments. It does not deal with assessment of individual nonprofit organizations, although that, too, is important since actual public support for nonprofits is typically not for abstractions but for specific organizations.
2. Little is known about whether the vastly larger use of volunteers by nonprofit, as compared with for-profit organizations reflects differential organization demand for volunteers or differential willingness of people to supply volunteer time. To the extent that differential demand is important, the nonprofit sector can be said to be providing greater opportunities and, in that sense, more valuable "outputs" than for-profit firms, other things equal.
3. Another source is donations, which is not examined in this paper, although the methods used to obtain them are relevant to the overall assessment of nonprofit sector behavior. Some imaginative new forms of appeals are being adopted. A recent advertisement by a charitable nonprofit stated, "Donate your car, truck, motorcycle, boat (any condition)," and it emphasized that it was tax deductible (Jewish United Fund News, 1995). Lollapalooza Tours, which organizes rock concerts, has added $1 to the price of tickets which they give to charities, and have raised $1.3 million in the past three years (Petersen, 1995).
4. If systematic behavioral differences were not observed, that would not imply that institutional form is irrelevant to public policy. It could be the case that competition forces all surviving forms of institutions to behave in similar ways (Hirth, 1993; Wolff & Schlesinger, 1994).

REFERENCES

Alchian, A., & Demsetz, H. (1972, December). Production, information costs and economic organization. *American Economic Review, 62,* 777–795.
Arenson, K. W. (1995, September 26). A small college's tax-exempt status challenged. *New York Times,* p. A14.
Becker, T. J. (1995, May 16). Opening door to synergy. *Chicago Tribune,* section 5, pp. 1, 7.
Ben-Ner, A. (1986). Nonprofit organizations: Why do they exist in market economies? In S. Rose-Ackerman (Ed.), *The economics of nonprofit institutions* (pp. 94–113). New York: Oxford University Press.
Blumenthal, D., Causino, N., Campbell, E., & Louis, K. S. (1996, February 8). Relationships between academic institutions and industry in the life sciences—An industry survey. *New England Journal of Medicine, 334,* 368–373.

Brannigan, M. (1995, September 18). Church-run tours collide with travel agents. *Wall Street Journal*, pp. B1–B2.

Christakis, N. A., & Escarce, J. J. (1996, July 18). Survival of medicare patients after enrollment in hospice programs. *New England Journal of Medicine, 335*, 172–178.

Cronin, A. (1995, August 9). Museums: The sluggers of the culture lineup. *New York Times*, pp. A1, B2.

Emshwiller, J. R. (1995, August 8). More small firms complain about tax-exempt rivals. *Wall Street Journal*, p. B1.

Glaberson, W. (1996, February 21). In era of fiscal damage control, cities fight idea of "tax exempt." *New York Times*, pp. A1, C17.

Goddeeris, J. (1988). Compensating differentials and self-selection: An application to lawyers. *Journal of Political Economy, 96*, 411–428.

Hancock, L., & Roberts, M. (1994). Fishing for freshmen. *Newsweek*, 104–105.

Hansmann, H. (1980). The role of nonprofit enterprise. *Yale Law Review, 89*, 835–899.

Herman, T. (1995, February 8). Tax report. *Wall Street Journal*, p. A1.

Herzlinger, R. E. (1996, March-April). Can public trust in nonprofits and governments be restored? *Harvard Business Review*, 97–107.

Hirth, R. A. (1993). Information and ownership in the nursing home industry. Unpublished doctoral dissertation, University of Pennsylvania, Philadelphia.

James, E. (1983). How nonprofits grow: A model. *Journal of Policy Analysis and Management, 2*, 350–365.

Jewish United Fund News (1995, December), p. 4.

Kramer, R. (1995). Is the sector concept obsolete? *Inside ISTR* (Bulletin of the International Society for Third-Sector Research, Johns Hopkins University), *3*(1), 6.

Kuttner, R. (1996, August 1). Columbia/HCA and the resurgence of the for-profit hospital business: First of two parts. *New England Journal of Medicine, 335*, 362–367.

Lambert, B. (1996, August 2). Adelphi U. failed to file I.R.S. report. *New York Times*, p. A16.

Lewin, T. (1994, October 25). Dehydrated-food plant in Texas is dedicated to effort to feed the hungry. *New York Times*, p. A14.

Mauser, E. (1993). Organizational form important to consumers and managers: An application to the day-care industry. Unpublished doctoral dissertation, University of Wisconsin-Madison.

Mervis, J. (1996, July 5). Agencies scramble to measure public impact of research. *Science, 273*, 27–28.

MIT wins a new trial in price-fixing case. (1993, September 18). *New York Times*, p. 6.

Nudelman, P. M., & Andrews, L. M. (1996). The value added of not-for-profit health plans. *New England Journal of Medicine, 334*, 1057–1059.

PARKProgress. (1995, Summer). Northwestern University-Evanston Research Park.

Pearce, J. L. (1993). *Volunteers*. New York: Routledge.

Petersen, A. (1995, September 7). Charities bet young people will come for the music, stay for the pitch. *Wall Street Journal*, p. B1.

Preston, A. E. (1988). The effects of property rights on labor costs of nonprofit firms: An application to the day care industry. *Journal of Industrial Economics, 36*, 337–350.

Roomkin, M., & Weisbrod, B. A. (1999). Managerial compensation in for-profit, nonprofit, and government hospitals. *Journal of Law, Economics, Organization, 15*(3), 750–781.

Salamon, L. M., & Anheier, H. (1995). The emerging sector: A statistical supplement. Working Paper. Baltimore: The Johns Hopkins Comparative Nonprofit Sector Project.

Schiff, J., & Weisbrod, B. A. (1991). Competition between for-profit and nonprofit organizations. *Annals of Public and Cooperative Economics, 62*, 619–639.

Schlesinger, M. (1998). Mismeasuring the consequences of ownership: External influences and the comparative performance of public, for-profit and private nonprofit organizations. In W.

Powell & E. Clemens (Eds.), *Private action and the public good*, chap. 6 . New Haven, CT: Yale University Press.

Schlesinger, M., Dorwart, R., Hoover, C., & Epstein, S. (1997). Competition and access to hospital services: Evidence from psychiatric hospitals. *Medical Care, 35*(9), 974–992.

Schmitt, R. B. (1995, July 27). Uncharitable acts: If donors fail to give, more nonprofit groups take them to court. *Wall Street Journal*, pp. 1, 5.

Schuster, J. M. D. (1994). Arguing for government support of the arts: An American view. In O. Robison, R. Freeman, & C. A. Riley Hanover (Eds.), *The arts in the world economy* (pp. 42–55). Salzburg Seminar. New Hampshire: University Press of New England.

Sills, D. L. (1968). Voluntary associations. In D. L. Sills (Ed.), *International encyclopedia of the social sciences* (Vol. 16, pp. 357–379). New York: Free Press.

Simon, J. (1987). Tax treatment of nonprofit organizations. In W. Powell (Ed.), *The nonprofit sector: A research handbook* (pp. 67–98). New Haven, CT: Yale University Press.

Sinclair, M. (1996, July). Chao declines "gift" from UWA board members. *NonProfit Times*, pp. 1, 10.

Steinberg, R., & Weisbrod, B. A. (1996). To give or to sell? That is the question. Or, . . . price discrimination by nonprofit organizations with distributional objectives. Working Paper, Indiana University/Purdue University at Indianapolis, and Northwestern University.

Svarstad, B. L., & Bond, C. A. (1984). The use of hypnotics in proprietary and church-related nursing homes. University of Wisconsin–Madison, School of Pharmacy.

Swarns, R. L. (1996, August 10). Unknown "charity" appeals for TWA victims, but many are wary. *New York Times*, p. 18.

Symposium on contingent valuation. (1994). Articles by P. R. Portney, W. M. Hanemann, and P. A. Diamond and J. A. Hausman. *Journal of Economic Perspectives, 8*, 3–64.

Thurow, R. (1995, November 17). Shoe companies, tongues out, buy up college teams wholesale. *Wall Street Journal*, p. B10.

U.S. Small Business Administration. (1983). *Unfair competition by nonprofit organizations with small business: An issue for the 1980's*. Washington, DC: U.S. Small Business Administration.

Walsh, S. (1996, July 23). Charity's ex-chief faces fraud charges. *Washington Post*, pp. C1, C10.

Webster, A. (1994). University-corporate ties and the construction of research agendas. *Sociology, 28*, 123–142.

Weisbrod, B. A. (1975). Toward a theory of the voluntary nonprofit sector in a three sector economy. In E. S. Phelps (Ed.), *Altruism, morality and economic theory* (pp. 171–195). New York: Russell Sage Foundation.

Weisbrod, B. A. (1983). Nonprofit and proprietary sector behavior: Wage differentials among lawyers. *Journal of Labor Economics, 1*, 246–263.

Weisbrod, B. A. (1988). *The nonprofit economy*. Cambridge, MA: Harvard University Press.

Weisbrod, B. A. (1998). Institutional form and organization behavior. In W. W. Powell & E. S. Clemens (Eds.), *Private action and the public good* (pp. 69–84). New Haven, CT: Yale University Press.

Weisbrod, B. A. (1997).The future of the nonprofit sector: Its Entwining With Private Enterprise and Government. *Journal of Policy Analysis and Management, 16*(4), 541–555.

Winslow, R. (1995, August 29). Getting down to business at Duke's medical school. *Wall Street Journal*, pp. B1, 6.

Wolff, N., & Schlesinger, M. (1994). Changes in ownership-related differences in hospital performance in response to intersectoral competition. Working Paper. Newark: Rutgers University, Institute for Health, Health Care Policy, and Aging Research.

Wuthnow, R. (1995). *What it means to volunteer: Lessons from America's youth*. Washington, DC: Independent Sector.

Young, D. R. (1994, Summer). Through the looking glass: When businesses and not-for-profits act alike. *Advancing Philanthropy*, 13ff.

Index